D1591776

Simply Natural
Health

HARNESSING THE
HEALING POWER OF NATURE

ACUPRESSURE · AROMATHERAPY · FOOD AS MEDICINE

Juliet Kelly-Wong

Marshall Cavendish
Editions

© 2017 Marshall Cavendish International (Asia) Private Limited

Designer: Lynn Chin Nyuk Ling
Editors: Renata Kelly, Jane Vanlanschot Hubrecht and Jill Birch
All photographs by Kate Drewer except pages 70, 134, 140 and 163 by Karl Henz

Published by Marshall Cavendish Editions
An imprint of Marshall Cavendish International

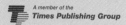

A member of the
Times Publishing Group

Other Marshall Cavendish Offices:
Marshall Cavendish Corporation. 99 White Plains Road, Tarrytown NY 10591-9001, USA
• Marshall Cavendish International (Thailand) Co Ltd. 253 Asoke, 12th Flr, Sukhumvit 21
Road, Klongtoey Nua, Wattana, Bangkok 10110, Thailand • Marshall Cavendish (Malaysia)
Sdn Bhd, Times Subang, Lot 46, Subang Hi-Tech Industrial Park, Batu Tiga, 4,0000 Shah
Alam, Selangor Darul Ehsan, Malaysia

Marshall Cavendish is a registered trademark of Times Publishing Limited

National Library Board, Singapore Cataloguing-in-Publication Data

Name(s): Wong, Juliet Kelly, author.
Title(s): Simply Natural Health : harnessing the healing power of nature /
Juliet Kelly-Wong.
Other title(s): Harnessing the healing power of nature / Juliet Kelly-Wong.
Description: Singapore : Marshall Cavendish International (Asia) Pte Ltd, [2017]
Identifier(s): OCN 982042301 | ISBN 978-981-47-7195-5 (paperback).
Subject(s): LCSH: Naturopathy.| Alternative medicine. | Medicine, Popular. |
Holistic medicine.
Classification: DDC 615.535—dc23

Printed in Malaysia by TWP Sdn. Bhd.

Dedication

This book is dedicated to my
husband Nicholas and to our two children
Christopher and Sophia, who have been my willing guinea pigs
for many of the following remedies, and for this I thank you.
They have made my life complete in so many ways.

Contents

Acknowledgements

There are so many people I would like to thank and who have helped me to finally get this book off the ground. Firstly to Kate for all the beautiful pictures! You have made the book exactly what I had in my head. Thank you for your patience, good humour and pure talent – four more to go!!

To Anita who didn't realise what she was getting herself into by offering to help me at the clinic. Thank you for your time and friendship.

To my wonderful parents who have always been there for me, thank you for all your love, encouragement and advice. Thank you Dada for that raised eyebrow when I announced I was writing a book – that pushed me to keep going.

To my sister Jane who has always been encouraging me to follow the natural route, from Soho to Singapore. Jane, I have sheer admiration for your ability to always be positive and find humour in all situations. I wish you so much luck in all that you do.

To my soul sister Isabelle who started Bunny & Monkey with me so many years ago – I am eternally grateful!

To Dr. T.T. Ang – who healed and taught me. Thank you for sharing your amazing knowledge and passion for acupressure with all your students.

To Farida and Marc who have been so encouraging over the past few years, thank you for your friendship and shared moments. Marc, I will always credit you for your comment in the kitchen that motivated me to finish the book!

To Melissa, Lynn and Lydia at Marshall Cavendish for actually allowing to make this happen – a million thank yous.

To Judith Lea who started me on this path – your gentle touch changed my life.

A huge thank you to all my patients (especially Jo Bush, my first ever patient and friend) for trusting me with your health – without all of you, 'The Natural Clinic' and this book wouldn't be.

An eternal gratitude to God, the Universe and all my angels who guide me in everything I do – it is your work not mine that I do.

Preface

I started practicing as a natural therapist in 2007 with the combination of different therapies – namely acupressure, cupping, moxibustion, aromatherapy and nutrition. At that time, I did not realise the healing powers that I had in my hands.

As I now learn and have expanded my knowledge and continue to work with my patients, it has become evident to me that there are definite holes in the world's conventional medical knowledge. Don't get me wrong, medicine is now able to do the most amazing things but with all its complex machines, diagnostic tools and amazing drugs, it has also failed to embrace the simplicity of how the body works. Our bodies are always telling us something but medicine sometimes fails to listen, and instead relies on machines and drugs to give us the answers.

As natural therapies gain strength, the time has come for doctors to learn to embrace and incorporate their vast medical knowledge and diagnostic tools with the simplicity of nature as well as the ancient 5000-year-old diagnostic system of acupressure and acupuncture to truly understand what our bodies are trying to tell us. At this juncture I would like to quote a portion of the Hippocratic oath that doctors were and still are historically made to take before they start to practice: "I will remember that there is an art to modern medicine as well as science, and that warmth, sympathy, and understanding may outweigh the surgeon's knife or the chemist's drug. I will not be ashamed to say "I know not" , nor will I fail to call in my colleagues when the skills of another are needed for a patients recovery". Based on the original writing of Hippocrates, this was written in 1964 by Louis Lasagna, Academic Dean of the School of Medicine at Tufts University, and is used in many medical schools today.

Introduction

Congratulations on embracing the
simply natural approach to healing yourself,
your family and friends! I hope that what you will
read in this book will change
the way you look, feel, and perhaps live –
all for the better.

Adopting these few simple, straightforward – yet often neglected – ways of treating yourself may make as profound a difference to you and your loved ones as they have to me and mine.

If you have read the preface, you will know what I, was up against prior to investigating alternative treatments and simple ways of treating myself. The success I had – with myself as a guinea pig – led me to become who I am today. A healthy and happy wife and mother, not to mention a fully qualified natural therapist practicing in Singapore. I am qualified in the Traditional Chinese Medicine (TCM) art of acupressure, in aromatherapy, nutrition, kinesiology (Touch for Health) and the Bach flower remedies. The combinations of these remedies in the treatment of my patients and the results that have been realised have been more than encouraging. Many of my patients can attest to this!

None of these methods are new or different, but what I believe in is the combination of them. Never is there one method that is 'better' than the other, but it's the synergy and combination of these different areas working together where we see positive and lasting results.

I work with my patients in a very physical way, encouraging and restoring flow and balance with the use of acupressure points, which I combine with essential oils. I also explain how different foods can positively and negatively affect our systems and then instruct my patients how to use various foods as medicines.

I strongly believe that the emotional side of healing is crucial and I deal with this again through a combination of acupressure, essential oils and Bach flower remedies (more on all these methods in Part 2 – Mother Nature's

Medical Kit). From the common to the complex, this combination of methods has proved to be highly effective. My only frustration as a therapist is that I wish more people could learn and experience this simple, natural system of healing, which is why I decided to write this book.

THE AIM OF THIS BOOK

Through and with this book, I want to empower and encourage you to realise that "we all have a physician inside us" and when it comes to our health, we can do more than we think to help our families and ourselves through nature and trusting our instincts.

This is really the crux of this book: giving you the tools to start and support healing without immediately reaching for conventional medicines, which can frequently be both harmful and avoidable.

The book is divided into three parts:

Part One will look at our health and the aspects of modern life that may be damaging our health and our immune system. Here, I encourage you to start asking questions about all the different elements that are affecting the health of individuals in this modern world, but at the same time give you confidence and knowledge that we still have the chance to make better decisions for our families and ourselves when it comes to health.

Part Two is called "Mother Nature's Healing Kit". Here, I describe in detail all the ingredients that I use in my treatments: e.g. why you are being asked to drink cabbage juice and baking soda on an empty stomach to help your heartburn? This is to help people understand the varied and effective healing properties of foods, herbs and essential oils, so that you can perhaps use them in many other ways outside of this book.

Part Three is an A–Z list of health concerns, which includes many of the conditions I have treated hands-on at my clinic as well as some standard conditions that I manage to treat by advice alone (e.g. lice and athlete's foot). The preponderance of the latter examples is what actually inspired me to write this book – realising that each of us has the possibility of becoming a healer with a little help and expert guidance. Particularly if the guidance is followed. Just as reading this book will not qualify you as a natural health practitioner, not following the steps I recommend correctly will not alleviate a condition.

The step-by-step instructions are important, as they are the key to making nature work for you.

For example, it's easy to be told that manuka honey is great for colds or burns but how do you actually use it? My aim is to help you follow the same procedures that I use and give to my patients, along with time frames and specific instructions, to make sure that nature works for and heals your condition.

On this note I wish you luck with your endeavour to follow 'an alternative choice in health'.

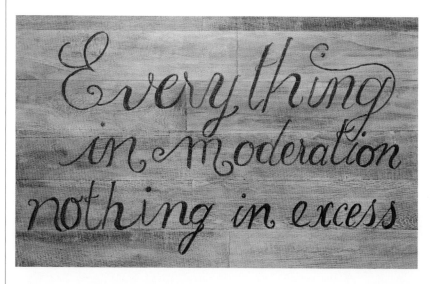

This sign hangs on my clinic wall and I refer to it daily. I truly believe that "everything in moderation, nothing in excess" is how we should all strive to live, and I am not alone. The reference to moderation has been expounded on by Plato, Aristotle, Mark Twain, Benjamin Franklin and found inscribed in the temple of Apollo at Delphi, and is even referenced in the Bible, so, as you read this book, I want you to keep this in mind.

This book is about providing information and allowing you to take what you need and figure out what works for you. Remember too that all the life changes you might want to make can't be achieved in a day, so relax and just do what you can and the rest will follow.

Finally, I want to say, this book is not a guarantee. I can't guarantee you will never need antibiotics again, but I can assure you that if you follow the steps and start this natural journey early, you will find you may be able to cope without them. If you feel something is beyond your capability do not feel guilty. Follow your instinct and seek medical advice. Never put a family member, yourself or anybody at risk.

What I really want to teach is that we can't be perfect, but we can always do something. The key to good health is moderation and knowing what to do.

Part One

OUR
HEALTH

Since the start of my clinic in 2008, I have seen a huge increase of interest
in approaching health through more natural means. I attribute this to a few different
reasons: the worry of drug resistance is very real and being talked about more and more,
people are finding that medicines often only help temporarily, and that they are
just not getting the answers they want from modern conventional medicine.
Why exactly are cancers, autoimmune diseases, diabetes and autism so much on the rise?
Why are our guts becoming so sensitive? What else can I do to keep myself healthy
besides popping pills? These questions are what I get asked all the time and
it is these questions that I will try to answer in this book.
What you are about to read are just my honest observations together with simple research
and first-hand experience from my own health issues and from working with my patients
over the past 10 years. I hope some of your questions get answered or
at least start you on a natural path to your own health.

In these very modern times, we are actually a generation of people that are becoming less and less healthy each year. Here are some of the factors that have contributed to our decline in health.

CANCER

Cancer is the number one killer in the world[1]. Fourteen million new cases of cancer are diagnosed every year, and there are 8.2 million deaths from cancer a year[2].

Around one third of cancer deaths are due to the five leading behavioural and dietary risks: high body mass index, low fruit and vegetable intake, lack of physical activity, tobacco use and alcohol use.

The number of new cases is expected to rise by about 70% over the next two decades.

DIABETES

The number of people with diabetes has risen from 108 million in 1980 to 422 million in 2014.

The global prevalence of diabetes among adults over 18 years of age has risen from 4.7% in 1980 to 8.5% in 2014. Diabetes prevalence has been rising more rapidly in middle- and low-income countries. Almost half of all deaths attributable to high blood glucose occur before the age of 70 years. World Health Organisation (WHO) projects that diabetes will be the 7th leading cause of death in 2030.

AUTOIMMUNE RELATED DISEASES

Autoimmune diseases are now the number two cause of illnesses after cancer. Over the past fifty years, multiple sclerosis (MS) rates have nearly tripled in many countries such as Finland, the UK, the Netherlands, Denmark, Sweden, Norway, Germany, Italy and Greece. In many developed countries, MS diagnosis has been rising at nearly 3% a year. Rates of increase of the numerous other autoimmune diseases – scleroderma, Crohn's disease, Addison's disease and polymyositis – show the same alarming pattern.

The rapid increase in these numbers is being blamed on environmental factors.

AUTISM SPECTRUM DISORDER

Autism spectrum disorder (ASD) is the fastest growing neurobiological condition in the world.

In his 2009 article, *Autism Statistics*, Dr. Arthur Schoenstadt states that "experts estimate that 2 to 6 children out of 1000 will have autism in the coming years. The impact on education, families, and the healthcare system will be staggering. Autism is considered a lifelong disability. As these children grow, they will require continued long-term care as adults."

ALZHEIMER'S AND DEMENTIA

Nearly 44 million people have Alzheimer's or a related dementia in the world[4].

The global cost of Alzheimer's and dementia is estimated to be $605 billion, which is equivalent to 1% of the entire world's gross domestic product[5].

There was an estimated 46.8 million people worldwide living with dementia in 2015. This number will almost double every 20 years, reaching 74.7 million in 2030 and 131.5 million in 2050. Much of the increase will be in developing countries. Already 58% of people with dementia live in developing countries, but by 2050 this will rise to 68%[6].

OBESITY

Worldwide obesity has nearly doubled since 1980.

In 2008, more than 1.4 billion adults, aged 20 and older, were overweight. Of these over 200 million men and nearly 300 million women were obese.

Overweight and obesity are the fifth leading risk for global deaths. At least 2.8 million adults die each year as a result of being overweight or obese. [7]

---

[1] The World Health Organisation [2] Cancer Research UK [3] World Health Organisation
[4] Alzheimer's Disease International [5] Alzheimers.net [6] Alzheimer's Society
[7] The European Association for the Study of Obesity

SOMETHING TO THINK ABOUT!

The above statistics are based on a number of "worldwide statistics" that I have found in my research. The most frightening statistics are coming out of the "developed" world. Whether this is because the information is just not as readily available in "underdeveloped" countries, or is it that the said "underdeveloped" countries are just not getting these 1st world diseases? Could this be due to the less frequent availability of medicines and over the counter drugs, the eating of simpler foods with less chemicals added, the necessity to eat food that is readily available from the land as opposed to treated and imported or the inability to afford highly processed foods – the list could go on.

WHAT IS MAKING US SO SICK?

Following on from the above statistics, it is 'simply natural' to question what is happening to our health. Why, in such a scientifically sophisticated modern world, with diagnostics and medicine more advanced than ever before, are we falling ill more so than ever?

Many scientists, doctors and everyday people like you and me have tried to answer this question but there is simply no exact answer to this. In my opinion, our health is all about balance. We are throwing ourselves off balance and falling ill not due to one factor, but to a combination of many.

Here are the main factors that I feel are affecting our internal balance and ultimately our health:

- The overuse of chemical medication and especially antibiotics
- Too many vaccines
- Eating too many "foods" that harm us and that our bodies don't recognise as foods
- Being exposed to too many chemicals in our food and our environment
- The fact that we tend to over sanitise our environment
- Our ever-growing impatience

Here's how these factors may be hurting our systems.

TOO MANY ANTIBIOTICS AND DRUGS

Antibiotics are very necessary and have helped the world immensely, but they should also be used with caution. Unfortunately, some doctors are too quick to prescribe antibiotics when they're not necessary and that becomes a problem.

Antibiotics only kill bacteria and only certain bacteria at that. They don't kill viruses, they don't kill worms, they don't kill fungal infections; in fact, they can make some fungal infections worse. They should never be used in a "just in case" scenario or as a prophylactic, which they so often are.

We have been led to believe that antibiotics can be a quick one-stop-fix and have overused this powerful medicine to such an extent that they are becoming almost completely ineffective. The more we rely on antibiotics, the more the bacteria in our bodies develop resistance to them, which makes treating infections increasingly challenging. A telling example is the resurgence of tuberculosis (TB) in many parts of the world. TB used to react quickly and effectively to antibiotics, making it a much less dreaded disease. The resurgent strain of TB seen in 2016 is non-reactive to antibiotics, as the bacteria has become drug-resistant.

Antibiotic resistance is now one of the top health concerns of the 21st Century.

> *"The global emergency of extensively drug-resistant tuberculosis heralds the advent of widespread, virtually untreatable tuberculosis,"* writes Tracy Dalton of the Centres for Disease Control.

The medical and scientific worlds are also increasingly concerned about the fact that antibiotics wreak havoc on the natural balance of good bacteria that is present in our guts and is crucial for good health. With the overuse of antibiotics, not only present in medication but in foods as well, we have depleted the necessary, life-giving, good bacteria that is so essential for good health. The compromise of this "good" bacteria is now being linked to many of the health issues I described in the previous section such as autoimmune diseases, cancers and autism as well as digestive respiratory and skin issues.

The food and agricultural industries are both falling under heavy criticism from governments for using too many antibiotics in the production of meat, fish, poultry and dairy products as well as using them on fruit and vegetable crops. These industries use antibiotics as a prophylactic to ensure that their crops and livestock don't get sick. Unfortunately, these antibiotics then come into our human diet when we eat the treated animals or crops. These industries are under great pressure to look for alternatives to reduce the hidden antibiotic overload that the world is getting, which then directly contributes to the antibiotic resistance crisis that we are facing today.

So by allowing these unnecessary antibiotics into our systems, environment and food chain – not to mention frequent overprescription of antibiotics by doctors – we are directly hurting our stomachs. One of the very first things that I was taught, when studying acupressure, was that the key to good health and balance always came from the stomach. My acupressure master would always say, "strong stomach, strong you".

HOW TO RECOGNISE WHEN YOU NEED ANTIBIOTICS

Antibiotics are not bad in themselves; it is just the overuse of them that has become harmful to us and our world. We need antibiotics – without them the world would be an even more dangerous place. So the question is how do we stop overusing them?

We must be able to recognise when to use them and when not to use them.

- Most things start virally, and normally one can be quite sick with fever for about five days. However, if a fever or a cold is getting worse after five days, you should seek medical assistance as you may need antibiotics.
- Fevers, however, are not only viral or bacterial but could also indicate dengue, malaria and meningitis. **Never ignore a fever**.
- If a fever starts, goes away, then returns, this may mean that something has become a bacterial infection and you might need antibiotics. In such a case, seek medical advice from the doctors.
- When you have cut yourself or a foreign object has entered your system and you see the following symptoms happen to your wound – the appearance of pus, the wound turning hot and red and the redness spreading, seek medical advice immediately.
- Post-operatively, doctors like to give antibiotics as a prophylactic, in case there is an infection from the hospital. Discuss your individual case with the doctor. Often the warning signs for bacterial infection can be monitored as opposed to pre-treated.

- Certain parasites and other diseases (like tropical sprue) can affect the stomach and will often need to be treated with antibiotics. Beware: they each need a specific type of antibiotic, not broad-spectrum antibiotic. Doing a stool test is imperative to be able to isolate the antibiotic that will actually work.
- It is always wise to seek a doctor's advice in any situation that you are concerned about, but do try to discuss your options with the doctor before you start a course of antibiotics and keep him posted about the development of your situation.
- If you also start using the advice from this book at the start of any 'illness' or problem, you will be giving your system a head start even if you do finally need antibiotics. However, in most situations you might be able to avoid them altogether.

Alternatives to antibiotics

There are many natural alternatives to antibiotics. You just need to know how to use them. Below is a list of antibiotic foods that can help fight off bacterial infections. I go into more details on these foods in Part 2 and Part 3 and guide you how to use them effectively.

Antibiotic foods:
- Apple cider vinegar
- Cabbage
- Cinnamon
- Cloves
- Echinacea
- Extra virgin coconut oil
- Fermented foods such as kombucha tea, kefir, miso, sauerkraut, kimchi, yoghurts and tempeh
- Garlic
- Ginger
- Manuka honey UMF +15 (or higher)
- Oregano (herb and oil)
- Thyme

Getting these foods in your diets on a regular basis will help to boost your immune system against viral and bacterial infections.

TOO MANY DRUGS

Antibiotics are only one part of the problem. There are, however, other medications that are routinely offered by doctors that help alleviate symptoms of a disease or illness. We must also be aware and wary of these.

For example, decongestants, cough syrups, fever and pain suppressants, steroids, antihistamines, anti-inflammatories, anti-nausea and anti-diarrhoea medicines are all usually available without prescription and easily bought over the counter, but many of them can hinder your body's natural healing process.

I am not saying that all these medications are bad and should never be used, but they are often handed out without any warnings that they can, and sometimes do, have serious side effects.

These medicines can stop our bodies' natural immune response to a virus or bacteria. When our noses run or our throats are sore, glands are swollen, tummies upset or our skin reacts, it is our bodies' way of telling us that something is wrong and is asking us to help. Yes, these symptoms can be uncomfortable, but they are also our bodies' natural response to a problem that has entered our system; so, the last thing we should probably do is suppress them – which is just what most medicines do. Instead, we should support our system and try to alleviate our symptoms without harmful drugs. In that way we help our bodies to heal themselves.

Cough suppressants – These suppressants can override the body's natural instinct to cough, which can damage the development of the respiratory tract in young children. It is now widely advised in many parts of the world that cough suppressants should not be given to children under the age of six and in some countries under the age of 12.

Fever and pain suppressants – Prolonged use of fever and pain suppressants can increase the risk of conditions like stroke, renal failure and gastrointestinal bleeding.

Anti-inflammatory or Non-steroidal Anti-inflammatory Drugs (NSAIDS) – Prolonged use of these drugs can cause stomach problems like bleeding ulcers and stomach upset, irritable bowel syndrome (IBS), high blood pressure, fluid retention (causing swelling especially around the lower legs, feet, ankles and hands), kidney problems and failure, heart problems and rashes.

Steroids – Prolonged use of steroids can cause acne, blurred vision, cataracts or glaucoma, easy bruising, difficulty sleeping, high blood pressure, increased appetite, weight gain and increased growth of body hair.

TOO MANY VACCINATIONS

This is a contentious topic and many people have very strong opinions on this issue.

I believe we do not need as many vaccinations as we are told and we do not need to give them to our children when they are very young. We do have a right to ask questions and if we choose to vaccinate, we should be able to choose a schedule with which we feel comfortable with. Arguably the reason why we have the luxury to choose to vaccinate or not is probably due to the fact that most people have been vaccinated and therefore don't have to face the fear of epidemics like smallpox; and rarely do we come across victims of polio in our schools. This is a direct result of the vaccination which has controlled and overtime has nearly eradicated this horrible disease. We should not shun vaccinations, instead ask questions, do research and do not get pressured into a decision by doctors or school governing boards.

Do your research

Do we need to vaccinate at all? Again, this is really a personal decision. Nobody can tell you which way to go. But I would suggest that if you want to vaccinate, do some research first. There are many wonderful books published on the subject. Here are a few:

- *"Germs, Biological Warfare, Vaccinations"* by Gary Null
- *"Raising A Vaccine Free Child"* by Wendy Lydall
- *"Vaccinations – A Parent's Dilemma"* by Greg Beattie

Your choices when it comes to vaccinations

- Choose a doctor who will listen to you and discuss alternative choices and schedules. Discuss with the doctor the last time there was an outbreak of measles or whooping cough in your area and calculate the risks you are taking by not giving your child that vaccination.
- Discuss and research which shots can be split up as opposed to being given in a combination: i.e., measles, mumps and rubella can be given in three different shots with a space in between; you just need to ask.
- Go at a pace suitable for your own child. If your child is a delicate and physiologically sensitive child with various allergies, stomach and even skin issues, then you do not need to give your child a 6-in-one vaccination at age 2 months or even at 1 year. It can be delayed until later. Discuss this with your doctor.

- Know the risks in the country where you live.
- Make a conscious effort to keep your child's immune system healthy and strong. Most of the diseases that we are being vaccinated against are not deadly diseases; it's only when your immune system is down or compromised that there is a danger.
- Always boost up the immune system, especially with good bacteria, before a vaccination by giving probiotics and eating fermented foods regularly (please see Part 2 – Mother Nature's Medical Kit for a list of fermented foods). Our guts and immune system need good bacteria to be strong and there is now good concrete evidence that a gut that is low on good bacteria is much more likely to have an adverse reaction to a vaccine.
- Never give a vaccine to a child who is sick, slightly sick or has just been sick – particularly if they have just had a tummy bug or a course of antibiotics which will have depleted all the good bacteria in their stomachs. If your child is due for a vaccine and has been sick, delay it. Boost them up with immune-boosting foods as well as multi-strain probiotics and fermented foods for about 2–4 weeks before you even think of giving them the vaccine.
- Get full information of the possible side effects of the vaccination and know how to identify a vaccine reaction.
- Ask your doctors if they are a member of Vaccine Adverse Event Reporting System (VAERS) or the equivalent in your country.
- Following a vaccination, consider homeopathic remedies that can help with some of the side effects children suffer after a vaccination. The side effects are listed below.
    - Frequent infections/lowered immunity
    - Mood change
    - Mucus buildup
    - Onset of allergies
    - Swollen glands
    - Recurrent fevers

These homeopathic remedies help reverse the above side effects from vaccinations but still leave you with the immunity that you were aiming for through the vaccines.
- Follow the steps to boost up the immune system before – and how to detoxify after – the vaccination.

Saying no to certain vaccinations

A few words of advice to those who say no to certain, or all, vaccinations for their children:

- Read, research and discuss so you know why you are not vaccinating. Make an educated decision not an emotional one.
- Know how to support your child through the various diseases that you are not vaccinating your child against. Though most of them are not deadly, there can be side effects like encephalitis, blindness, disfigurement, hearing loss and fertility issues.
- Be socially responsible towards other parents and children. If your child does come down with a disease, keep them away from others, let others know, even tell your local doctor – and keep the child at home. There are some adults and children who, due to certain conditions and lowered immune response, are not able to be vaccinated and these diseases can be fatal to them.
- Consider the science of homeopathy as there has been a lot of success with homeopathic "vaccinations" that have a 100% success rate.

What about booster shots

So you've vaccinated your child and now it's time for the booster shots. Do they really need booster shots? Not always. There is a very simple way to find out. Ask for a blood test to check if the antibodies are present in the system; if the antibodies are positive you do not need the booster. If the antibodies are negative, your child does not have the immunity and then you decide.

PROCESSED FOODS
WHY THEY ARE BAD FOR US

The term processed foods is rather misleading, as technically any food that has been altered slightly could fall under the term "processed". For example, freezing a home-cooked meal could be termed "processing". The processed foods that are harming our health, however, are those that are pumped full of refined sugars and flours, preservatives, conditioners, artificial flavours, colours, herbicides and pesticides. These foods are extremely dangerous because they are full of harmful chemicals many of which even the FDA is aware could cause cancers, disrupt thyroids contain endocrine and digestive disrupters and could trigger other diseases.

Another reason why processed foods are dangerous is that they taste good, are fast and easy to prepare and make our lives simple whilst sadly, they are just not good for us.

The top main artificial ingredients (and those that cause the most problems) are:
- Refined sugars and high fructose corn syrup (HFCS)
- Artificial colours
- Artificial flavours (the term artificial flavour on a label may include 10 or more chemicals)
- Preservatives
- *Texturants* and conditioners (chemicals that add a texture to food)

These chemicals overload our digestive system, and it takes our detoxifying organs longer to process or deal with them. This means they remain in our bodies or are stored as fat, either of which is quite toxic for our system.

More details on these ingredients and others can be found under the list of additives at the end of this section.

PROCESSED FOODS CAN BE AS ADDICTIVE AS DRUGS

Addicted to junk food? Unlike whole foods, which contain a mix of carbohydrates, fats, proteins, fibre and water to help you feel satisfied, processed foods are imbalanced in their composition and have added chemicals which stimulate dopamine. Dopamine is a neurotransmitter that makes you feel good even though the food lacks nutrients and fibre. This artificial dopamine stimulation can lead to excessive food cravings and, ultimately, food addiction. Another example of a dopamine stimulant is cocaine.

PROCESSED FOODS CAN MAKE YOU INSULIN RESISTANT

Refined carbohydrates like breakfast cereals, bagels, waffles, pretzels and most other processed foods quickly break down into sugar in your body. This leads to rapid spikes in blood sugar and insulin levels and can give you sugar cravings a few hours later when blood sugar levels go down again. This phenomenon is also called the 'blood sugar roller coaster'; it in turn increases your insulin and contributes to insulin resistance. What is insulin resistance? Insulin resistance is a condition in which the body produces insulin but does not use it effectively. When people have insulin resistance, glucose builds up in the blood instead of being absorbed by the cells, leading to type 2 diabetes or pre-diabetes.

PROCESSED FOODS HAVE NO NUTRITIONAL VALUE

Processed foods often have the real food, and therefore nutrition, processed right out of them. The nutrients that have been taken out of the food are sometimes added back in the form of synthetic vitamins and minerals. These synthetics nutrients do not fool your body, however, and will not provide the whole, synergistic nutrition that eating whole food will.

Furthermore, there's no way that a lab can provide the thousands of phytochemicals and trace nutrients found in whole foods. Science hasn't even begun to uncover all of them. The best way to ensure your body gets the benefits of all the vitamins, minerals, antioxidants, and more that nature has to offer is to eat whole, unprocessed foods.

LIST OF CHEMICAL ADDITIVES IN PROCESSED FOODS:

Refined Sugar and/or High Fructose Corn Syrup (HFCS) – These refined sugars damage your liver in the same way consuming too much alcohol does. HFCS actually "punches holes" in your digestive track, which leads to the leaky gut syndrome and therefore allergies. In addition, HFCS is well-documented to contain high levels of mercury. Refined sugar overrides your system's natural regulators, which tell our brain and stomach we are full. Thus we overeat – which leads to obesity and facilitates various inflammatory conditions.

MSG (E621) and Artificial Flavours – Artificial flavours enhance the flavour of foods. They trick our taste buds and our nervous systems whilst depleting us of important vitamins and minerals which then causes deficiencies that lead to many health issues. Some scientists claim that artificial flavouring can be directly linked to fibromyalgia, obesity, fatty liver, high insulin and blood sugar, high cholesterol, metabolic syndrome, high blood pressure, and disturbances in the gut-brain connection which can impact neurological and brain health.

Caution: There are many different names for MSG: yeast extract, anything "hydrolysed", soy protein, whey protein isolate, glutamic acid, glutamate, monosodium glutamate, mono potassium glutamate, calcium glutamate, mono ammonium glutamate, magnesium glutamate, natrium glutamate, any hydrolysed protein, calcium caseinate, sodium caseinate, yeast food, yeast nutrient, autolysed yeast, gelatin, textured protein, soy protein isolate, whey protein isolate, *vetsin* and *ajinomoto*.

Trans fat – Trans fat are used to enhance and extend the shelf life of food products and is amongst the most dangerous substances that you can consume. Numerous studies show that trans fat increases LDL (bad) cholesterol levels while decreasing HDL (good) cholesterol, which then contributes to a higher risk of heart disease, strokes and general inflammation.

Sodium Sulphite (E211, E220-228) – According to the FDA, approximately one in 100 people are sensitive to sulphites in food. Most of these individuals are asthmatic, suggesting a link between asthma and sulphites.

Sodium Nitrate/Sodium Nitrite (E250 and E251) – These chemicals are used as preservatives, colouring and flavouring, and are highly carcinogenic once they enter the human digestive system. In our digestive system they begin to form a variety of nitrosamine compounds that enter the bloodstream and wreak havoc with a number of our internal organs: the liver and pancreas in particular. Sodium nitrite is widely regarded as a toxic ingredient. The United States Department of Agriculture (USDA) tried to ban this additive in the 1970s but was vetoed by food manufacturers who complained they had no alternative for preserving packaged meat products. Why does the industry still use it? Simple: this chemical just happens to turn meats bright red. It's actually a colour fixer, and it makes old, dead meats appear fresh and vibrant.

BHA and BHT (E320 and 321) – This common preservative keeps foods from changing colour, changing flavour or becoming rancid. It also affects the neurological system of the brain, alters behaviour and has the potential to cause cancer(s). BHA and BHT are oxidants which form cancer-causing reactive compounds in your body. These chemicals are the same chemicals found in airplane fuel. BHA and BHT keep your potato chips nice and crisp.

Sulphur Dioxide (E220) – The appearance of food would be very different if sulphur dioxide was not added – it would be brown in colour and would have a much shorter shelf life. Sulphur dioxide destroys Vitamins B1 and E and is not recommended for consumption by children. The International Labour Organization says to avoid E220 if you suffer from conjunctivitis, bronchitis, emphysema, bronchial asthma or cardiovascular disease. In some countries like Australia and New Zealand, sulphur dioxide is totally banned. In the US the use of sulphur dioxide on raw fruit and vegetables is banned. Sulphur dioxide is commonly used in most other parts of the world and is currently on the EU approved list of additives.

Potassium Bromate (E924) – An additive used in baked goods and breads. It is used to increase the volume in breads, making them fluffier and whiter. Potassium bromate has been linked to thyroid issues and thyroid cancer. It is banned in the United Kingdom, Canada, Brazil and the European Union. Even small amounts in bread can create problems for humans.

Potassium *Sorbate* (E202) – Potassium *sorbate* is used to prevent mould growth in foods. In a study done in Turkey, potassium *sorbate* was found to cause damage to the DNA of unborn children.

Benzoic Acid (E 210) – Benzoic acid is used as a preservative in cereals, low-sugar products, meats and drinks. It can inhibit the digestive enzyme functions and lessen glycine levels in the body. It is particularly bad for people who have food allergies that manifest in the forms of hives, asthma and hay fever.

Calcium Sulphate (E226) – This additive also functions as a preservative. It makes a product look fresh all the time even though in normal circumstances it would be almost rotten. It may cause low blood pressure, flushing, bronchial problems and anaphylactic shock.

Potassium Nitrate (E249) – Potassium nitrate is used to prolong the shelf life of canned meats. This additive has the ability of lowering the blood's capacity of carrying oxygen around the body. It also has the tendency to combine with other substances and form carcinogens known as nitrosamines.

Artificial colours – For years the effects of artificial food colourings on our health have been under investigation. Food colouring has conclusively been linked to the following cancers – thyroid, adrenal, bladder, kidney and brain cancers as well as to syndromes like attention deficit disorder (ADD) and attention deficit hyperactivity disorder (ADHD) as well as a huge quantity of common allergies and skin conditions.

FOODS WE THINK ARE GOOD BUT ARE NOT

So, in general, there are very few people who are not aware that processed foods are not that good for us, but what about the foods that we consider 'healthy' but are not quite good for us? What are these foods and how are they detrimental to our health?

MILK / DAIRY PRODUCTS

For many years I have been trying to convince people of the dangers of milk and dairy products. It is probably one of the most difficult things for most of them to hear as we have all grown up with the idea that milk was the healthiest thing we could drink. We have been led to believe by excellent marketing campaigns worldwide, in the 'health' benefits of milk and that milk and dairy products are the best source of calcium to make our bones strong and our teeth even stronger.

- Milk does have lots of calcium in it but we, as humans, cannot absorb it. For us to absorb calcium we need magnesium at a specific ratio of 2:1. Thus to absorb 500 mg of calcium, we need 250 mg of magnesium to do this, but in cow's milk the ratio is 10:1; so we can't absorb the calcium even if we wanted to. This could be why osteoporosis is on the rise. We have been told the best source of calcium for bones is from milk; but, in fact, the incorrect calcium/magnesium ratio might actually promote the calcium to be leached from our bones making them more brittle.

- In numerous studies, the findings are incontrovertible that higher dairy intake is linked to increased risk of prostate cancer and ovarian cancer.

- There is now substantial evidence that protein from cow's milk may play a role in triggering type 1 diabetes through a process called molecular mimicry.

- It is well-documented that the populations that consume more dairy products have higher rates of MS than those populations that don't.

- In studies on both humans and animals, dairy protein has been shown to increase Insulin-like Growth Factor-1 (IGF-1) levels. IGF-1 is a growth hormone that we normally have and our bodies control with their own hormones. When you get a dose of this extra IGF-1, it prompts not only the person to grow unnaturally but can also encourage cancer cells and tumours to grow at a rapid rate.

- Dairy products and milk can increase LDL cholesterol.

NOTE

It is important to note that a glass of nut milk or 1 tablespoon of blackstrap molasses will give you more absorbable calcium than any cup of cow's milk.

- The primary milk protein (casein) has, in experimental animal studies, been seen to promote cancer.
- D-galactose, one of the ingredients in milk and dairy products, has been found to be pro-inflammatory and a factor that accelerates the aging process.
- Higher milk intake is linked to acne and obesity.
- Milk intake has been implicated in constipation and chronic ear infections.
- Milk is perhaps the most common self-reported food allergen in the world.
- Milk is full of hormones and antibiotics.
- It was reported recently that if milk wasn't pasteurised it actually could poison us due to all the pus and blood found in it. This is because the cows from large dairy farms are all on constant hormones to make them produce more and more milk. Over milking causes major mastitis in cows' udders.

What are your options?
- Replace cow's milk with alternative milks like almond, macadamia, walnut, cashew, hazelnut, pistachio, oat, rice or quinoa milk. Try a variety and see which ones you like.
- If you can't give up milk, buy organic milk – one that you have good evidence has not had any hormones and antibiotics added.
- Buy raw milk – but only from good sources.
- Find humane dairy farms that care for the cows and do not give them chemicals.

WHEAT AND GLUTEN

Wheat has received such bad press over the years as more and more people become wheat or gluten intolerant. The main thing in wheat that is causing problems is gluten. Gluten is the protein that is found in wheat. It helps bread to become softer, more fluffy and chewy.

Unfortunately, the wheat that we are eating today is a totally different wheat to that which our ancestors used to eat even 50 years ago – and here is where the problem arises. Wheat manufacturers have cross-bred and modified wheat to make it a hardier and a better growing crop. They have done this by introducing some compounds to wheat that aren't meant to be there and are not entirely beneficial for humans. In fact, wheat should be called hybridised wheat. Our bodies just don't recognise it, don't break it down and don't react well to it – and this is causing an abundance of problems in our systems.

So what is wheat – or rather this hybridised wheat – doing to our systems?

- It is raising our blood sugar levels and is linked to type 1 diabetes.
- It increases our gut autoimmunity: this means it makes the gut more permeable, so all kinds of particles can get into the bloodstream which can then trigger the immune system to overreact and cause allergies to flourish.
- It inhibits the absorption of important minerals, the lack of which has been linked to many different conditions.
- It aggravates our intestines and can cause abdominal pain, swelling and discomfort, constipation, diarrhoea, Crohn's disease and ulcerative colitis.
- Wheat is addictive – the more you eat the more you want to eat.
- Wheat and gluten are highly acid-forming and cause inflammation in the body. Inflammation is the key trigger to most diseases.
- Most breads have bromated flours in them. Bromates are highly toxic and can create big problems within our system. (Please read about bromated flours in the previous section.)

Unfortunately, wheat plays a big role in diets throughout the world, so how do we reduce wheat in our own diet?

- Avoid highly processed and refined wheats. So pre-packaged sliced white breads should be a definite no-no.
- Buy breads from a reliable baker who, ideally, uses bromate-free, organic or unbleached (not heavily refined) flours.
- Opt for breads or baked goods made from different flours like coconut, buckwheat, oat, almond, tapioca, chickpea, sorghum, teff, cassava, amaranth or rice flours.
- Buy or make sourdough breads whenever you can. Sourdough breads are made from wheat flour but the flour has been fermented. This breaks the gluten down which makes it more digestible than standard bread and more nutritious too. How does it do this? During the fermentation process, lactic acids are produced which break down the hard to digest gluten as well as help to neutralise the phytates in flour. Phytates inhibit the absorption of certain vitamins. This process makes the vitamins and minerals in the flour more available to the body. Some people with coeliac disease (the condition where one has lost the ability to break down gluten, which in turn makes gluten a real poison for that person) can actually eat sourdough breads.

- Even if you are not intolerant to wheat and gluten, avoid becoming intolerant by only eating wheat-based foods 2–3 times a week. This can dramatically slow down your chances of ever becoming wheat intolerant.

SUGAR – THE NUMBER 1 KILLER

Where should I start? To be clear, what we are talking about here is refined sugar. Sugar actually starts out somewhat healthily and not at all white. So, what happens to it and what makes it so unhealthy?

Sugar starts off as a plant – either a sugar cane or a beet. These plants get boiled which starts the separation of the sugar from the fibre. The sugar liquid is then spun, leaving little white crystals; ironically, it is the liquid that is left behind that is the good stuff – full of minerals and vitamins – whilst the white crystals, or 'white gold' as it was called in the 16th Century, that is left is devoid of any nutritional value whatsoever. In spite of the lack of nutritional value, the white crystals taste good and are very addictive.

My personal belief, and the belief of some others, is that because refined sugar has been so stripped of nutritional value, it is constantly on the hunt to find the nutrients that it has lost. Therefore when we eat sugar, it actually leeches vitamins and minerals from our systems in its attempt to become "whole" again.

According to a 2016 study on sugar, an individual consumes an average of 130 pounds or 286 kg of sugar per year. Imagine the damage done by that amount of white sugar going into your bodies hunting for vitamins and minerals? This then in turn leaves our bodies stripped of essential minerals and vitamins, and thus open to a whole host of diseases.

How exactly does sugar harm our bodies?
- Sugar feeds cancer cells and helps them to multiply.
- Sugar has the same impact on our liver that alcohol does.
- Sugar affects our hormones – it impacts our kidneys and our cortisol levels which then leads to hormonal imbalances which can affect fertility and mood: i.e., depression and anxiety.
- Sugar affects our brain and how it functions. You might feel it through depression, brain fog, memory loss and Alzheimer's.

- Sugar has unique fat-promoting effects. As the calories are empty calories, this can translate into an increased calorie intake which leads to weight gain and obesity.
- Sugar causes massive dopamine releases in the brain, which makes sugar highly addictive – so we just want more and more and more.
- Sugar can cause insulin resistance, a stepping stone towards metabolic syndrome and diabetes.
- Sugar raises your cholesterol and plays a big role in heart disease.
- Sugar is inflammation's best friend. Inflammation is the key to most major diseases. So, the bottom line is to reduce your refined sugar intake.

If you find that you crave sugar then your body is telling you a few things:
- You've probably had too much sugar and you are slightly addicted to sugar.
- You may have a condition called candida or thrush, which makes you crave sugar.
- Your chromium or magnesium mineral levels are low and you need to start supplementing.

Here are some good sugars you can consume, in moderation:
- Organic un-sulphured blackstrap molasses
- Raw organic honey
- Raw maple syrup
- Raw coconut sugar

Recommended daily sugar intake:

Females	25 g	5–6 teaspoons a day
Males	36 g	9 teaspoons a day
Children	12–16 g	3–4 teaspoons a day

An example of how much sugar there is in our foods:

A can of coke will have 36 g.

A chocolate chip will have 5 g.

A Mars bar will have 68 g.

MEAT

Humans have been eating meat since they began to roam the earth so why does meat now have such a bad reputation? Often people assume that I must be vegetarian (which I am not) and then they proudly say that they never touch the stuff. But why? Over the years, meat, especially red meat, has been lambasted in the press as it has been linked to heart conditions, high bad cholesterol levels and making our digestion more acidic. Meat is known to be hard to digest and is said to rot in the colon. It is accused of causing some cancers and has even been linked to diabetes.

Yes, meat can cause all the above problems if it is eaten in excess and if we don't know what kind of meat it is that we are eating. However, if we ate meat the way we were supposed to, not every day and more as a treat then as the norm, none of the above problems would apply.

Bear in mind that meat is a great source of Vitamin B12 and iron – two very important nutrients that we need constantly, especially growing children. Actually one of the most absorbable ways of getting B12 is through meat. The problem is twofold: we are eating too much meat – especially too much 'bad' meat – and the 'meat' that we are eating is not the same meat our ancient ancestors ate.

KNOW YOUR MEAT

So, to reiterate, humans have been eating meat since we began to walk the earth, but the meats we are now eating are vastly different – know your meat before you eat.

There are four different categories of meat:

Conventional Red Meat – This meat is completely different from the meat that our ancient ancestors chased or reared, killed and ate. Though derived from the same animal in name, the animals we eat now are usually born and raised in a factory and fed grain-based feed (feeds which are predominantly genetically modified organisms- GMO) and they will undoubtedly have received growth-promoting hormones, steroids and antibiotics. This makes for a much less healthy form of meat, which can cause problems.

White Meat – White meats include meat from poultry (chicken and turkey), veal and rabbit. Often seen as the healthier meat, nothing could be further from the truth. Not as high in fats, these meats are also fed foods that are not naturally eaten by the animals (mainly from GMO crops) and are given massive doses of antibiotics because of the conditions that they are raised in – not to mention the well-known fact that they are given growth hormones and steroids that force them to reach maturity in half the time that they would have naturally.

Processed Meat – Today, our meat products go through even more processing after the animals are slaughtered – they are smoked, cured, then treated with nitrates, preservatives, food additives, flavourings and often stuck together with meat glue. There is now concrete evidence that these meats cause cancers, especially pancreatic cancer.

Grass-fed, grass-finished or free-range organic meat – This is the type of meat we should all be eating, in moderation. This meat comes from animals that have been naturally fed and raised organically, without drugs and hormones. They have no artificial chemicals added to their food and can eat what they naturally are meant to eat, predominantly grass, shrubs, flowers or insects.

IS ORGANIC FOOD ALWAYS BETTER?

Organic fruits and vegetables that are produced locally are fantastic. Organic fruits and vegetables that have flown halfway around the world to hit your shelves – questionable. It's a matter of logic.

The meaning of 'organic' 15–20 years ago was very different to what it is today. Organic has become quite a big marketing buzzword in the food industry, and organic food often comes with a hefty price tag. Put the word "organic" on packaging and we feel the content is automatically healthier than processed alternatives. But be warned. Even if something has the word 'organic' on its label, it doesn't automatically mean that it is organic.

Often it will mean that a few choice items might have been organically grown, but most of the other ingredients will not be organic. A few organic ingredients do not mean that there aren't preservatives and additives in your expensive purchase. Sadly even if a fruit or vegetable has been grown organically in order for it to travel half way around the world and still look edible, it has to be sprayed and the spray is not organic.

If you want to choose the healthiest option, source for organic farms near you and try to buy locally. If there is no organic farm nearby, go for local products. Just make sure you wash them well in baking soda and vinegar – instructions in the next section.

DO WE REALLY NEED VITAMIN SUPPLEMENTS?

The sad truth is that as the world has become more globalised and we have become more to accustomed to berries and tomatoes all year around, our foods contain less vitamins and minerals and can no longer be a viable and reliable source of nutrition.

How do fruits and vegetables make their vitamins? They make vitamins from good fertile soil and sunshine. These are exactly the two things that we are not giving to our fruit and vegetable crops. Soil is not being allowed to rest and to re-fertilise itself by natural means: i.e. animal faeces and rotten vegetation. Instead, soil is being pumped full of artificial fertilisers and chemicals again and again to force crops to produce their yield faster and with greater abundance.

These crops are also being heavily sprayed with herbicides and pesticides. The run-off from these sprayed crops goes into the soil. This soil will then not be allowed to rest and detoxify itself, resulting in a 'tired soil' that becomes depleted of the nutrients that it needs to give the plants. Fruits and vegetables also need the sun to make their vitamins and minerals, but because of the need to ship them around the world, they are often picked before they are ripe which does not allow their vitamins and minerals to reach their full potential. Once picked, the vitamins and minerals of the product slowly start depleting. Frequently, the product is then ripened with "artificial sunlight".

Not only are fruits and vegetables devoid of nutrients, some, not all, are also pumped full of chemicals and colours which give the fruit a healthy long-lasting appearance, but ultimately can harm our health.

I am not saying do not eat fruits and vegetables, quite the opposite. Our diets should be full of the fruits and vegetables that are good for us. How do we do this?

• Ideally buy locally grown organic fruits and vegetables whenever possible.
• In general opt for locally grown fruits and vegetables even over organic

if the organic produce has come from too far away (just make sure you soak them).
- If you have the luxury to live near farms, choose produce from small farms that do not have a high yield reputation.
- Buy fruits and vegetables that are in season.
- Soak fruit and vegetables in a mixture of baking soda and vinegar to remove any chemical residue that may be in the skin. Into 1 litre of water put 120 ml of vinegar and 2 tablespoons of baking soda.
- Many people, though, do not always have the choices I recommend nearby or on a daily basis. Supplementing then does become necessary to get the vital nutrients that our bodies need to be strong and healthy.

So yes we do need to supplement but we need to be careful – even with supplementing. Here are some guidelines we need to follow when choosing vitamin supplements:
- Choose liquid or powder supplements as opposed to capsules or pills.
- Only choose supplements that are derived from foods, herbs and plants.
- Check that there are not too many additives. The additives that are found in supplements that you want to stay away from are: magnesium stearate, sodium benzoate, titanium dioxide, artificial colours, hydrogenated oils, cupric sulphate, boric acid and ascorbic acid.
- Steer away from the mass-produced vitamins – those made by huge conglomerates (often owned by pharmaceutical companies) and opt for smaller businesses that you have researched about first.
- Research and look for a company with a philosophy that reflects their genuine interest in improving the health of the world.

WHAT ARE THE IMPORTANT NUTRIENTS, MINERALS AND VITAMINS WE NEED TO SUPPLEMENT?

Do we need to take millions of supplements? The short answer is no but due to a lack of nutrients from our diets, we should be aware that we can become depleted in some vitamins and minerals due to a deficiency in our diets. The supplements that I would advice you to take to keep your immune system strong would be the following:
- Vitamin B (complex)
- Vitamin C

- Vitamin D3 (if you have no access to the sun)
- Minerals – potassium, sodium, magnesium and zinc
- Omega-3 oils
- Probiotics

I am not saying that other vitamins and minerals aren't necessary. The ones listed above are the bare necessities that we need to be healthy, we use most rapidly and become most depleted in.

Do note, though, we should not be relying solely on pills or powders to get our "healthy" vitamins and minerals, whilst our diets are terrible. Most of our nutrition, vitamin and mineral intake should be obtained through good healthy whole unprocessed foods. There are many wonderful foods which will give us the essential vitamins and minerals and which we can use as medicines. I go into more detail on this in Part 2 and 3.

A 2004 report by the Institute of Medicine and the National Research Council stated "Adverse health effects from genetic engineering have not been documented in the human population, but the technique is new and concerns about its safety remain".

GENETICALLY MODIFIED (GM) FOODS – FOODS OUR BODIES DON'T RECOGNISE.

In 1994 the first genetically modified (GM) food substance was approved for release. It was a type of tomato that was called the Flavr Savr (which eventually failed and is no longer in existence). I read an article in TIME magazine discussing what exactly a genetically modified food was. It talked about these foods and what they could do for the world, but at the same time it also mentioned that, although the tomato was visually identical to a normal tomato, there was about a 5% genetic difference between a "normal" tomato and a GM tomato. The article went on to explain that there was only a 1% genetic difference between an ape and a human. This figure astounded me. Look at what a huge difference there is between an ape and a human. This made me pose the question that many are asking: are GM foods really safe to eat and do we actually know what we are eating? Twenty three years after the invention of genetically modified foods, this question is still not answered. What we do know, however, is that the world in the past 23 years has seen a huge rise in the occurrence of food intolerances, diabetes, cancers, autism, obesity, heart conditions and autoimmune diseases. Is this a coincidence?

As always there are two sides to the argument. Science argues that the modification of foods has helped certain food industries from extinction (due to certain viruses as in the case of the Hawaiian Papaya) as well as enabling us to feed more of the world's population with more fortified and nutritious food. However, the claim that we need GM crops to feed the world ignores the real, root problem: hunger is caused by poverty and inequality, not from a lack of food.

The truth is that we already produce enough food to feed 10 billion people, which is the number our population is predicted to reach by 2050. A third of this food produced around the world is wasted every year. People are generally hungry not because of insufficient food production, but because they do not have the money to buy food, do not have access to land to grow food, or because of poor food distribution systems and a lack of reliable water and farming infrastructure. GM crops do not help solve these causes of hunger. In fact GM crops have done very little of what they had promised to do.

- GM crops have not increased yields.
- GM crops have not increased farmers' incomes. In fact, quite the opposite is true as farmers are forced to buy their seeds annually as opposed to using the seeds from the previous crops.
- GM crops are patented and owned by large companies which now control 98% of GM acres.
- GM crops have increased the use of herbicides and pesticide by 24% worldwide.

So not only do we not know exactly what we are eating, we are also eating foods that are more contaminated with herbicides, which is not a good combination for our health. Are all foods modified? No.

The following foods are genetically modified:
- Corn
- Papaya
- Rapeseed/canola
- Rice
- Soy
- Sugar beet (where sugar comes from)
- Yellow squash
- Zucchini (courgette)

WATER

We all know water is important, but I think many don't realise just how important water is and just how many elements of our life water affects. For example, inadequate water consumption can directly be linked to back pain, depression, hormonal imbalances, skin issues and every single metabolic process in our bodies. Without food we can survive for weeks, but without water our bodies would cease to function in days.

Here are just some of the ways water helps us:
- Water is vital in helping our body to detoxify. Toxins we take in from our environment, through our foods and from various medicines need to be eliminated from our bodies otherwise the toxic overload becomes too much for our systems and we can get very sick. Water is what our detoxifying organs need to work more effectively.
- Water is crucial for our kidneys and liver but not only for detoxification; it also helps to keep our hormones balanced. Without water, blood can become quite thick and harder to "clean", which can lead to hormone imbalance and toxic overload.
- Water helps to moisten the mucous membranes of our respiratory and digestive systems.
- Water helps to aid our digestive process and prevent constipation.
- Water helps to maintain the skin's texture and appearance; it helps slow down the ageing process.
- Water carries essential nutrients and oxygen to our cells. These nutrients and oxygen are crucial in our fight against so many diseases, especially cancers.

- Water serves as a shock absorber inside the eyes, spinal cord and in the amniotic fluid sac surrounding the foetus in pregnancy.
- Water helps reduce fluid retention. The body will retain fluid if there is too little water in the cells. If the body receives enough water on a regular basis, there will be no need for it to conserve water and this will reduce fluid retention.

Quite an impressive list. So water is vital to everything. Unlike camels, however, our bodies have no way to store extra water, so we must replenish our water throughout the day, on a regular basis. So how do we do this and how much water do we really need to be healthy? Are all waters created equally? No. There are waters that are more helpful when maintaining balance in your body and there are waters that can actually throw you off balance. Here is a guide to good water sources and some sources that you should avoid, if you have the luxury to do so. But remember in the case of dehydration, don't be too picky about which water source it has come from.

GOOD WATER

Spring water bottled at source – Spring water is full of naturally occurring minerals and is at the top of the list.

Artesian spring water – Artesian spring water comes from a natural source but is bottled off-site and is processed and purified.

Mineral water – Mineral water could be natural spring water or artesian water but it comes from an underground source and contains at least 250 parts per million (ppm) of dissolved solids, including minerals and trace elements. Mineral waters are good but watch the sodium levels in mineral water, as they can be high and lead to fluid retention and high blood pressure. Limit the amount of mineral water or choose low-sodium varieties (less than 30 mg sodium per 100 ml).

Well water – Well water comes from a hole drilled in the ground that taps into a water source. A pump brings it to the surface. If you do not have access to city water, then you would need a well. Always make sure that well water has been tested properly for chemicals that might have leached from surrounding farms etc.

Filtered tap water – Filtered tap water normally comes from a municipal source and is generally deemed safe. However, additives like chlorine which is linked to respiratory ailments and cancer, and fluoride which is linked to autism and thyroid issues are added. So if you do drink tap water, you must invest in a good filter that removes not only bacteria and pathogens but also chlorine, additives and even metals.

WORST SOURCES OF WATER

Unfiltered tap water – Depending where you live, unfiltered tap water often contains toxic heavy metals such as lead, mercury, copper, cadmium and aluminium. It also can have volatile organic chemicals (VOCs) such as pesticides and herbicides, hormones, pharmaceuticals, chemicals from irresponsible manufacturers, as well as thousands of untested chemicals from our personal care and household cleaning products.

It is also full of 'water treatment additives' such as chlorine, fluoride and other toxic chemicals that are put into the water to kill off "nasty things" and which make the tap water 'drinkable'.

Reverse osmosis (RO) water – Unlike tap water, RO water is too clean, as everything has been stripped out. By drinking RO water, you can become seriously deficient in magnesium and calcium. This water could potentially leach other important minerals out of our system leaving us extremely mineral deficient. If you have to drink RO water, make sure you add in your own minerals.

Deionised water – Deionised water is more susceptible to attracting the metals found in your plumbing than mineralised water because it is a less stable form of water and could put you at risk of toxic metal contamination. The calcium and magnesium in regular water may help prevent the accumulation of toxic substances in your drinking water by stabilising the water and acting as antitoxic substances.

Distilled water – Free of dissolved minerals, distilled water has the special property of being able to actively absorb toxic substances from the body and eliminate them. However because this water is so quick to absorb toxins it can also absorb minerals from your system, especially potassium, magnesium, sodium and chloride. If we become deficient in these minerals it has quite an effect on our bodies from irregular heart beat to high blood pressure, just to name a few. Be warned that cooking with distilled water will lower the nutritional value of your food.

HOW MUCH WATER DO WE NEED?

While water from herbal teas, diluted juices and even milk can account for 20% of the daily amount of water, they should not replace water. For instance, eight glasses of juice or nut milk should not replace eight glasses of water.

These adequate intakes include all fluids, but it is preferable that the majority of intake is from plain water (except for infants where fluid intake is met by breast milk or infant formula).

Sedentary people, people living in cold environments, or people who eat a lot of high-water content foods (such as fruits and vegetables) may need less water.

Can we drink too much water?

Drinking too much water can also damage the body and can cause hyper hydration (water intoxication), which can be fatal. Drink water but don't drink it all at one go and don't drink too much.

If you find that you drink and urinate immediately afterwards then you would need to check your kidney health as the kidneys might not be holding on to the water. This means even though you are drinking you can still be dehydrated or your mineral levels might be compromised.

If you're not used to drinking water daily, be sure to only increase your intake by one cup at a time so you don't overload your kidneys.

"In medicine, the hygiene hypothesis states that a lack of early childhood exposure to infectious agents, symbiotic microorganisms (e.g. gut flora or probiotics), and parasites increases susceptibility to allergic diseases by suppressing the natural development of the immune system. In particular, the lack of exposure is thought to lead to defects in the establishment of immune tolerance.

It is now also recognised that the "reduced microbial exposure" concept applies to a much broader range of chronic inflammatory diseases than asthma and hay fever, which includes diseases such as type 1 diabetes and multiple sclerosis, and also some types of depression and cancer."

– David P. Strachan, MD, PhD of St George's University of London, 1989

The "hygiene hypothesis", which states that we have over-sanitised our living environments, interests me profoundly. One of the reasons that it struck a chord with me was that it sounded very familiar to something my teacher told us when I was studying acupressure. Our teacher said that if you wanted to gain the best immunity you should take a spoonful of dirt from any country that you lived in or travelled to and mix this into some water and drink it. This would give you immunity to most of the diseases that were present in this new environment. Like Strachan's hygiene hypothesis, I loved the concept of this, but have not been brave enough to try it. However, the concept makes sense.

Following from this, my family and I were recently in some very basic schools in rural Cambodia and Indonesia. I couldn't help but notice that there was not one sign on a classroom door indicating it was a nut, milk, wheat, strawberry, kiwi-free zone. Whereas every other door at my children's swanky, modern, private school has food-free zones everywhere and the nurse's office is piled high with EpiPens. What's the difference?

Of course, some may argue that in the underdeveloped world, these allergies aren't documented or picked up as easily or readily as in the developed world.

One of my good friends agrees with me on the hygiene hypothesis ever since she and her family moved from hygienic Singapore to rural Argentina. Her children now attend the local school there. She noticed that allergies were almost non-existent at the school compared to the school that her children had attended in Singapore, where every other room had allergy warnings on the door. When I asked her what she thought the difference was, she said that kids were allowed to be kids – they were outside a lot, they didn't eat as much processed foods (as they weren't available) and when kids got sick, they were allowed to be sick and not rushed off to a doctor.

This again is in line with the findings of Strachan's "hygiene hypothesis". Could the reason we are having more health issues, especially in the developed world be caused by the fact that we don't let our children get dirty enough or allow them to get sick? And if they do get sick, we step in with powerful and damaging chemicals which override their immune system? On top of this, our homes have become too clean, too hygienic and we have been taught to become bacteria phobic. This theory follows the findings of many microbiologists who are concerned that the good bacteria in our environment, the bacteria that we need and which can help us fight off many illnesses are being destroyed, resulting in us succumbing to more and more serious diseases.

The thing is, we need to get sick with coughs, colds and stomach bugs from viruses and bacteria to gain immunity from them and possibly to gain strength to fight off more serious disease like cancers, diabetes and autoimmune issues later in life. This is especially true of children. We all started as children and children need to get sick to strengthen and build their immune systems. An average child should get sick a maximum of four times a year. For adults, we look at a healthy adult getting sick 0–2 times a year. We shouldn't be afraid to get sick. We should acknowledge the sickness and realise that our body is doing something it is naturally made to do. Take a step back and support yourself through the illness, rest and let your body heal.

PRACTICAL ADVICE FOR HEALTH

HOW TO CHOOSE A DOCTOR

Here we must again follow the wise words from Hippocrates and the Hippocratic oath that all medical doctors are made to take before they become a fully-fledged doctor.

Always remember medicine is not an exact science but "an educated guess". Doctors go through years of training to analyse and evaluate but at the end it is an educated guess that they are giving you. Doctors can be wrong and you have the right to ask questions and challenge a diagnosis. A good doctor will listen and work with you.

If you go to a doctor and he/she gives you medicine, don't be surprised – this is what doctors are fundamentally taught to do. If you are looking for a doctor who will also give you choices and alternatives, then try to find a doctor who has also studied alternative medicine. If your doctor is one to dismiss alternative medicine, and if this is not what you want, change your doctor.

A doctor is someone who:
- You can trust and has your and your family's best health interests at heart.
- Has time for you, will listen to your concerns and is willing to discuss alternatives.
- Will allow you to discuss altering the immunisation schedules or allow you to wait till the fever has run one more day before insisting on medicating, or will encourage tests before medicating for a 'just in case' scenario.

FEVERS

I believe the greatest injustice that conventional medicine has done is to make us fear and look negatively at fevers. Fevers are one of the most important healing tools our bodies have; the last thing we should do is to suppress them.

We have been taught by conventional medicine to think that fevers are dangerous, dreaded and to be immediately suppressed by drugs. This is not how the body was made to work. Fevers are the best thing we can have when it comes to fighting diseases. Again, I will quote Hippocrates here. He said, "Give me a fever and I can cure any illness". For if we could actually make fevers happen in our bodies, we could pretty much help most diseases. Unfortunately, as soon as we have fevers, people panic and try to stop this incredible curative power.

"Contrary to popular belief, a fever is not a symptom to be treated but a sign of a healthy, functioning immune system naturally working to heal the body. The rise in body temperature is caused by the intensification of efforts by the body's defences as they fight microbes and purify the internal terrain. Lowering a fever through the use of drugs counters the body's ability to fight illness, infection, or poisoning and can greatly lengthen recovery time."
– Christopher Vasey ND, *The Healing Power of Fevers*

In my opinion, we should not suppress a fever but work with its curative powers. Of course, you should never leave a fever and lie in bed feeling horrible or leave a family member to just suffer through his or hers. What you should do is work with the fever and support whoever is having the fever. Know that you can give a bit of relief and comfort naturally, at the same time, benefit from this very natural healing power. In Part 3 on pg 170, I will go through the steps on how you can both relieve the discomfort and support the healing power of fevers.

DETOXIFY TO BALANCE

As you may have understood by now, the keys to good health lie in a combination of many things, with the ultimate goal being balance. We should eat as healthily as possible, avoid medicines whenever we can, reduce our chemical exposure, drink lots of water and detoxify.

One of the most important ways our bodies achieve balance is through detoxification. Our detox organs (liver, kidneys, intestines, colon, lungs, and skin) work 24 hours a day to rid our bodies of the harmful toxins and sticky waste products that accumulate in our cells.

The practice of detoxification has been used for centuries by cultures around the world, not to mention that every religion has a history of fasting and "purification" which plays a big role in helping people reach a higher level of understating of their faith.

Detoxification is about resting, cleansing and nourishing the body from the inside out. Removing and eliminating toxins through detoxification and feeding your body with healthy nutrients can protect you from disease, renew your ability to maintain optimum health and even bring you to a higher level of spirituality.

Does this mean you have to go on a crazy detox diet for weeks or months on end, starve and drink only liquids? No. What I am talking about is a sensible way of living and eating that allows your body to take a break from the constant barrage of chemicals and toxins encountered in your environment and foods. This gives our body and our detox organs a well-deserved chance to rest and regenerate.

Doing a detox for a week or 10 days every six months to a year is optimal and you should plan to do this when it suits you. However there are also lots of things one can do on a regular to almost daily basis to support and continuously detox your system. Here are a few tips that you can add daily or weekly into your routine, which will help ease the burden on your organs and system.

- Start your day with water. The first thing that should enter your system should be water. Optional: Squeeze ½ a lemon or add 1–2 teaspoons of apple cider vinegar into the water.
- Eat as many fermented foods as possible. There should be at least one fermented food or drink in your diet on a daily a basis – kombucha tea, kefir, sauerkraut, miso soup, yoghurt.
- Eat plenty of fibre through organically grown fresh fruits and vegetables and various fibrous foods. Adding 1 tablespoon of psyllium husks into your morning water or juice really helps to scrub out the colon and intestines.
- Add detoxifying foods into your diet on a daily basis. A list of detoxifying foods is provided in Part 2 – Mother Nature's Medical Kit.
- Cleanse and protect the liver by taking herbs such as dandelion root, burdock, milk thistle and green tea – you can take these as supplements or infusions.
- Take Vitamin C, which helps the body produce glutathione, a liver compound that drives away toxins.
- Drink at least two litres of good quality water a day (see pg 42 for more information on good sources of water).
- Spend 15 minutes a day breathing deeply to allow oxygen to circulate more completely through your system. Help your body produce more oxygen by taking iron-rich foods – blackstrap molasses is my favourite.

- Practice hydrotherapy by taking a very hot shower for five minutes, allowing the water to run on your back. Follow with cold water for 30 seconds. This stimulates the circulation and the lymphatic system.
- Sweat in a sauna so your body can eliminate waste.
- Daily dry skin brushing is a way to remove toxins through your pores. Start with your feet and brush upwards towards the heart. Always brush towards the heart (so downwards from above).

- Choose one day a week, I prefer a Friday or Saturday, for a weekly detox bath. Into a warm, verging on hot, bath, add either 340 g Epsom salts (for a more mild detox) or 170 g Epsom salts, 85 g baking soda and 120 ml apple cider vinegar, plus one of the following detoxifying essential oils: thyme *vulgaris*, lemon, mandarin, juniper, rosemary or grapefruit. Add 10–15 drops of your chosen oil to your bath. Make sure you do this before bed as you will feel tired after this.
- One of the most important ways to detox is to exercise on a regular basis. Thirty minutes to one hour every day is optimal or a minimum of three times a week. The best detoxing forms of exercise are yoga, stretching, qigong and martial arts, but any form of exercise is better than none at all.
- Do not become detox obsessed. Our bodes are made to detoxify, so if you do have things that are not good for you (in moderation), don't worry, your body will know what to do.

Finally, I'd just like to say have faith – our bodies are made to heal. We just need to give ourselves the time and support. We are such an impatient society that we want instant and quick fixes. Thus, we end up taking medicines that tend to mask a problem. The alternative way will take longer and may not be the most comfortable – sometimes requiring lifestyle changes – but the results are long-term and can be life-changing.

Part Two

MOTHER NATURE'S MEDICAL KIT

Now is the time to share all the tools that I use to treat the conditions I detail in Part 3. Creating your own Mother Nature's Medical Kit is neither difficult, expensive nor perplexing. In fact, it is simply rewarding.

There are four, very important, sections here:

CREATING YOUR HEALING PANTRY

how to use foods, herbs and natural products for health, most of which can be found in your kitchen cabinet or local supermarket.

HEALING WITH ESSENTIAL OILS

how to use and combine essential oils to optimise healing.

HEALING POINTS

how to use acupressure to support healing.

HEALING THE EMOTIONS: THE BACH FLOWER REMEDIES

how to use the Bach flower remedies
to restore emotional health.

The beauty of using the tools that Mother Nature has given to us in the forms of food, plants, herbs and acupressure points is that you are working with your body and nature to heal yourself. As a result you can get rid of bacteria, fungus, viruses and parasites with no harmful side effects. Your system is left stronger and healthier by these problems are gone. This is very different from conventional medicine, which can upset the body's balance and sometimes create a new problem as a side effect.

The following list of foods, herbs, essential oils and Bach flower remedies are all the ingredients that I use to treat the conditions described in detail in Part 3.

I personally use these on my patients, family and friends and have had excellent results time and time again.

CREATING YOUR HEALING PANTRY

TIP

If you have sunburn or have burnt yourself on something hot, apply the gel on your skin for instant relief.

ALOE VERA

Whether you drink it, eat it or use it as a gel, aloe vera has a multitude of healing properties. It contains high levels of Vitamins A, C, E, B12, folic acid and choline – all of these vitamins are crucial for a strong immune system and support the antibacterial properties of aloe. Aloe vera also contains an enormous amount of enzymes, which help to fight inflammation. Packed full of essential minerals like potassium, magnesium, sodium, chromium, calcium, selenium and zinc, just drink a shot of aloe vera juice first thing in the morning if your mineral balance needs a boost. High in antioxidants, it accelerates healing of all kinds due to its high mineral content: it was also used as a means to control diabetes for centuries.

ASPARAGUS

Asparagi are loaded with fibre, folate, Vitamins A, C, E and K as well as the mineral chromium. This vegetable is also a rich source of glutathione – a detoxifying compound that helps break down carcinogens and free radicals. Asparagus has been found to help our brains fight cognitive decline. It helps delivers folate, which works with Vitamin B12, to help prevent cognitive impairment.

It's also known to help with liver drainage. The liver is responsible for filtering out the toxic materials from the food and drinks we consume. Often toxins can block up the drainage and, as the drain gets "blocked up", asparagus has a bit of a *draino* effect as it unblocks 'that drain".

Asparagus also contain high levels of the amino acid asparagine, which serves as a natural diuretic. Being a diuretic, this not only helps the body to release unnecessary fluids but it also gets rid of excess salts which can really help those with oedema, high blood pressure and kidney stones.

AVOCADOS

Avocados are full of Vitamins K, C, B5, B6, E, folate (which helps us absorb B12) and potassium. They used to have a bad reputation as they are, indeed, high in fat. However, this fat is a good fat, which we now know, is incredibly important for us. Good fats provide essential fatty acids, keep our skin soft, help our bodies deliver fat-soluble vitamins and are a great source of energising fuel. Avocados also help our bodies to reduce LDL (bad cholesterol), raise HDL (good cholesterol) and are key in reducing high triglycerides. Avocados are also one of the most potassium-rich foods we know of – even higher than bananas. Therefore avocados will also help to regulate our blood pressure.

BAKING SODA OR BICARBONATE OF SODA

Throughout this book you will find it hard not to find a remedy that does not have baking soda (bicarbonate of soda) in it. Baking soda is one of my all-time favourite remedies. Baking soda comes from the earth and should be viewed as one of the most useful substances in the world as it can actually save lives. How? By drinking a small amount of baking soda, this helps to alkalise our bodies and our cells – rapidly. Most of our health problems (indeed most diseases in general) are a result of our systems being too acidic. Most of the modern foods we eat encourage this acidity and leave us susceptible to diverse problems. Baking soda can correct this acidity within seconds and turn us into balanced alkaline people. Fungus, viruses, bacteria and even cancer cells do not like alkaline surroundings so the benefits are immediate.

BEETROOT

Beetroots are high in immune-boosting Vitamin C, folate, fibre, potassium, iron and manganese. They also contain something called betaine, a nutrient that helps protect cells, proteins and enzymes from environmental stress. Beetroots are also known to help fight inflammation, protect internal organs, and improve

TIP
Drink a glass of beetroot juice before physical exercise. This has been documented to increase athletic performance.

vascular risk factors – and, as if that was not enough, they help lower blood pressure and enhance physical performance.

Beetroots are also high in the phytonutrient department – this is what gives them their beautiful crimson colour. These phytonutrients are now recognised to help fight off cancer. Research has shown that beetroot extract can reduce multi-organ tumour formations in animals and it is now being studied for use in humans – particularly those being treated for pancreatic, breast and prostate cancers. Beetroots don't just protect us and enhance our well-being – while possibly killing off cancer cells – but they are also incredibly good at detoxing. Beetroots help to bind toxins to other molecules so that they can be excreted from your system. This will help to purify your blood and your liver – who can argue with that.

BLACK PEPPER

Black pepper is a rich source of manganese, iron, potassium, Vitamin C, Vitamin K, chromium, calcium and dietary fibre. Black pepper stimulates the taste buds in such a way that an alert is sent to the stomach to increase hydrochloric acid secretion, thereby improving digestion. Hydrochloric acid is necessary for the digestion of proteins and bicarbonates. When the body's production of hydrochloric acid is insufficient, food may sit in the stomach for an extended period of time, leading to heartburn or indigestion. Not only does black pepper help you derive the most benefit from your food but the outer layer of the peppercorn also stimulates the breakdown of fat cells and stimulates your metabolism.

Finally, and most importantly, black pepper helps us to absorb and activate various nutrients such as Vitamins A, C, B12, selenium, beta-carotene and the *curcumin* from turmeric. So, basically, we can take or eat huge amounts of these vital nutrients but may not absorb or access their benefits. Thank goodness for black pepper, which helps us to do this in such a pleasant manner everyday.

BROCCOLI

Broccoli is so packed full of vitamins and minerals that it should be looked at as a multivitamin food, as it really has a little bit of everything we need. Of the many nutrients that broccoli has, the two things that really stand out to me are the levels of chromium and sulforaphane.

TIP
With a pepper grinder, grind black pepper into all your food and even into your juice in the morning.

SIMPLY NATURAL HEALTH

Broccoli is an excellent source of chromium, which helps prevent and even can reverse the onset of diabetes.

Sulforaphane is thought to have protective effects against various types of cancers, but also, specifically, helps the body to work with the enzymes in the liver to turn toxins into something your body can eliminate easily.

CABBAGE

Forget oranges. Cabbage is one of the vegetables that is most packed full of Vitamin C – one cup of cabbage will give you 75% of what you need every day – and if you drink it in a juice this doubles its potency.

Sulphur compounds found in cabbage have natural antibacterial properties as well as effective cancer-fighting properties. Cabbage's antibacterial properties work inside the body's cell processes and aid in detoxifying major organs. These same properties help to boost the immune system, which increases the body's resistance to invading bacteria and viruses.

Naturally antibacterial, eating shredded raw cabbage in your salad, as a side dish in the form of coleslaw, or drinking fresh cabbage juice (with manuka honey added to sweeten it) is an excellent way to fight bacterial infections, detoxify your system after any medication, improve digestion, heal your stomach lining and help to heal stomach ulcers.

CAYENNE PEPPER

The active ingredient in cayenne pepper is called capsaicin and is what gives the heat and power to the pepper. Cayenne is a powerful and pure stimulant; it increases the power of the pulse and helps to carry blood to all parts of the body, which improves circulation and therefore benefits the cardiovascular system. As it has such a powerful effect on the circulation, it is well-documented that cayenne is a cardiac tonic that can actually help to rebuild the heart. Even more importantly, it can actually stop a heart attack. It does this by forcing the circulation to flow and restoring balance to the circulatory system.

Cayenne pepper is also a haemostat, which means that, applied topically, it can stop the flow of blood from a wound in seconds, and so it would be ideal to have cayenne pepper in your first-aid kit.

Cayenne pepper also breaks down mucus buildup and helps the body to flush mucus from the system. Once the mucus is removed, general relief from head cold and flu-like symptoms usually follow quickly.

TIP

If it's the time of time year where lots of sweets are being served (e.g. holiday seasons or birthdays), make sure you serve lots of broccoli as the high levels of chromium in broccoli will help to counteract the bad effects that sugar has on our bodies.

To top it all off cayenne is also a vermifuge – which means it gets rid of worms and parasites. It actually paralyses intestinal worms, which allows them to be expelled through the gut.

CHAMOMILE

There are two types of chamomiles – German and Roman. Chamomile Roman is commonly sold as a calming tea which is good for insomnia and stomach aches. However, the real power behind both chamomiles is *apigenin*, which is the bioflavonoid that they contain. *Apigenin* helps to reduce anxiety and panic. It is excellent to take if you are nervous or prone to panic attacks. It also calms and clears inflammation in the respiratory system. Respiratory inflammation triggers an increase of mucus production. During hay fever season, chamomile can greatly reduce the symptoms of hay fever.

Perhaps the most important new research into the healing powers of chamomile concerns its ability to reduce the possibility of suffering strokes. Studies have indicated that people who drink chamomile tea on a regular basis are less likely to have a stroke than those who don't.

CINNAMON (STICKS AND POWDERED)

Cinnamon is very high in antioxidants, which protect the body from oxidative damage caused by free radicals.

It has huge antifungal, viral and vermifugal properties – it both protects, fights off and kills worms and parasites in the body.

Regular consumption of cinnamon has been linked to reduced heart disease, the world's most common cause of premature death. This may be because it also reduces levels of total cholesterol, LDL (bad) cholesterol and triglycerides – while leaving or even increasing HDL (good) cholesterol levels stable. A dose of just 120 mg of cinnamon per day could have all of these beneficial effects.

Cinnamon is well-known for its blood sugar lowering effect and can dramatically reduce insulin resistance, which is often the precursor to type 2 diabetes. For people with type 2 diabetes, 1 g of cinnamon per day has been proved to have beneficial effects on their blood markers. How does cinnamon do this? It interferes with numerous digestive enzymes, which in turn slows the breakdown of carbohydrates in the digestive tract. This ensures that not as much sugar is floating around in the bloodstream all at once.

Cinnamon also has a huge effect on neurodegenerative diseases such as Alzheimer's and Parkinson's disease. This is due to cinnamon's apparent effect on the buildup of a protein called "*tau*" in the brain. This buildup of *tau* in the brain stops the synapse from working properly, which contributes to memory loss. Cinnamon not only inhibits the buildup of this protein but also protects neurons, normalises neurotransmitter levels and improves motor function in the brain.

CLAY – ZEOLITE

There are many clays available but I use zeolite as it is quite safe, easy to use and effective. You can use it topically, as a poultice or in the bath. I, personally, like to drink it in water.

Zeolites are effective at absorbing heavy metals such as mercury, lead, aluminium, cadmium, and arsenic. In the 21st century these toxins are quickly accumulated in our bodies due to the overuse of chemicals in our food, household products, personal hygiene products, water and medical treatments. These heavy metals are highly toxic and create massive free radical stress in the brain, liver, kidneys and gut.

Zeolite has been shown to create an osmotic effect that helps pull these metals out of the tissue structure and into the zeolite matrix. It is a slow and steady process that could be used daily. Continually dislodging and removing heavy metals is absolutely essential for optimal health.

CLOVES

Cloves have played a huge role in many ancient medicines. Mostly known for their pain reducing benefits due to their anti-inflammatory properties, they have recently gained recognition for their powerful antiseptic, antiviral and antibacterial properties.

Not only are we finding cloves in conventional pain medication for toothaches but we are also now finding the active ingredients of clove being used in hospitals in antiseptic washes to help clean medical instruments and operating theatres.

Cloves also have the capacity to relieve upper respiratory infections. This is particularly true for sinusitis and any condition where there is great buildup of phlegm. Cloves help to break down phlegm, fight infection and are a strong expectorant, helping us to expel the phlegm from our system.

You can use clove oil to massage sore muscles and some people even use it to ease arthritic and rheumatic pain.

Cloves relax the smooth lining of the gastrointestinal tract, so therefore help to alleviate vomiting, diarrhoea, intestinal gas and even worms and stomach aches. Just be careful: cloves are strong; they can sometimes irritate the stomach and can build up in the liver. Only use cloves when you need them, not as an everyday prophylactic.

COCONUT OIL (EXTRA VIRGIN)

I cannot say enough about the benefits of coconut oil. It has three main wonderful ingredients: caprylic acid, *lauric* acid and *capric* acid – three very healthy fatty acids that our bodies need. Coconut oil is packed full of antioxidants that you can't find anywhere else in nature. Once in the body, these healthy fats convert into antiviral, antibacterial, and anti-protozoal monoglycerides, which can destroy viruses such as HIV, herpes, candida, influenza and various pathogenic bacteria (including listeria *monocytogenes*, H. Pylori) as well as protozoa and parasites such as *giardia*.

Research is underway as to how coconut oil can play a role in the fight against Alzheimer's and how it can help enhance memory in general.

Studies are also being done as to the role coconut oil may play in fighting certain cancers. When digested, coconut oil produces ketones in the system and a ketogenic diet is now thought to help patients recover from cancers faster.

Coconut oil can also be used to boost your immune system, balance your thyroid, lower bad cholesterol (LDL) and increase good cholesterol (HDL), stabilise blood sugar levels. It is safe to use internally and externally. Many people use coconut oil to moisturise their skin and fight off dandruff, I personally use it in my home-made sunscreen as it has a decent SPF factor.

CORIANDER

Coriander is an unassuming herb which adds delicious flavour to any meal. I personally think that coriander should have a much higher standing on the superfood herb list. It is full of Vitamin A, calcium, beta-carotene, phosphorus and Vitamin C – a veritable cocktail for health.

Coriander has a very strong antibiotic-like component which is said to be strong enough to actually kill the salmonella virus.

Fascinatingly, coriander is very commonly served with fish in South East Asia. Could this be because fish are known to pick up certain pollutants from the sea – like mercury – and coriander actually binds to mercury and helps us to expel it from our system?

DANDELIONS

Dandelions are often looked at as pesky herbs but they are anything but that. Dandelion leaves and roots are where the magic lies in this small weed. I tend to supplement dandelion in my diet by either drinking the leaves as a tea or the roots as a coffee; however, you can even add the fresh leaves to salads. Dandelions are full of calcium, magnesium, iron, zinc, Vitamin C, beta-carotene, phosphorus, a range of Vitamin Bs and are one of the rare foods that have Vitamin D in them.

The liver is one of the most overworked organs in our body. Dandelions are magnificent in helping to tone, strengthen and even repair the liver. The liver affects so many elements of our health that we should definitely be picking and eating dandelions instead of consigning them to the compost heap.

It is in our interest to keep our liver healthy especially for women. The liver affects how our hormones work. It keeps them in balance, from mood swings to sore breasts all the way to menopause. The liver also has a lot to do with cholesterol levels (both good and bad), blood pressure levels and has a role to play in stabilising sugar levels. Can you imagine – our anger and emotional levels have a lot to do with the state of the liver too.

Dandelions are very helpful, not just for the liver, but for our kidneys too. They clean out waste from the kidneys, therefore helping people who suffer from water retention and bloating not to mention other kidney-related problems.

After a heavy meal, dandelion tea encourages the production of stomach acids, which can relieve that feeling of being extremely full. As our three main organs – the liver, kidneys and stomach – work so harmoniously together, it is worth working this little weed into our lives on a daily basis.

ECHINACEA

With similar effects to garlic, echinacea stimulates the immune system by naturally boosting infection fighters in your blood stream. Echinacea is antibacterial, antifungal, antiviral and is most effective when used at the first signs of illness.

EPSOM SALTS (MAGNESIUM SULPHATE)

We need magnesium for every organ and for every function in our body, yet, we are becoming more and more deficient in this vital nutrient. Mankind's magnesium levels have dropped by half in the last century due to changes in agriculture and diet. One can supplement magnesium, however, it is well-

TIP

If you suffer from water retention whilst flying, or after the flight, this is an excellent tea to take on the flight or right afterwards as it brings the swelling right down.

CAUTION

Echinacea should not be taken long-term or for more than three weeks at a time as it can harm your liver if overused.

documented that magnesium is poorly absorbed through our digestive tract due to the presence of specific foods or drugs, certain medical conditions and what is happening in an individual's stomach, and is better absorbed through the skin.

This brings us to Epsom salts. Known scientifically as hydrated magnesium sulphate, Epsom salts are rich in both magnesium and sulphate. While both magnesium and sulphate can be poorly absorbed through the stomach, studies show that they are both *very* effectively absorbed through the skin, so soaking in a bath with Epsom salts is the ideal way to get both magnesium and sulphate.

Why are magnesium and sulphate so important to our bodies?

- Sulphate plays an important role in the formation of brain tissue, joint proteins and the proteins that line the walls of the digestive tract. They stimulate the pancreas to generate digestive enzymes and are thought to help detoxify the body of medicines and environmental contaminants.
- Magnesium is needed for every single function of our body from bowel movements to how we sleep and how our heart beats. We can never get too much magnesium.

Not to mention, soaking in an Epsom salt bath or footbath is incredibly relaxing and pleasant especially when you add in some of your favourite essential oils.

GARLIC

Raw garlic, when crushed or chewed, contains a compound called allicin – which has similar properties to penicillin. This superfood member of the onion family is antibiotic, anti-inflammatory, antiviral, anti-parasitic, antifungal and an antioxidant (mopping up nasties that have been proven to cause cancer). Garlic is also an excellent source of manganese, Vitamin B6 and Vitamin C.

Back in the 19th century, the French chemist and microbiologist Louis Pasteur examined the use of raw garlic juice as a potential antibacterial agent and found garlic to be capable of killing bacteria in the same way as penicillin does. Over the past few years, many medical journals have published studies that have confirmed the antibacterial and antiviral properties of garlic. In addition to its ability to control bacterial and viral infections, garlic has been shown to fight and heal infections caused by other microbes and worms.

Garlic is also known to reverse and repair liver damage. Packed full of the mineral selenium – which increases the action of antioxidants, garlic helps with liver detoxification and liver repair.

Garlic is also known to help repair eye disorders, dementia, rheumatoid arthritis, cardiovascular problems, diabetes, atherosclerosis, an impaired immune system, certain types of cancer and even Alzheimer's disease.

GINGER

Gingerol is the main bioactive compound in ginger and is responsible for its medicinal properties. It has powerful anti-inflammatory, antioxidant, anti-phlegm, antifungal and antibacterial effects. Major studies are also now being done on ginger and the possible cancer-fighting properties that it may have – principally against pancreatic, colorectal, ovarian and lung cancers.

Ginger is full of magnesium, potassium, manganese, sodium, phosphorus, Vitamins E, C, B1, B2, B3, B6, folate, calcium and zinc. It has been reported that the combination of calcium, magnesium and zinc, when given to growing children makes them grow taller.

Ginger also has anti-blood clotting abilities and therefore can help protect us against strokes and heart disease as well as help to relieve indigestion and stomach issues. Interestingly, ginger actually relaxes the smooth muscle in your gut lining which helps move food through the system more effectively. This is why it can help with nausea, constipation, gas and bloating.

In cases of coughs and colds – where there is a lot of congestion and phlegm – it helps to break down and dry up phlegm.

GRAPEFRUIT SEED EXTRACT (GSE)

GSE is effective against more than 800 forms of viruses and bacteria as well as more than 100 strains of fungus and many parasites. High in many antioxidants, GSE boosts immunity, alkalises the body naturally and aids in digestion by improving your beneficial gut flora. GSE is also one of the most effective ways of treating the incredibly stubborn and hard to treat condition of candida.

Scientific and medical studies now accept that GSE is very effective when it comes to treating antibiotic resistant strains of bacteria. For example, for some urinary tract infections that are resistant to antibiotics, GSE is able to get rid of the bacteria after only one "course" – where many courses of antibiotics have failed in the same circumstance.

Farmers and vets are even beginning to use GSE to treat animals as a safe and effective alternative to antibiotics and antifungals not to mention for general immune-boosting.

I use GSE in situations when immunity is lowered – particularly due to fungal sensitivities. These can be either environmental sensitivities to mould or internal sensitivities such as candida or fungal infections on the skin, hands or feet.

It can be taken internally but also externally too. GSE is not an essential oil but I add it into blends for fungal infections and it has never let me down.

LEMONGRASS

Lemongrass is full of Vitamins A and C, folate, folic acid, magnesium, zinc, copper, iron, potassium, phosphorous, calcium and manganese.

Lemongrass helps digestion by killing off bad bacteria and parasites and can relieve gastroenteritis. It can help reduce absorption of cholesterol from the intestines and actually helps to oxidise and reduce LDL (bad cholesterol). As it is high in potassium, it helps to regulate blood pressure, so lemongrass is a must for our overall heart and circulatory health.

The two properties that impress me most about lemongrass are how it helps with joint pain and what it does to cancer cells. For any joint pain – from arthritis to gout – lemongrass helps to suppress certain enzymes, which causes the inflammation in joints.

Now, here's the most impressive thing about lemongrass: an element found in lemongrass called citral actually encourages cancer cells to commit suicide. Cancer patients all over the world are being encouraged to drink lemongrass tea for this reason. The tea is very easy to make: just pour hot water over the lemongrass stalks (bruise them slightly) and let them steep for a good few minutes. It couldn't be simpler or healthier.

MANUKA HONEY

The "Queen" of honeys, in my book, is manuka honey. How is manuka honey different from other honeys? The bees that make this honey take nectar purely from the manuka tree, trees which only grow in New Zealand. The manuka plant is a relative of the melaleuca family – basically, it is a close relative of the tea tree plant – thus it carries almost the same properties (if not more) of the amazing tea tree oil. Basically, when you are eating manuka honey, you are

CAUTION

Not all honey is the same. The antibacterial quality of honey depends on the type of honey as well as when and how it's harvested. Some kinds of honey may be 100 times more potent than others.

eating an edible form of tea tree. Manuka honey has been proven scientifically to have the highest level of antioxidants and curative powers of any honey; however, it has different levels of power itself. These are called the honey's unique manuka factor or UMF. For medicinal reasons I suggest you use a manuka honey with a UMF of +15 or higher. Manuka honey does not come cheap, but believe me, it is worth it's weight in gold.

MILK THISTLE

Glutathione is one of the most powerful antioxidants that we are aware of and our wonderful body is the one that produces it. It is a protein that is produced by every cell in our body, and actually, we couldn't survive without it. We can't take glutathione as a supplement as only our cells can produce it. But what we can do is take foods that encourage our cells to increase the production of glutathione. What does glutathione do and how is it related to milk thistle?

Milk thistle contains high levels of a flavonoid called *silymarin*. *Silymarin* encourages our cells to increase the production of glutathione which helps to protect and regenerate liver cells, restores kidney health, benefits our heart, and has a huge effect on our brain health (including helping with brain cancers) and helps with the symptoms of Alzheimer's.

Milk thistle is also highly effective in detoxifying our bodies in the following highly toxic situations – overuse or overexposure to analgesics (pain relievers), iron, mercury, radiation and alcohol. Milk thistle is highly effective when used during chemotherapy.

MOLASSES

Many of my patients tease me about my obsession of molasses, as there are very few who walk through my clinic door who don't get 'prescribed' molasses at one stage or another and it's with good reason. Molasses is so packed full of vitamins and minerals that I see it as a super superfood. And here's why: molasses is the crude by-product of the production of white sugar; sugar is made from the sugar cane and sugar beet plants. Once all the minerals and nutrients (and all the good things) have been removed from these plants you have white sugar, devoid of all nutrients. Everything good is left in the molasses. Ironically, molasses has the lowest sugar content of any sugar cane product and the goodness lies in all the vitamins and minerals that are left behind: huge amounts of iron, calcium, magnesium, selenium as well as manganese,

NOTE

Milk thistle is best extracted and absorbed by our bodies if it is an alcohol or glycerine-based tincture.

CAUTION

If you have a ragweed allergy, avoid milk thistle and if you have any estrogen-based issue like fibroids, endometriosis, breast, uterine or ovarian cancers, avoid milk thistle.

potassium, copper, phosphorous, chromium, cobalt, sodium, Vitamins B6, B3 (niacin), B1 (thiamine) and B2 (riboflavin). *Extra*: Growing children need lots of extra iron during their growth spurts.

Because of all of these nutrients, molasses can help with the following issues: menstrual problems (from irregular periods to cramps), stress, cancer, enlarged prostate, acne and other skin ailments, constipation, depression, headaches, anaemia, electrolyte imbalance, hair care (it has been known to turn grey hair back to it's original colour by eating it, not rubbing it on the hair), sexual health, compromised nervous systems, wound healing and strengthening the immune system. It also helps maintain healthy levels of haemoglobin and aids in the function of new cells in the body.

MUSTARD

Whether it is in powdered or seed form, mustard is power packed with phytonutrients. Phytonutrients are found in plants and help protect the plants against damaging environmental effects like ultraviolet radiation, predator pests, toxins and pollution. When we eat plants, herbs and spices with phytonutrients, these phytonutrients then protect us against the same nasties.

Due to these phytonutrients, mustard seeds are a great way to prevent and slow the progress of cancers – especially cancers of the gastrointestinal tract. They can also restrict the growth of already present cancer cells and prevent the formation of new cancers.

Mustard seeds are also high in selenium and magnesium. Both these components give it a unique anti-inflammatory property. Consumed regularly, mustard is known to both control and keep at bay many of the symptoms of asthma, colds and chest congestion. When applied to the body, the paste heats the area it is applied to and helps to loosen muscles – leading to relief from

many pains (e.g. rheumatoid, arthritic and muscle pains).

Due to high levels of B3 (niacin), mustard protects arteries from plaque buildup, helps to regulate blood flow and prevent hypertension.

Mustard also encourages good digestion as it encourages production of saliva as well as helps to speed up our metabolism.

TIP

To ease a pain, place a small bundle of the mustard seeds in a muslin cloth, and add it to warm bath water. Either have a long relaxing bath or soak your tired and aching feet for instant relief. Another great way to reap the benefits is to apply the seed paste onto the painful area for a few minutes.

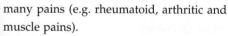

TIP

A good way to add mustard into your daily life is to make a home-made salad dressing with mustard, olive oil, garlic and vinegar.

SIMPLY NATURAL HEALTH

NETTLE TEA (STINGING NETTLE)

Nettle stimulates the lymph system to boost immunity, relieves arthritis and osteoarthritis symptoms as well as promotes a release of uric acid from joints and thus help with gout. Nettle tea also helps to support the kidneys and adrenals for people with adrenal and chronic fatigue. It can help break down kidney stones, reduce hypertension as well as strengthen the lungs and respiratory tract for people with asthma and allergic rhinitis. For those with sensitive and fragile gums, it prevents gingivitis and plaque when used as a mouthwash.

Nettle tea has also been shown to be helpful in the treatment of Alzheimer's disease and can help relieve neurodegenerative disease like MS, amyotrophic lateral sclerosis (ALS/Lou Gherigs disease) and sciatica. On top of this, it destroys intestinal worms and parasites as well as support endocrine health by helping the thyroid, spleen and pancreas. You might look differently at that field of stinging nettles next summer.

OATS

Oats are a rich source of soluble fibre. Soluble fibre has been conclusively linked to good heart health. How does it help our heart? Oats and their soluble fibre help to reduce bad cholesterol and, due to their high amount of calcium and potassium, help to reduce blood pressure. Low cholesterol and stable blood pressure crucial for good health – particularly for a healthy heart.

Oats help subdue cravings as the soluble fibre keeps blood sugar levels even so one can avoid "sugar crashes". This means that oats can help reduce the risk of diabetes by keeping blood sugar levels even. Oats are also amazing for the skin. Due to the proteins and lipids in oats (once they are in contact with water), they can reduce itchiness and inflammation when used actively as they draw moisture into the skin.

OIL OF OREGANO

Oil of Oregano is considered antimicrobial, antibacterial, anti-parasitic, antiviral and antifungal. It can be used internally and externally in the treatment of respiratory problems (especially the very stubborn and hard to treat mycoplasma). It is a fantastic aid in healing wounds, calming digestive upsets and alleviating the symptoms of the common cold. Packed with antioxidants known as phenols and flavonoids, it also heals and strengthens your immune system.

TIP

Wrap a generous handful of oats in a muslin cloth and add to your bath to help moisturise your skin.

OLIVE LEAF EXTRACT

Olive leaves have resisted bacterial attacks for thousands of years – which is a good indicator of the strength they hold. One of the main active ingredients (*oleuropein*) of this natural antibacterial extract breaks down the cell walls of a wide range of pathogenic bacteria, thus destroying them. Olive leaf extract is also a natural cure for sinusitis and is one of the best natural cold and flu remedies.

OLIVE OIL

There has been much written on the health benefits of the Mediterranean as it has been well-documented by many health experts that the incidences of all heart disease and strokes are much lower in these areas: this has been attributed to the high consumption of olive oil. It has now also been realised that Alzheimer rates are lower in these countries too. Again the link to olive oil consumption has been made.

Olive oil also helps protect against ulcerative colitis, thrombosis, protects your liver from oxidative stress and in general reduces inflammation in our bodies. On this note, I suggest to start your day with 1 tablespoon of olive oil into a cup of water with ½ a squeezed lemon or lime just to make sure you get this elixir of life into your daily routine.

ONIONS

Red onions, in particular, contain folate, thiamine, calcium, magnesium, potassium, chromium, manganese and Vitamins C, K and B6.

Red and yellow onions are one of the best natural sources of quercetin, a bioflavonoid that is particularly well suited for scavenging free radicals. Aside from its antioxidant properties, quercetin has been found to possess cancer fighting, antifungal, antibacterial and anti-inflammatory properties. It has shown promising potential for preventing and controlling the formation of intestinal polyps. Onions can suppress the rhinoviruses that are the underlying cause of most common colds.

In addition to quercetin, red onions provide high levels of allicin, a potent health-promoting compound. They can only be accessed when the plant is crushed or chewed. Allicin has been shown to promote cardiovascular health, prevent and treat cancer, and reduce high blood pressure.

*"Red onions encourage the bronchial passage
to open up and break down phlegm in the lungs."*

PROBIOTICS AND FERMENTED FOODS

Probiotics are one of the most incredible discoveries in the last decade. They work to boost and preserve the natural gut flora (good bacteria) found in your digestive system. In Traditional Chinese Medicine (TCM), one is taught that the stomach is the seed of health: "strong stomach, strong you". Research has proven that a balanced gut is one of the keys to overall wellness and even cancer prevention.

When using a probiotic supplement, make sure it is multi-strain and either freeze-dried and activated on contact with saliva or a live active source (this has to be kept in the fridge).

One of the best and most effective ways of getting an easily absorbable probiotic is through fermented foods. Fermented foods are packed with antioxidants and microorganisms that your body processes far better than supplements.

Here are a list of probiotic foods – unpasteurised sauerkraut, kombucha tea, apple cider vinegar, raw pickles, probiotic yogurt, kefir, kimchi, miso and natto. They are excellent ways to improve the balance in your intestines.

PSYLLIUM HUSKS

Psyllium husks are an increasingly popular food supplement used for weight control and intestinal health.

Pysllium is the husk of the plantago plant; it contains a spongy fibre that reduces appetite, improves and cleanses the digestive system. When combined with water, psyllium husks form a gel that will bulk and form a mass in the colon, this is transported through the intestinal tract – taking waste with it – the husks will 'scrub' the intestines clean as they move along. This will relieve constipation and encourage regular bowel movements. Pysllium also helps to reduce cholesterol and plaque buildup in your arteries.

TIP

Make sure you always buy raw honey as the pasteurisation process often kills its medicinal values.

RAW HONEY

Raw honey is one of the best natural antibiotics, antimicrobials, anti-inflammatories and antiseptics known to man. An enzyme found in honey releases hydrogen peroxide, which helps your body fight infection and prevents the growth of bacteria. Soothing to the digestive system, honey removes toxins from the blood and helps your liver operate more efficiently.

Honey also stimulates production of special cells that can repair tissue damaged by infection. In addition, applied topically, honey has an anti-inflammatory action that can quickly reduce pain and inflammation.

SAGE

My knowledge of sage first started on the hillsides of Greece where sage grows in abundance. I was taught to use it as a tea to clear up even the most stubborn of chesty coughs or to use it as a menstrual regulator and to keep menopausal symptoms at bay.

The benefits of sage are, however, further reaching than this. The saying of 'wise old sage' encapsulates one of the most interesting uses for sage as a brain booster. By drinking a sage tea, chewing the leaves or adding it into foods, you can increase not only your memory but also your concentration and recall ability.

Sage is also packed full of antioxidants which help slow ageing and protect us from cancers. It also contains Vitamin K which is hard to come by in nature, but is crucial for good health and bone density. If you are an osteoporosis sufferer or have low bone density start eating this wonderful herb. It will strengthen the bones and at the same time you may be warding off diabetes as well. It has been documented that sage contains certain extracts and chemicals that mimic the drugs typically prescribed to manage diabetes. Sage inhibits and controls the release of sugars from the livers. These releases are what causes major sugar fluctuations and can trigger the onset of type 2 diabetes.

TIP

If you are pregnant, it is not advisable to use sage in high levels of concentration.

THYME

Thyme has been regarded as one of the top healing herbs for centuries due to its extremely high Vitamin C levels. It is most effective against infections, specifically respiratory and digestive infections. It has a relaxing effect on muscles in the bronchi and helps to relieve asthma, whooping cough, laryngitis, bronchitis and dry coughs. Through inhalation therapy, it can help those who suffer from chronic sinus infections. On the digestive side, it helps with diarrhoea, parasites and fungal infections.

TURMERIC (POWDERED OR FRESH)

What we are looking for in turmeric is *curcumin* – the main active ingredient. It has powerful anti-inflammatory effects and is a very strong antioxidant. More famously, it is now known to have the ability to shrink tumours and leads to several changes on the molecular level that may help prevent and perhaps even treat cancer.

Unfortunately, *curcumin* is poorly absorbed into the bloodstream so it needs help. The two things that help our bodies absorb this wonder spices are fat and black pepper. So either crack black pepper onto anything you eat that has turmeric in it or make sure you are eating a fat alongside it. For a fat, I recommend coconut oil – although traditionally it was taken with full fat milk or butter, but coconut will do.

Curcumin has powerful antioxidant effects. It neutralises free radicals and stimulates the body's own antioxidant enzymes to work at full force.

FOODS THAT CAUSE INFLAMMATION

Wheat, eggs, milk, soybeans, yeast and meat are among the most common inflammatory foods. Meat contains inflammation-promoting arachidonic acid; beef has the highest content, double the amount found in lamb, pork, or chicken. Eggs and dairy products also contain arachidonic acid but in lower amounts.

Antibiotic Foods – garlic, raw honey, manuka honey, cabbage, grapefruit seed extract (GSE), apple cider vinegar, coconut oil, echinacea, fermented foods, oil of oregano, turmeric, cayenne pepper and ginger.

Anti-inflammatory Foods – chamomile, bok choy, celery, beetroots, broccoli, blueberries, cabbage, pineapples, salmon, bone broth, walnuts, coconut oil, chia seeds, turmeric and aloe vera.

Anti-phlegm Foods – all leafy green vegetables, thyme, rosemary, sage, oregano, peppermint, cauliflower, broccoli, celery, asparagus, bamboo shoots, onions, garlic, ginger, turmeric, citrus fruits (lemon, grapefruit, limes), pineapples, berries, Brussels sprouts and hot peppers – chilli, cayenne, paprika.

Calcium-rich foods – watercress, kale, dandelion, arugula, cabbage (red, white and Chinese), okra, broccoli, beans, almonds, sardines, anchovies, leeks, molasses, figs, black currants and Brussels sprouts.

Cold/Cool foods – tomatoes, watermelons, bananas, pomelo, grapefruit, persimmon, star fruit, seaweed, kelp, sprouts, watercress, lettuce, salt, soya sauce, millet, barley, wheat, buckwheat, eggplant, cucumber, celery, peppermint, broccoli, cauliflower, spinach, pears, apples, pineapples, coconuts, strawberries, oranges, tangerines, mangoes, papayas, cream, yoghurt and cheese.

Detoxifying Foods – Artichokes, asparagus, avocados, beets, broccoli, cabbage, dandelion, garlic, grapefruit, green tea, kale, lemongrass, lemons, olive oil, seaweed, turmeric, water, wheatgrass, hibiscus tea, white tea, Brazil nuts, goji berries, onions, sesame seeds (tahini), basil, pineapples and cinnamon.

Gut-healing Foods – Sauerkraut, kimchi, kefir, kombucha, beet kvass, sourdough bread, psyllium, sweet potatoes, yams, yuccas, squash, pumpkins, parsnips, broccoli, cauliflower, avocados, coconut oil, olive oil, ginger, turmeric, peppermint, oregano, fennel, liquorice, dandelion root, chamomile and bone broth.

Hot/Warm foods – black pepper, cinnamon, ginger, chilli peppers, mustard seeds, coriander, onions, leeks, asparagus, sweet peppers, pomegranates, apricots, peaches, cherries, lychees, longan, pumpkins, fennel, garlic, onions, nutmeg, rosemary, basil, dates, walnuts, pine nuts, carp, lobster, chicken, ham, goat's milk, clove, coffee, vinegar and wine.

Magnesium-rich foods – dark green leafy vegetable (kale, spinach, chard, *kang kong*), pumpkin seeds, avocados, yoghurt, bananas, dried fruits, dark chocolate, figs, black beans, kefir, almonds, cashews, coriander, goats cheese and artichoke.

Omega-3 rich foods – flaxseeds (oil and seeds), chia seeds, walnuts, fatty fish (mackerel, sardines, herring, tuna, salmon), seafood, spinach, egg yolk, hemp seeds, cod liver oil, Brazil nuts, hazelnuts, kale, Brussels sprouts and watercress.

Potassium-rich foods – avocado, spinach, sweet potatoes, potato (with skin), coconut water, kefir, yoghurt, white beans, black beans, banana, butternut squash, apricots, mushrooms, salmon, tomato, watermelons (with seeds), beetroots, edamame and chard.

Vitamin C-rich foods – cabbage, thyme (fresh and dried), parsley, citrus fruits, peppers (green, red and yellow), kiwis, broccoli, Brussels sprouts, cherries, cauliflower, strawberries, papayas and blackcurrants.

Zinc-rich foods – beef, lamb, chickpeas, yoghurt, *keffir*, garlic, ginger, pumpkin seeds, cashews, cocoa powder, spinach, seafood, watermelon seeds and wheatgerm.

HEALING WITH ESSENTIAL OILS

Aromatherapy is a healing therapy based on the use of pure essential oils for physical and emotional health and well-being. These all-natural oils are a powerful form of herbal medicine and have been used for centuries and in some societies as the only form of medicine. However, unlike allopathic medicines, aromatherapy is safe and non-toxic to the system. The oils will enter your body and only target the problem at hand, leaving other organs untouched or strengthened. Aromatherapy is the safest, and possibly the most powerful, herbal medicine that nature has to offer.

Essential oils, derived from the flowers, leaves and other parts of plants, are highly concentrated and need to be used with great respect. Aromatherapy works in great synergy with the acupressure meridians, organs and acupressure points.

With aromatherapy, one has to be a little bit more careful than with acupressure as the strength of these oils are intense and too much can cause some irritation so they must be used carefully. They should be treated as a medicine. You would not overuse a prescription medicine – would you? Treat these oils the same way.

INGESTING OILS

Just a quick note on ingesting essential oils. There are many companies at the moment advocating the ingestion of oils, which I do not advocate. Good quality oils can be ingested but, due to their strength, you must know how to do this safely and not randomly. If you want to ingest oils, see a certified aromatherapist or naturopath for guidance.

There are over 60 essential oils that I use in my clinic. I have only chosen a select few for this book, as they are readily available, easy and safe to use. The oils that I use in this book and suggest you have on hand in your home are the following:

BASE OILS

- **Almond oil –** A very lubricating and gentle oil that is good for delicate skins, almond oil is very high in protein so it nourishes the skin at the same time while softening it.
- **Avocado oil –** A very nourishing and penetrative oil. It is high in proteins, lecithin and essential fatty acids, as well as in Vitamins A, B and D.
- **Calendula oil –** A strong germicide and an antiseptic oil, calendula helps to seal broken blood vessels and promotes healing without the formation of scar tissue.
- **Carrot oil –** Carrot oil is extremely high in Vitamin A so it helps with complex and sensitive skin conditions, as well as immune issues.
- **Evening Primrose oil –** High in gamma linolenic acid, evening primrose oil is useful in treating dry and mature skin, eczema and psoriasis.
- **Jojoba oil –** A highly penetrative oil, jojoba oil can be used on all skin types as it helps to regulate and remove excessive sebum.
- **Rosehip –** High in Vitamin C, this oil is excellent at encouraging healing of skins and tissue, even helping to minimise wrinkles, heal scars and at the same time boosting the immune system.
- **Sunflower oil –** One of the most versatile oils used. High in Vitamin E, it is safe for most skin types.

ESSENTIAL OILS

Basil – An excellent oil to use in any situation of stress and/or anxiety, basil helps to calm down your nervous system and at the same time can repair damaged nerves. If you are suffering from nervous exhaustion and indecision, this oil will strengthen you and your mind. It is also antispasmodic and helps with tired and sore muscles.

Benzoin – Benzoin is a very gentle yet strengthening oil. It has a rich and resinous smell that improves as it ages, even in a blend. It can be used for mouth ulcers, dry cracked heels and on sores that are taking a long time to heal. It helps the respiratory system by calming coughs, bronchitis, asthma, general congestion and laryngitis. If you combine benzoin with frankincense, it will strengthen the lungs, which is extremely important to do if your lungs have been weakened by illness.

Black Pepper – Black pepper is mainly known for its help with digestive issues. It stops the buildup of gas in the intestines and encourages the absorption of nutrients. It is also an antispasmodic oil which helps with cramps and muscle strain and can help relieve joint pains such as rheumatism and arthritis. Black pepper also strengthens the energy system when you are exhausted due to illness, stress or overexertion and is an aphrodisiac.

Cardamom – Cardamom is tonifying and helps with deep-seated issues like mental fatigue and lack of interest in life, low sexual response and mental illnesses. As it works on the stomach, cardamom helps colic, stomach cramps and constipation, and is also very tonifying for the immune system. This means that cardamom may provide beneficial support for the very complicated immune crises arising from cancer and HIV.

Chamomile German – Chamomile German is a very calming oil that has sedative properties. It helps to calm "inflammation of the mind" manifested through anger, bitterness, hatred and irritability. It helps with insomnia, especially when the insomnia is related to emotional turmoil. It works wonders on any skin inflammation (e.g. eczema, psoriasis, rashes and chicken pox). It helps heal wounds and has strong antifungal and antiparasitic properties. Due to its anti-inflammatory properties, chamomile German can also help soothe osteo and rheumatoid arthritis, gout and neuralgia and can give relief to sufferers of hay fever and allergies.

Chamomile Roman – Chamomile Roman can be used for both emotional and physical healing. On an emotional level, it can be used when there is over sensitivity and ceaseless thinking. On a physical level, it is excellent in treating insomnia, anxiety, tension and fear. Its anti-inflammatory properties help with relieving pain from osteo and rheumatoid arthritis and spondylitis, and calms any inflammation of the skin.

Clary Sage – Clary sage is a strong euphoric oil as well as an aphrodisiac. It is one of the main ingredients that I use for menstrual disorders and for depression. It is also excellent to use as a post-pregnancy oil. It works directly on the kidneys and strengthens them when they are weak.

Clove Bud – Clove bud is used a lot in pharmaceutical medicine now due to its antibacterial, antiviral and antiseptic properties. In fact, clove is even being used in hospitals to help fight superbugs. It is a stimulating and immune-boosting oil that relieves the pain of sore and strained muscles. Besides being an antispasmodic, clove bud also has anaesthetic properties and has been used by dentists for years. Clove oil also helps with sinus infections and digestive disorders.

Cinnamon – Cinnamon is a very strengthening oil which helps with mental and physical exhaustion or lack of focus. It helps boost the immune system, improves circulation and can aid a sluggish digestion. It is very useful in fighting the common cold or flu. It also helps to regulate blood sugar levels and can get rid of worms.

Cypress – Cypress is a clean and clear oil that helps with broken veins, haemorrhoids, varicose veins, fluid retention and can also help fight psychic blocks. It is good to use to dispel negative energies.

Eucalyptus *Globulus* – Eucalyptus *globulus* is a cleansing and stimulating oil. It is most well known as a powerful expectorant and is widely used for coughs and colds. It also has the ability to fight off viruses, bacteria and microbes. Interestingly, eucalyptus *globulus* has the ability to recognise when one needs to be cooled down or warmed up, so it will warm you up in the cold and cool you down if you are feeling heated.

Eucalyptus Radiata – Eucalyptus radiata is a slightly gentler version of eucalyptus *globulus*. This eucalyptus helps to breakdown buildups of phlegm but, as its expectorant levels are lower than eucalyptus *globulus*, it tends to be gentler. It can also be used in cases of chronic fatigue, fever and sinusitis.

Frankincense – Frankincense is a mentally rejuvenating oil that helps to oxygenate our blood stream. Excellent in times of mental exhaustion and even spiritual depression or stress, frankincense helps to strengthen our energy system, allowing us to become calm and strong in times of adversity. It boosts our immune system to help us fight off ailments from colds to cancer. In ancient Egypt, they used frankincense to embalm mummies because it was known to stop cells from breaking down. Consider adding it into your facial routine as it not only preserves your skin but also encourages new cells to grow. In addition, frankincense helps to dispel poisons from various insect or animal bites, heal ulcers and wounds that are hard to heal, and will help dispel tumours (you should rub the pure oil directly on and over any tumours you have).

Geranium – Geranium is a harmonising oil that works directly on the kidneys and adrenal glands to help keep us in balance. With antispasmodic, antifungal, antiviral and hormonal balancing properties, it makes for an excellent treatment against many kinds of viruses including the herpes simplex and zoster virus. Geranium is also a powerful bug repellent and is crucial for the treatment of sore throats.

Ginger – A warm and comforting oil, ginger is antispasmodic and works incredibly on any strained or tired muscles. It is a carminative oil as it works directly on the stomach, dispelling wind and encouraging digestion. It also encourages good circulation and breaks down phlegm.

Juniper – A very protective oil, juniper helps to dispel negative energy around you and your home. It also helps with detox by working on our lymphatic system as it promotes drainage. Juniper is also excellent to use for gout, oedema, poor circulation, cystitis, urinary stones and UTIs.

Lavender – Lavender is one of the most versatile and safe oils you can use as it is gentle on the skin and can be used neat, straight from the bottle. Not only does it smell divine, lavender has antiseptic properties and is excellent for burns, cuts and scrapes. It encourages new cells to grow and is also fantastic at helping the healing process and reducing the risk of scarring. It can reduce stress and hysteria, helps with sleep, calms nerves, deters mosquitoes, reduces itching, breaks up poisons and can alleviate headaches. Lastly, it has anti-inflammatory properties that can help relax aching muscles.

Lemon – Using lemon oil is like adding a little bit of sunshine into your life. It is the most uplifting and cleansing oil you can use. It boosts the immune system, detoxifies the liver and helps with the aches and pains of fever. Lemon oil can also be used to disperse cellulite, keep the wrinkles at bay and zap stubborn spots. It is fantastic to use when you have a headache and tones the lymphatic and digestive systems.

Mandarin – One of the most gentle of oils (and an excellent one to use on babies). Mandarin helps with digestion; it calms stomachs as well as induces appetites so it can help fussy eaters to eat. The soothing smell of mandarin can improve circulation and help the most troubled minds to sleep. Used on the skin, it helps with stretch marks, wrinkles, hydrates the skin and at the same time helps decongest clogged pores. Be careful when using on children under six months, ask guidance from the aromatherapists before using.

Myrrh – Most famously known from the biblical story of the Three Wise Kings at Christmas who come bearing gifts of gold, frankincense and myrrh (all three of these 'gifts' are used in this book by the way). Myrrh has an abundance of incredible healing properties. On a deeper level, it uplifts 'spiritual' depression and helps give those that have lost direction in life some direction. Myrrh is one of the most strengthening oils that I work with. It strengthens our immune system by stimulating the production of white blood cells, it also strengthens our stomach, lungs and even our gums. It can be used for gum infections, chronic bronchitis, laryngitis, coughs with lots of mucous, pharyngitis, mouth ulcers, thrush and haemorrhoids.

Peppermint – Peppermint oil is mainly known for its help in the digestive area as it helps the stomach to digest foods as well as gives us relief from painful stomach issues like bloating, stomach spasms and gas. It is also extremely effective at relieving headaches that are related to food intolerances and what I call a 'stomach headache' (see under Headaches in Part 3). Peppermint can also give huge relief to the digestive system. I use it in all my sinus blends and inhalations as it helps to dry up stubborn thick phlegm. It also calms down hay fever and allergic rhinitis due to allergies, relieves coughs and asthma and on top of all this, it is also an excellent way of keeping ants and little crawly bugs out of your house forever.

Pine – Another oil that works on many different levels is pine. Pine is said to be one of the most protective oils and is used not only for protection against illness but also negativity. It is also the best oil to use when you are recovering from an illness or operation and are still feeling weak. Pine has an affinity with the lungs and is highly recommended when there is a cough. It also helps to detoxify the kidneys and can be used in cases of pneumonia, cystitis, candida, gout, flu, psoriasis and prostate problems.

Rosemary – Known for its clearing and energising properties, rosemary has been used in folk medicine for years. It's most known for it's ability to encourage new hair growth as well as to strengthen hair and is often used in shampoos. Hair aside, what it does under the hair is truly amazing. Rosemary stimulates the brain and enhances memory. It helps improve concentration and recall, which is excellent if you are taking an exam. It can also help with osteo and rheumatoid arthritis, bronchitis, mental fatigue and sore muscles.

Sweet marjoram – This is the oil I always reach for when I need an anti-inflammatory. It has such strong antispasmodic and anti-inflammatory properties and also works really well for painful and swollen muscular aches and pains: back pains, shoulder pains and ankle pains etc. Sweet marjoram is also good in times of panic or hysteria, hypertension, migraines, constipation, asthma, emphysema, and can regulate the heart.

Tea Tree – Used for centuries by the Aboriginals in Australia, the healing powers of tea tree are legendary. It is said to be more powerful than carbolic acid yet not poisonous to humans. Hospitals around the world now use tea tree oil as their chosen disinfectant as it is one of the few substance that can deal with the superbugs of today. A very powerful immune stimulant, tea tree encourages the body, when threatened with an infection, to respond naturally. Its antifungal, antiviral and antibacterial properties make it useful for a wide range of conditions. It can be used to treat sore throats, warts, candida, mouth ulcers, lice, ringworm, acne, athlete's foot and gingivitis.

Thyme *vulgaris* **–** One of the greatest benefits of thyme oil is that it has a very detoxifying effect on the body. It helps to detoxify the body, mind and spirit. For mental fatigue and depression, it helps energise and move you on the next phase in your life. Thyme *vulgaris* can also be used as an expectorant for coughs, colds, flu and bronchitis and can even help alleviate snoring.

HEALING WITH ACUPRESSURE POINTS

Acupressure is a therapy that utilises the principles of acupuncture and Chinese medicine. In acupressure, the same points on the body are used as in acupuncture, but are stimulated with finger pressure instead of the insertion of needles. Acupressure is used to relieve many symptoms and pain. Unlike acupuncture, which requires a visit to a professional, acupressure can be performed by a layperson, you just need to know what to do. Acupressure techniques are fairly easy to learn, are very safe and have been used to provide quick, cost-free, and effective relief for many symptoms and have been around for centuries – 5000 to be exact.

The beauty with acupressure is that the worst thing that happens is that nothing happens. The best-case scenario, however, is that often diseases, illnesses and problems seem to just slip away as health is restored. In actual fact, the healing is so gentle and "natural" that I often have people who come back into my clinic, after having suffered from something for months or even years, and say "I feel better, but maybe I was getting better anyway". Sometimes the effects are immediate but at other times they may take more time. With acupressure, the issues just start to melt away in such a natural way that one wonders, was that because of the points or was I already on the mend?

HOW DOES ACUPRESSURE WORK?

Although acupuncture is more widely known, most sources suggest that acupressure actually predates acupuncture by about 2,500 years.

Acupressure (and acupuncture) are based on the concept of a person's energy, or life force called chi, qi (pronounced *chee*) or prana. Our energy, chi, travels along identified pathways called meridians. Each meridian starts from a certain organ and connects to other meridians and organs. Traditional Chinese Medicine (TCM) dictates that there are 20 meridians. However, in acupressure and acupuncture, most work centres around 14 meridians: the 12 regular meridians and two extra meridians known as the Ren meridian (conception vessel) and the Du meridian (governor vessel). A block in any of these meridians will stop the chi from flowing and will result in discomfort or even disease. To release the blocked energy, or to promote energy flow to a certain area, the acupressure practitioner presses an acupressure point. This sends signals to the brain and other parts of the body to say there is a blockage, which our body needs to correct. Naturally, our bodies start to do so.

An energy stream or meridian originates from each of our major organs. They connect to one another and the network runs all through our bodies. For example, the stomach, gallbladder and liver meridians run the full length of our bodies from our toes to our heads and visa versa. So, judging by the symptoms that people present and where the problems lie, one can quickly identify which meridians – and therefore which organs – are being affected.

What I have always found amusing – and occasionally exasperating – in my clinic is that often a patient will come to visit my clinic with a problem and I talk to them about what meridian and organs I thought were affected (for example the liver and kidneys). The next time they come to see me, normally a week later, they would come with a full report on their kidneys or liver. They have gone to the doctor for a check on the 'offending' organs I mentioned. They would then report that their beloved doctor had proclaimed their liver and kidneys were absolutely fine. I then explain that although the actual function of the organ is fine (for example, the kidneys are doing the job that conventional medicine recognises they need to do), the energy stream from the kidneys is not strong, or is blocked or has way too much energy. This is why the patient may have symptoms such as back pain, dizziness, depression or even tinnitus (to name only a few conditions that the kidney meridian flow can affect). Eventually they get it – it's a different way of working and it's a different system. And it can work miracles.

TUI NA MASSAGE

Tui na massage is massaging the meridian and encouraging the flow of energy in the correct direction. By massaging, kneading and tapping on the meridian, the energy/chi/prana will start flowing more strongly and will help to remove blockages along the meridians of the body, and stimulate the flow of chi and blood to promote healing from within.

HEALING THE EMOTIONS: THE BACH FLOWER REMEDIES

In order to start healing ourselves and our families fully, we have to understand how emotions and diseases work closely together.

Dr. Edward Bach (of the Bach Flower Foundation) discovered this link. He left his practise as a top immunologist in Harley Street to dedicate his life to researching the link between emotions and disease. Dr. Bach realised that emotions such as fear, guilt and anger etc. would eventually manifest themselves as a disease or an imbalance within the body if not dealt with properly. This could explain why out of two people who may have had contact with the same virus or bug, one may get sick and the other not. His findings and works are still being used around the world many years after his death.

I love working with the flower essences and they have become a regular part of my family's life. We often go through various moods and emotions even as the day progresses.

In my clinic, I have seen the most amazing transformations for people who have used these essences. The flower essences work gently but with such a strength that often people just come back only to get more of the Bach flower remedies.

I have summarised quickly how each remedy can be used to help with various emotions or states of emotions that we go through. You can just take one or combine up to seven – but no more than that.

HOW TO TAKE THEM

- You can add 2 drops of an individual remedy to water, tea or juice and sip at intervals.
- You can drop 4 drops straight onto your tongue.
- You can make up your own bottle of remedies by buying a 30 ml dropper bottle into which you put spring water and ½ teaspoon of either brandy or apple cider vinegar and then add 2 drops of the combination of remedies that you have chosen for yourself. You can only use seven different remedies into one mixing bottle, then take these 4 drops four times a day.
- It can be overwhelmingly transformational or so subtle and gentle that it is often only in hindsight that you can see how much they have changed you.

Agrimony – This remedy is for those who hide their feelings behind a brave cheerful face. These people are usually bright and happy but may be emotionally tortured beneath the surface.

Aspen – This remedy is for fear, but fear of unknown reasons. For example, people who are afraid of a room, or get a strange feeling that something is there but they don't know what. Fear caused by a known reason can be helped by mimulus.

Beech – This remedy is for people who are overcritical and lack tolerance and empathy. They can appear to be patient at times but underneath they are seething with irritation.

Centaury – This remedy is for those who find it hard to stand up for themselves. They are kind and always willing to help out, but are easily dominated or manipulated. They have a hard time saying no.

Cerato – This remedy is for those who do not trust their own judgement. Rarely will they make a decision without asking for advice or an opinion from others, and will sometimes take advice even if they know it is wrong.

Cherry Plum – This remedy is for people who are often on the edge of a nervous breakdown or are in danger of committing suicide. It is for those who have a desperate fear of their mind giving way to insanity or doing harm to others or oneself.

Chestnut Bud – This remedy is for those who just keep making the same mistake again and again and they just do not seem to learn from their first mistake.

Chicory – This remedy is for people who are the "mothering" type. They like to control all situations as they always think they know "what is best". Although their intentions are mostly always good (in their head), they tend to be overprotective and fuss a lot. They also have a tendency to feel sorry for themselves with a "nobody appreciates me" attitude when people don't want to do as they say.

Clematis – This remedy is good for people who appear dreamy and absent minded, as they do not live in the present but in their own dream world. They are inclined to lack concentration and become easily bored if something does not hold their interest for long enough. Sometimes these people are labelled ADD/ADHD. Clematis can be used when people are feeling faint or have lost consciousness.

Crab Apple – This remedy is known as the "cleansing remedy" and is used for those who always feel the need to clean or are obsessed with cleanliness. They often are very fussy about their living spaces and will not eat somewhere where they don't feel the hygiene is up to their standards. It is an excellent remedy to use on somebody who has obsessive-compulsive disorder (OCD).

Elm – This remedy should be used when people feel overwhelmed when there is too much to do or think about. This overwhelmed feeling can sometimes lead to panic and the general feeling of "not being able to cope".

Gentian – This remedy is for people who have gone into a state of discouragement or despondency. They can be feeling temporarily depressed if things aren't going their way e.g. after losing a job, doing badly at an interview or failing an exam.

Gorse – This remedy is for deep despair and depression. A person who needs this remedy is filled with utter hopelessness, refusing to try again and has given up on life.

Heather – This remedy is for people who just can't stop talking. They often don't have a good idea of personal space and love to constantly touch, nudge or grab your arm to make sure they have your attention. It's all about them, every situation is turned towards themselves with endless stories and moments or anecdotes about their lives.

Holly – This remedy is for people who have explosive personalities and are quite often viewed as being angry; whereas really the underlying emotion is not so much anger as one of jealousy, envy, hatred, revenge and suspicion.

Honeysuckle – This remedy is for people who always live in the past and dwell upon memories of times gone by. People in a honeysuckle state tend to miss out on the present life, as they are preoccupied with past events – both positive and negative.

Hornbeam – This remedy is for people who procrastinate and need emotional strength to face the day ahead. They can't seem to muster up the enthusiasm so they put things off and will find everything or anything to do but the task at hand.

Impatiens – This remedy is used when people are very impatient and short-tempered. People who need impatiens are quick in thought and in their actions and tend to speak quickly too. People just don't seem to move fast enough for them and they can get quite agitated, annoyed and snap unnecessarily.

Larch – This remedy is for people who lack self-confidence. They doubt themselves and their ability to achieve great things, so they often will miss out on chances in life.

Mimulus – This remedy is for fear, but fear of the known. So when people are fully aware of why they are scared, for example fear of flying, death and spiders. This remedy will help them overcome their fears. Mimulus can also be used to help shy people come out of their shells.

Mustard – This remedy is for people who suddenly feel that there is a dark cloud over their heads, and nothing feels right or good and they just can't see the joy in anything. It is normally a temporary state of mind that will pass.

Oak – This remedy is for people who are steady, reliable and hard-working but can get very tired. They are always willing to work and get their hands dirty. Even when they are sick and their bodies need a well-deserved rest they will soldier on with a brave face. However, deep inside they can be very sensitive and extremely tired – this is when they might lose their energy and will need to take the remedy.

Olive – This remedy is for people who are exhausted mentally or physically. Normally this tiredness is due to overwork or over-exertion and then just the simple things in life become hard work.

Pine – This remedy is for people who always feel guilty. It might be guilt from the past, from parents or even from religion. These people are always apologising for things they have done or felt they have done and will even apologise for what others have done.

Red Chestnut – This remedy is for those who constantly worry. I believe most mothers should take red chestnut on a regular basis. It's a worry that something bad is going to happen to the people they love. In every situation, they look for possible dangers and will worry until everybody is at home safely.

Rock Rose – This remedy is for terror and panic. These emotions may stem from a situation that instilled panic and fear in the person. It could have been a car crash, seeing somebody die, being attacked or even from being bitten by a dog when young – which transforms into a fear or phobia for life.

Rock Water – This remedy is for people who are very hard to reach. Unfortunately, the people who need this remedy rarely, if ever, will ask for it or be willing to take it – they are so rigid (and somewhat self-righteous) in their ways that they find it hard to see anything wrong with their characters. They are perfectionists and dislike it if things aren't up to their perfect standards.

Scleranthus – This remedy is for people who can never decide on anything, but will ping-pong backwards and forwards on a decision, simple or complex, and then finally, when they have made a decision, they are prone to changing their mind at the last minute.

Star of Bethlehem – This is the remedy for shock. Often, when we experienced a shock, our brain and our emotions have to find each other. So, if somebody has experienced something dreadful but has not been able to release it, Star of Bethlehem will help.

Sweet Chestnut – This remedy is for people who have somewhat lost the will to live and just cannot in anyway see that there is any light at the end of the tunnel. Despair and anguish are all they experience.

Vervain – This remedy is for people who hold very strong opinions. Whether it is about politics, the environment, religion, animal rights or poverty, you will soon know their thoughts. Don't dare stand in their way or try to impose your view. People who are in need of vervain are people who are active and on the go and will always look at life as a project to be completed, and will stop at nothing.

Vine – This remedy is for people who are natural leaders and will take control in any and every situation and can be very unbending. However, when they take control, they take complete control. Sadly, nasty dictators are often seen as having vine personalities. The vine character is super strong, slightly vain and totally confident that what he or she is doing is right.

Walnut – This remedy is for change. It can help in any situation where there is change such as moving country, house, job or school – even changes in life like childbirth, teething, puberty and menopause. Walnut will help break the ties to the old memories or previous states.

Water Violet – This remedy is for people who are usually very calm and extremely comfortable with their own company. They prefer to be with a handful of good friends rather than large social gatherings. Sadly, others find them aloof and slightly arrogant and see them as unfriendly, which is not true. By taking the remedy water violet, this will allow this person to reach out and be more warm.

White Chestnut – This remedy if for people who can't stop thinking. They just keep going over and over things in their own head and whether they want to or not, the mind just can't stop. Often this white chestnut moment can cause insomnia and exhaustion.

Wild Oat – This remedy is for people who are at any crossroads in life. It can be a time when you stop and think, "what is it I really want to do with my life". Wild oat can put you on the right path.

Wild Rose – This remedy is for people who find life difficult. They believe there is nothing that they can do about it. They lack the ability to feel any emotion – good or bad.

Willow – This remedy is for people who feel sorry for themselves. "Nothing is going my way, why is my life so hard and everybody else has it so easy?" is how they feel. Willow will help them realise that life is not so bad.

Bach rescue remedy – This remedy is a combination of five flower essences; rock rose, clematis, star of bethlehem, impatiens and cherry plum. The combination allows it to be very helpful in many situations where there are shock, panic, terror, irritation and worry. You can use Bach rescue remedy before you have to present a speech or after a car crash. It helps to calm and instill irrational or rational thoughts and fears.

Mother Nature's Medical Kit is about giving you a knowledge of the 'tools' that I use in my remedies (that follows in Part 3 – A–Z of Conditions). The reason to give you this information is twofold; one is so that you can understand more deeply why I am asking you to take huge amounts of garlic mixed with manuka honey and two is with the hope that the more you understand about foods, essential oils and Bach flower remedies, the more you can apply them into your daily lives or create your own recipes for health.

As I mentioned before, I have not included every medicinal food item and every essential oil here in this book. I am just trying to keep it as simple and as easy to use as possible. Just remember that half of healing is having faith in what you are doing, so with whatever tool you decide to use and have an open mind and believe you can heal.

Part Three

A–Z
HEALTH
CONCERNS

In this section, I will guide you through some of the most common
conditions that I have treated in my clinic. I couldn't put every condition
in this book but rest assured even if it's not here you might have the knowledge
from part 2 & 3 to treat it yourself. A word of advice, read the following section
on 'how to make these remedies really work'.

Good luck and good health.

HOW TO MAKE THESE REMEDIES WORK FOR YOU

Just as a doctor will prescribe an antibiotic to be taken three times a day, strictly before or after food, or an antihistamine may be prescribed every four hours, you need to follow a 'prescription' for natural remedies too. The fact that the remedies are foods, herbs, acupressure points or essential oils does not mean that instructions and guidelines don't have to be given and followed. These everyday foods and natural remedies can have immense healing powers when used correctly but you need to know how to make them work for you. For example, it's easy to be told that thyme tea is good for a dry ticklish cough but exactly how do you make it? Is it from dried thyme or fresh? How often do you take it, how much of it at a time and for how long? What can you add to make it more effective? This is what I want this book to give you: step-by-step instructions to really ensure you are taking your natural medicine correctly so that it will truly make a difference and work for you and your loved ones.

If prepared and administered correctly, consumed or used properly, the natural healing that can result is just astounding.

So here is how it works.

STEP 1 – Start quickly!

Crucial to making the natural way work best is to start at the very beginning. Prevention is always better than cure. At the first signs of an ailment start your cure. This will shorten the length you are down with the condition.

However, this does not mean that you cannot follow the recipes and if you haven't started from the first sign of illness. If you start midway through your developing condition, just give it a bit more time.

Be warned, unfortunately in some cases you will feel worse before beginning to feel better – this is commonly referred to as the healing crisis.

STEP 2 – Follow instructions

As you follow instructions from a conventional doctor, follow the instructions that are given with each condition. If you are instructed to take manuka honey UMF 15+ every three hours, do it. If you have to do an inhalation three times a day, do it. Many people, for some reason, tend to expect miracles from nature and will take 1 cup of tea or 1 spoonful of honey and expect it to work it's magic after just 1 dose. No medicine works like this – conventional or natural.

Just as with a prescribed course of antibiotics, when you start feeling better, don't stop. Often you can feel better quite quickly, especially, if you start treating yourself from the beginning of the ailment but even if you feel better or the condition seems to be clearing up, keep going for the required amount of time until you have been completely clear of symptoms for at least 2–3 days.

STEP 3 – The healing crisis

This is probably the biggest downfall of alternative medicine. Unfortunately, it is often during the healing crisis that you may feel like giving up and running to a doctor. As our bodies correct or purge the system of whatever you have, you often feel worse before feeling better. With most conditions, the 'healing crisis' lasts no longer than 12–24 hours. If it goes on for longer, then you need to seek medical help.

The healing crisis can be uncomfortable – splitting headaches, high fevers, aches, skin eruptions, diarrhoea, emotional crying or a new pain in a different location to the original pain you are treating. All these symptoms are typical of your body healing itself. Through the common use of conventional medicine we are taught to fear these symptoms and try to suppress them. Quite the opposite is in fact needed. Do not suppress them. Try to ride them out and follow the steps given to you in this book. When the healing crisis is over, the outcome and healing is often astonishing. However, I must repeat, if the 'healing crisis' lasts longer than 24 hours, seek medical advice. You may be treating the wrong base condition, started too late, or the infection has taken a stronger hold than expected.

STEP 4 – You can combine conventional and alternative medicines

If you feel that things are not going in the right direction, and you might need the help of conventional medicine, that's okay – you can actually use it alongside most of the natural treatments I have prescribed without side effects. However, not all alternative and allopathic treatments can be combined for example if you are treating a wart my way, and you get drops from the chemist, an interesting but painful chemical experiment may result. Use your best judgement. Do not mix topical treatments. Only use one solution in your bath at a time – mine or a medical one. Inhalations should not be used at the same time as a nose-spray, but should be used on an alternate basis. Acupressure points, however, can give relief no matter what method you are using. However, always inform your doctor that you are also using natural remedies.

STEP 5 – Allow yourself time to heal

We have become an instant gratification society – fast food, microwaves, the internet, mobile phones and high-speed trains all putting the world at our fingertips instantly. The natural approach to medicine is very effective but you must have a bit of patience. By patience I mean don't expect miracles. If you have a cold and it's not completely gone the next day, don't say 'oh this doesn't work'. Instead, let the bug, virus or bacteria work its way out of your body. You will be sick but probably not for as long as usual and your recovery will be much faster. If you took a commercial cold pill, you'd probably feel better instantly for a few hours before feeling lousy again. Then you would take the next pill, and the next. These pills mask the problem instead of healing and letting the body work at healing itself – which is what these natural remedies do.

HOW TO MAKE ACUPRESSURE WORK FOR YOU

In most conditions there will be acupressure points listed and shown. The points are a very crucial step to stimulating and instructing your body to heal. They are not complicated. Just look at the picture where the point is placed and find that same area on yourself. If you are unsure you have the exact point, do not worry, just rub the general area. Press or rub into it as deeply as you can for the count of between 30–60 seconds then release. Repeat for a total of 3–5 times (you can do more if you would like to, there is no limit). I will advise you to do them 1–3 times a day or every hour or until there is relief. This will depend on the issue at hand, but ultimately you do them when it is convenient for you. Just bear in mind pressing them just once might not have the same results as compared to doing so multiple times. The area where you are pressing can feel bruised but this is normal. Sometimes you may even see a bruise appear but do not worry this can actually be a good thing. Sometimes, I find the people who have bruised points tend to heal more quickly.

You will see with each point, there will be some letters and a number. The letters will indicate the meridian that is running through the area that is affected, or where the meridian stems from. For example, the large intestine (Li), gallbladder (Gb), liver (Liv) and stomach (St) meridians, all run through the sinus area, so the different points on those meridians will be indicated to be pressed or massaged. The number will indicate the location on the meridian.

Lu – Lung meridian
Li– Large intestine meridian
St – Stomach meridian

Sp – Spleen meridian

H – Heart meridian

Si – Small intestine

Ub – Urinary bladder

K – Kidney meridian

P – Pericardium meridian

Sj – Sanjiao meridian (SanJiao is also known as the Triple Warmer– TW)

Gb – Gallbladder meridian

Liv – Liver meridian

Du meridian is also know as the GV – Governing Vessel

Ren meridian is also know as the CV – Conception Vessel

Each meridian starts from an organ and will end at the next organ, except for the Du and Ren meridians, which are extra meridians and connect to each other. The combination of acupressure points in this book is predominantly based on Dr. T.T. Ang's method.

SUPPLEMENT GUIDELINES

With most conditions I give a list of advised supplements and amounts. This is a guideline for you to work with. As I am not aware of what is available in your area or where you will be sourcing your supplements from, you might want to speak to a naturopath or a store pharmacist to guide you further. My only condition on supplements is that they should be sourced from nature – foods, plants and herbs etc. and either in liquid or powder forms. Hard pills tend to have nasty fillers and these can actually harm us in the long run.

All the following supplement dosages are for adults. If you want to supplement for children, please follow the following guidelines:

For children age 0–3 years, seek professional advice.

For children age 3–6 years, take ¼ of the amount.

For children age 6–12 years, take ½ of the amount.

For children age 12 and above, follow adult dosage.

I am providing you with the methods and remedies with which I have successfully treated myself, my family and my patients, and I have no doubt that you too can treat yourself and your family with equal success. Take your time, heal gently and good luck.

Manuka Honey +15 UMF
Cayenne Tincture
Salt - Sea / Pink
Turmeric
Tea Tre
Frankinc
Cayenne Powder
Clay
Lavender

FIRST AID

Let's not beat about the bush – an emergency is an emergency. In any of the following situations, first call for an ambulance or doctor to come to your help.

You can then apply my emergency techniques whilst either waiting for medical assistance or on the way to seeking medical attention.

You need the following few items in your basic home Emergency First-aid Kit to treat the most common medical emergencies. It is worthwhile ensuring that you have all of them at hand as you never know when an emergency may occur.

EMERGENCY FIRST-AID KIT

Baking soda
Cayenne tincture
Dry cayenne pepper
Eucalyptus *globulus* essential oil
Frankincense essential oil
Lavender essential oil
Manuka honey UMF 15+
Sea salt or liquid minerals (sodium, potassium and magnesium)
Sterile cloths
Syringe (for oral use only)
Turmeric powder

Cayenne Tincture
170 g cayenne powder
470 ml vodka

Method
Combine cayenne powder and vodka in a jar. Mix well, seal the jar then put it in a dark cupboard. Let sit for 3–4 weeks, shaking it up every other day. Strain mixture through a muslin cloth, coffee filter or a nut bag. Place the tincture in a dark bottle or in a dark area. Use when called for.

HEART ATTACKS

Apart from administrating CPR, immediately give 1 teaspoon of the cayenne tincture (pg 97). If you can give this in a drink (ideally a little warm water, juice or tea), do so, otherwise, syringe it directly into mouth. Press acupressure point P 6 for 30 seconds at a time. Release for a second and then continue. Repeat this until the condition improves or until help arrives. Keep sipping the cayenne tincture.

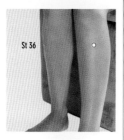

STROKES

Mix 1 teaspoon cayenne tincture into a little warm water and get the person to drink it if they are able – if not, syringe it directly into mouth. Make a very small incision with a sterilised needle on the top of the middle finger of either hand. This will relieve the pressure from the brain. Press on the acupressure point Du 26.

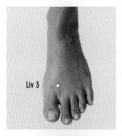

FAINTING

Press acupressure point Du 26 with your fingernail until the person starts to revive. Release and then hold again for another 30 seconds. Give 4 drops of Bach rescue remedy (pg 89).

SEVERE ALLERGIC REACTIONS

Allergic reactions can manifest themselves in many ways. Symptoms can appear as hives, swelling, breathlessness, sneezing, itching and watery eyes. Allergic reactions can come on very quickly.

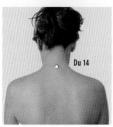

If the allergy is more of a reactive type (sneezing, hives, swelling, breathlessness etc.), quickly make a mixture of 1 teaspoon powdered turmeric with 1 teaspoon manuka honey UMF 15+. Either feed it to the person from the spoon, dilute it in warm water for him or her to drink or syringe it into his or her mouth.

As allergic reactions are known to quickly affect both a person's breathing and swallowing capacities, it is very important to get the person to rest until further help arrives.

While he or she is resting, press acupressure points Du 26, St 36 and Liv 3 for 30 seconds each.

ANAPHYLAXIS

Most people who know that they have a dangerous allergy (or anaphylaxis) will carry an EpiPen with them. If the allergy is a first off, or the EpiPen is mislaid, press acupressure points St 36 and Du 26. Try to keep constant pressure on the Du 26 point. Get emergency medical help as quickly as possible.

CUTS

For deep cuts that are bleeding uncontrollably, pour powdered cayenne pepper onto the cut. Cover with a clean/sterile cloth and apply pressure. This should stop the bleeding until you can reach medical attention or until it reaches you. If you are uncomfortable applying cayenne, drop 5 drops each of tea tree and lavender essential oils onto a sterile cloth, hold this over the cut and apply strong continuous pressure until you get help. The problem with not using the cayenne and using the latter method is that when you remove the pressure from the cut, it might start to bleed again. For Minor Cuts see pg 148.

SUNSTROKE

This condition is much more serious than is commonly believed: it can quickly become very dangerous for the vital organs. Firstly get the person out of the sun and heat as fast as possible. If you are at home get the person into a cool bath and add 170 g baking soda, 170 g Epsom salts, 2 drops each of peppermint essential oil and eucalyptus *globulus* essential oil. If there is no bath available, get them into a cool shower or get a bowl of cool water with some Epsom salts, baking soda, peppermint and eucalyptus oil and sponge them down with a cloth. Make them drink room temperature water with 1 teaspoon baking soda added to it or water into which you have added 1 teaspoon of minerals (magnesium, sodium and potassium). If you don't have any of the above, add 1 teaspoon of salt (preferably good quality rock, sea or pink salt – but any salt will do in an emergency) and 1 teaspoon of sugar or honey into water or juice and drink. Repeat every hour until the sunstroke victim is feeling better.

The best drinks to alleviate the symptoms of sunstroke, in addition to the rather salty concoctions above, are coconut water or mango juice – both of which contain heaps of healing electrolytes.

Rub acupressure point Du 14 in a clockwise direction.

A–Z LIST OF HEALTH CONDITIONS

KEEPING BALANCED = KEEPING HEALTHY

I know I am not starting with the letter A but I have decided to start on a positive note. Many people come to see me with problems for which they seek help, but only a few come to ask how they can prevent themselves from getting sick. As the saying goes, "prevention is better than cure". So let's start this section with prevention. What are some quick and easy steps we can take to keep ourselves generally healthy and hopefully keep us from falling ill?

- Sleep. Sleep is crucial to good health. If you aren't sleeping well, make it your number one priority to correct this situation. Sleep is the time when our body heals and everything fixes itself. To learn more about sleep, look under Insomnia (pg 198) to learn more about your own body clock.
- Avoid processed foods. Eat a healthy well-balanced diet with a variety of fruits, vegetables, fibre and proteins. Good quality meats can be consumed but only 1–3 times a week.

St 36

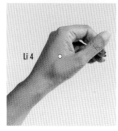

Li 4

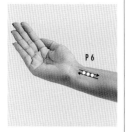

P 6

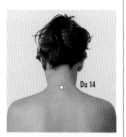

Du 14

- Add some variety to your diet. Our bodies love variety and need to have a break from certain food. For example, good quality breads, could be eaten without the usual side effects if only eaten 1–2 times a week even if you are intolerant to gluten.
- Always maintain a good mineral balance. Our essential minerals are magnesium, potassium and sodium. You can do this with a liquid mineral supplement, or by eating a spoonful of un-sulphured blackstrap molasses or by drinking a shot of aloe vera juice daily.
- Remember strong stomach, strong you. Keep your stomach strong by adding in probiotic foods to your meals and drinks on a daily basis.
- Try to avoid using conventional chemical medicine – always turn to nature first and see what you can do.
- Exercise. Do some form of exercise daily for a minimum of 30 minutes or a minimum of three times a week. One session should be in the form of stretching. Learn some simple yoga stretches even if you are a body builder.
- Detox – adding in detox foods regularly, doing a detox every six months or even a detox day every now and then will give your body a little holiday.
- Emotional health – all diseases start with the emotions. Looking after your emotional health is imperative. Explore both the Bach flower remedies (pg 84) and the essential oils to help support your everyday emotional needs or even to help you realise deep-seated emotions that may be affecting your life.
- In an ideal world we would be going for a massage every week, if not every month, however, this is not always possible. Learn the following four basic acupressure points to do on a regular basis to keep yourself strong and your system moving: St 36, Li 4, P 6 and Du 14.
- Stay hydrated. Water affects every organ, every cell and every aspect of our health. Learn to enjoy drinking water and retrain your brain to drink water on a regular basis.
- Breathe. Relearn to breathe. We all breathe, it's our natural instinct, but we don't breathe deeply. Spend five minutes a day just thinking about your breathing and breathe deeply.
- Laughter is the best medicine. We all love to laugh. Even if we don't have much to laugh at, there is always something funny in life. So don't take yourself too seriously, laugh a little.
- Boost your immune system by taking Vitamin C, zinc, probiotics and your essential minerals on a regular basis.

SIMPLY NATURAL HEALTH

ABSCESSES

An abscess is a pocket of pus under the skin that indicates that there is a bacterial infection present. This normally happens when a bacteria has entered the body either through a cut, scrape or scratch. The pus is made by the white blood cells trying to fight the bacteria. Abscesses can be nasty and painful but can be dealt with very quickly if treated as soon as they appear. An abscess normally starts as a very tender red lump that can grow to quite an alarming size if not treated properly. One must not squeeze an abscess as this can spread the bacteria further into the system.

Essential:

- At the first sign of an abscess, apply a little tea tree on the site. Reapply every two hours.
- Make a paste with 1 tablespoon Epsom salts, 1 tablespoon clay zeolite (or any therapeutic clay), 1 teaspoon manuka honey UMF 15+ and 1 drop each of the following essential oils: tea tree, thyme *vulgaris*, and lavender. Cover the abscess with the paste and then place a hot towel on top. Leave on for 20 minutes. Keep reapplying the hot towel when it has cooled.
- Mix 100 g manuka honey UMF 15+ with 4 garlic cloves and take 1 teaspoon of this every 2–3 hours.

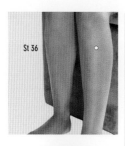

St 36

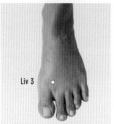

Liv 3

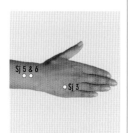

Sj 5 & 6

Sj 3

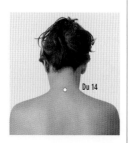

Du 14

Acupressure Points:

St 36, Liv 3, Sj 3, Sj 5, Sj 6 and Du 14. Put neat tea tree on Du 14 and rub in a clockwise direction).

Additional Information:

- Replace all teas and coffees with a thyme tea. To prepare thyme tea, place a handful of fresh thyme or 1 teaspoon of dried thyme into a mug and pour hot (not boiling) water over it. Let sit for 15 minutes then strain. Add 1 teaspoon of manuka honey UMF 15+. Drink three times a day. If you can't find thyme, use echinacea tea (which can be bought at most health food stores).
- Skin a potato and secure the potato skin to the abscess. Leave on overnight or however long you can.
- Prepare a blood cleansing juice and drink daily until the abscess clears up.

Supplements (take until symptoms disappear):

- Echinacea – ½ teaspoon (three times a day).
- Vitamin A – 6,000 ius.
- Vitamin C – 3–5,000 mg.
- Vitamin D3 – 4,000 ius.
- Zinc – 25 mg.

....

BLOOD CLEANSING JUICE

1 grapefruit, peeled
1 green apple
½ bitter gourd or 1 lemon
1 clove garlic, peeled
340 g blueberries

Place all ingredients in a juicer or high-speed blender. Add 235 ml water if using blender.

....

ACNE

What is acne? The human skin, especially on the face, neck, back, and chest is covered in hundreds of thousands of microscopic hair follicles called pores.

These follicles sometimes overproduce cells and become blocked. Sebum (oil), which normally drains out of the surface of the skin, gets trapped and bacteria begins to grow.

One of the reasons why acne may occur is because there are too many toxins in the system. These toxins can come from food intolerances or hormones. They can also come from imbalances in the liver, kidney, stomach and spleen areas. When these four areas are weak or "blocked", our system isn't able to detoxify properly and toxins buildup and try to exit through the skin.

Food-related acne (for acne on forehead or cheek area):

Many people who suffer from acne suffer from food intolerances or allergies. The main foods that cause problems within our systems are the usual culprits: wheat products, all milk and dairy products, sugars, refined foods and heavily fried greasy foods. If you suffer from acne, you should try to remove the aforementioned foods for three weeks and see what happens to your skin. The results can be quite astonishing.

Hormones (for acne on chin and nose area):

When our hormones are out of balance, our skin can be out of balance. As the body tries to get rid of an excess of hormones that haven't been cleaned up by the kidneys and liver, these toxins may, again, try to exit through the skin. Hormonal changes (adolescence, pregnancy or menopause) also promote the skin to produce more sebum, which can clog up pores. Once the hormones are under control, the skin should clear up.

Essential:

- Take 8–10,000 mg of Vitamin C per day. (If this prompts diarrhoea then lower the dosage slightly. Don't worry about overdosing on Vitamin C; you can't in the short term – you will just pee out the excess).
- Take 200 billion cells of probiotics daily. 100 billion in the morning and 100 billion in the evening before bed.
- Start your day with the juice of either ½ a freshly squeezed lemon or with 1 tablespoon apple cider vinegar and 1 tablespoon psyllium in a glass of water.
- Adding fibre (psyllium) into the diet is crucial. This helps clean out the gut which is where toxins can be lurking, creating more and more toxicity. Psyllium is a good source of pure fibre.
- Water is essential for hormonal health and aids the body in detoxifying. Drink at least two litres of good quality water a day.
- Avoid using harsh facial scrubs and foaming facial washes. These strip our skin of its natural PH balance and may, contrary to promises on their labels, actually encourage more spots to appear. The following simply natural facial scrub has worked wonders for spots and acne.
- Blend 170 g oats with 1 tablespoon of baking soda and 1 tablespoon pure Vitamin C powder in a blender. Add some water to obtain a paste. Scrub the face gently, leaving the paste on for a few minutes before washing it off. Store paste in a clean jar and use daily until the spots calm down or use it a minimum of once a week as a preventative measure.
- Tone the face with apple cider vinegar and water. Make a small bottle of toner by adding 1 teaspoon of the apple cider vinegar into 200 ml water and add 2 drops each of tea tree and lemon essential oils (optional: 1 drop patchouli). Shake well before each application and use with a small cotton ball or square.
- Prepare a spot gel of 1 teaspoon of baking soda mixed with a small amount of water and 1 drop of tea tree or 1 tablespoon aloe vera gel and add 1 drop tea tree and 1 drop lemon essential oils. Dab onto spots and leave overnight.
- Not strangely, acne tends to rear its ugly head around the same time that young adults start to use deodorants. As your body is busy trying to get rid of excess toxins through sweat, using an antiperspirant can actually make the spots worse. I would suggest using a natural deodorant instead. The rock deodorants are great and can also be used on spots. Potassium alum (the main ingredient in the rock deodorant) kills bacteria and zaps spots.
- For adults, it is important to take digestive enzymes to make sure that food is being digested properly.

 **CAUTION**
Make absolutely sure you drink lots of fresh water when taking psyllium as it has a tendency to constipate.

- Contrary to popular belief, using oils on a face with acne helps the condition rather than hurts it. Make a mixture of 1 teaspoon jojoba oil (this helps to control the sebum), 1 teaspoon evening primrose oil, 1 teaspoon rosehip oil and 1½ teaspoon almond oil. Add the following essential oils: 2 drops geranium, 2 drops tea tree, 2 drops lavender, 2 drops lemon and 1 drop patchouli.

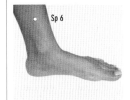

Acupressure Points:

Liv 3, Sp 6, St 36, St 44 and Li 4. Extra points Li 1, Li 11 and St 6 (see pg 235).

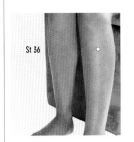

Additional Information:

- Going for a lymphatic drainage massage can help get rid of the toxic load in the system.
- Dry skin brushing is also a great way to stimulate the lymphatic system to detoxify and encourages toxins to leave the skin.
- Make sure you add lots of fresh garlic to your food. Drinking a detox drink of garlic, lemon and manuka honey is an excellent way to clean out your system and get rid of acne. Drink at night before bed or make a natural antibiotic of 100 mg manuka honey UMF 15+ with 5 crushed garlic cloves, 1 teaspoon turmeric powder and $^1/_8$ teaspoon of black pepper. Take 1 teaspoon three times a day.

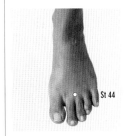

- Once a week, take a warm bath with a handful of Epsom salts, adding 5 drops each of geranium and lemon oil. This helps to detoxify your skin and balances the kidneys and liver.
- Use jojoba oil to remove make-up.
- Use zeolite clay mixed with water or a dilution of water with apple cider vinegar to make a mask or dab on individual stubborn spots.
- Honeysuckle tea helps to clean out toxins from the blood.

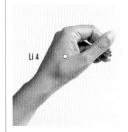

- Use the following Bach flower remedies: gorse (for despair), crab apple (for toxins and impurities), larch (for confidence), mimulus (for shyness and self-consciousness). Either drop each remedy individually into any drink four times a day or get a 30 ml bottle with a dropper, fill it with spring water and add 2 drops of each of the remedies. Take 4 drops four times a day.
- Blood cleansing foods: apples, avocados, beets, blueberries, cabbage, celery, cranberries, garlic, grapefruit, lemon, limes and bitter gourd.
- Drink the clear skin juice.
- To get rid of blackheads, rub pure jojoba oil on the area daily.

Supplements:

The following vitamins and minerals are extremely beneficial to help clear up, prevent and repair the damage done by acne:

- Omega-3 – evening primrose oil works on both skin and hormones.
- Probiotics – 200 billion cells a day (for this I prefer the ones that are freeze-dried and activated by saliva, not the ones that need to be kept in the fridge).
- Selenium – 200 mcg.
- Vitamin A – 10,000 ius (do not use if pregnant).
- Vitamin E – 400 ius.
- Zinc – 25 mg.

....

CLEAR SKIN JUICE

1 green apple, peeled
1 grapefruit, peeled
½ bitter gourd or 1 lemon
1 lime, peeled
170 g blueberries
A handful of mint
1 clove garlic, peeled
1 teaspoon zeolite clay

Place fruits and garlic in a juicer.
Add zeolite clay. Stir.

....

ADRENAL FATIGUE AND CHRONIC FATIGUE

Your adrenal glands are two thumb-sized organs that sit above your kidneys and are part of the endocrine system. Also known as the suprarenal glands, they're involved in producing over 50 hormones that drive almost every bodily function, many of which are essential for life. Hormones affect every function, organ and tissue in the body directly or indirectly. They react to each other as well as respond to conditions in the body in an intricate and highly sensitive balancing act. The adrenal glands work closely with the hypothalamus and the pituitary gland in a system known as the hypothalamus-pituitary-adrenal axis (HPA axis).

Adrenal glands play a huge role in stress response. Your brain registers a threat — whether it's emotional, mental or physical. The adrenal medulla releases adrenaline hormones to help you react to the threat (the fight or flight response), rushing blood to your brain, heart and muscles. The adrenal cortex then releases corticosteroids to dampen processes like digestion, immune system response and other functions.

Adrenal fatigue can occur due to many reasons: high levels of stress (emotional, work-related or family-related), post-virally, after a serious illness, excessive exercise, after exposure to continuous toxins, can be a reaction to long-term medication, a response to too much air travel or a result of chronic insomnia, poor diet and lack of exercise.

The main areas we need to heal are the kidneys (the adrenals lie on top of the kidneys), the stomach and the liver.

Essential:

- Cut out all alcohol, caffeine, teas, coffees and soft drinks. Replace with dandelion root, rooibos, thyme or liquorice teas. However, if you suffer from high blood pressure, do not drink too much liquorice tea.
- Cut out all refined sugars and replace them with manuka honey UMF 5+ (for sweetener), raw unpasteurised honey, pure maple sugar, organic un-sulphured blackstrap molasses or coconut sugar – all in moderation.
- Remove all gluten and wheat products from your diet. The only exception is wholewheat sourdough bread.
- Cut out all refined and processed food.
- Raw foods and adrenal fatigue do not mix. Raw foods take up too much of our system's energy to break down once eaten and require a lot of energy from the kidneys. Lightly steam or stir-fry most vegetables before juicing or blending them.
- To strengthen your kidneys and adrenals, make a blend of the following oils: add the following essential oils into a base of 1½ teaspoon of olive oil: 2 drops geranium, 2 drops ylang-ylang, 2 drops pine, 2 drops black pepper, 1 drop myrrh and 1 drop cardamom.
- Using a small amount of the oil, rub the area where the kidneys lie on the back (either side of the spine above the buttocks), along the spine and on the acupressure points.
- If you feel that your adrenal fatigue is due to emotional stress, explore the Bach flower remedies on pg 84.

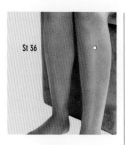

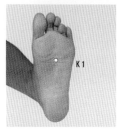

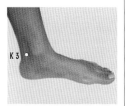

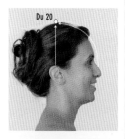

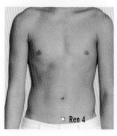

Helpful tips for adrenal fatigue sufferers:

- Try to eat breakfast within an hour of getting up to restore blood sugar levels that were depleted during the night. For example, if you wake up at 8 am, have breakfast by 9 am.
- Eat a healthy snack an hour later (9 am). Aim for a snack that has a balancing effect on your sugar levels – veggies and hummus, sugar-free oatmeal biscuits, apple slices with a nut or seed butter.
- Try to eat lunch between 11–12 pm to prevent a large dip in cortisol levels.
- Eat a healthy snack between 2–3 pm to help offset the natural cortisol dip that occurs around 3–4 pm. Many people notice this dip every day and reach for extra caffeine or carbohydrate-loaded snacks. These will actually impede hormonal balance. Choose to eat the divine delight.
- Try to eat dinner between 5–6 pm and, although it may be difficult at first, try to eat a light meal. Eventually your body will get used to digesting less food in the evening.
- Eat a nutritious, light snack an hour before bed but be sure to avoid refined sugars. Replace all refined sugars with organic raw coconut sugar (very high in magnesium), raw organic honey (ideally manuka), pure maple syrup or an organic un-sulphured blackstrap molasses (packed full of Vitamin B6, magnesium, calcium, iron and potassium).
- Take an Epsom salt bath with 2 drops each of lavender, chamomile Roman and geranium oil.
- It is natural to crave sweets when you have low blood sugar. Fighting adrenal fatigue is exhausting and reaching for quick, easy, and even tasty snacks such as cookies, doughnuts, candy, colas and coffee drinks are common.
- Unfortunately, the energy we get from these types of foods is short-acting and will spike sugar levels.
- As the sugar hits and leaves quickly, it messes with our cortisol levels, which results in a 'crash' after a short-lived burst of energy.

Acupressure Points:

St 36, K1, K3, Du 20 and Ren 4. Extra points Du 4, Ren 6, Ub 23 and *ying tang* (see pg 235).

Supplements:

- Digestive enzymes with every meal to aid digestion and make sure all the nutrients are being absorbed.
- Liquid Multi B complex – which must include Vitamins B12, B5 and B6. Take 1 teaspoon each morning for about 3–6 months or until your energy levels

come back (though a good liquid Multi B is something we should have on a regular basis).

- Magnesium – 200 mg in the morning and 200 mg before you sleep.
- MSM – 100–500 mg (three times a day). MSM helps with stress, increases energy levels and fights fatigue.
- Probiotics – 100 billion cells.
- The adaptogenic herbs of *ashwagandha* and Rhodiola are very helpful. You can often find these in a mix together or individually. Only take them in the morning as directed.
- Vitamin C – 3,000 mg in the morning and 3,000 mg in the afternoon.

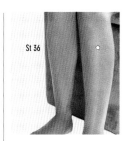

St 36

DIVINE DELIGHT

1 tablespoon un-sulphured blackstrap molasses
1 tablespoon pumpkin seed butter or tahini

Mix together and eat as a treat or when you
feel your energy level is low.

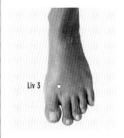

Liv 3

ALLERGIES / HAY FEVER / ALLERGIC RHINITIS

Allergies can be caused by pollen, dust, moulds, plants, grasses and animal dander. When allergies strike, the mucous membranes of the eyes and nose become inflamed, causing sneezing, runny nose and watery or itchy eyes.

The aim here is to teach the body not to react and to reteach the body that what it considers an enemy is actually okay.

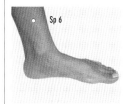

Sp 6

Essential:
- For immediate relief do the acupressure points in order St 36, Liv 3, Sp 6, Li 11 and Li 1–Li 4 (press along the ridge of finger).
- Prepare an oil blend of 1 tablespoon base oil with the following essential oils: 2 drops each of chamomile German, peppermint and geranium. Rub on the spine, over the points and on the sinus area.
- Drinking chamomile tea reduces the inflammation quickly and calms the system down. You may also drink peppermint tea if your nose can't stop running.
- If it is a pollen-based allergy, try to get honey made from local beehives, this will have traces of local pollens. By having 3–4 teaspoons a day, you are gently teaching your body to get used to the pollens. This is highly effective.

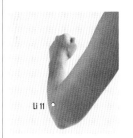

Li 11

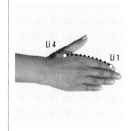

Li 4
Li 1

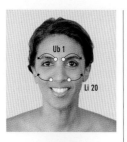

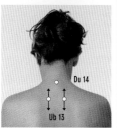

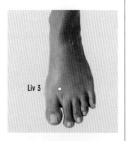

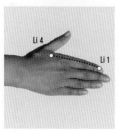

- As soon as the allergies start, get 100 mg of your local honey (if there is no honey produced in your region, use manuka honey UMF 15+ or above) and add 1 teaspoon (either dried or fresh) turmeric and 1 teaspoon of coconut oil. Take this three times a day.
- Take a milk thistle tincture (pg 65) or a dandelion root tea three times a day. This will encourage your liver to clean itself out, allowing the allergen to move through faster.

Acupressure Points:

- For immediate relief press Du 14, St 36 (see pg 113), Liv 3, Sp 6 (see pg 113), Li 11, Li 1–Li 4. Press along the ridge of the finger from the tip of finger ending at Li 4. Hold here for a few seconds.
- For a runny nose press Li 20 and Ub 1, rubbing in a half circular motion.
- For allergic rhinitis rub up and down along Ub 13.

Supplements:

- Glutamine – 1,000 mg.
- Olive leaf extract – 500 mg (daily; 250 mg two times a day).
- Probiotics – 50 billion cells.
- Vitamin C – 2,000 mg (two times a day).

ANAEMIA

Anaemia develops when your blood lacks healthy red blood cells that are known as haemoglobin. Haemoglobin is the protein in our blood that binds to oxygen. This oxygen is then carried to our organs. If your red blood cell count is low or your haemoglobin is abnormal – the cells and organs in your body will not get enough oxygen.

Symptoms of anaemia are principally: fatigue, dizziness, poor concentration and easy bruising. These symptoms occur because organs aren't getting what they need to function properly.

The most common cause of anaemia is blood loss. However, other reasons which may also cause anaemia are poor diet, haemorrhoids, gastritis, digestive disorders, certain medications (non-steroidal anti-inflammatory drugs such as aspirin and ibuprofen), alcohol abuse, tropical sprue, coeliac disease, hypothyroidism, cancer, lupus and overconsumption of caffeinated drinks.

Vegetarians and vegans run a higher risk of anaemia due to possible folate and Vitamin B12 deficiencies. B12 and folate are needed to make red blood cells.

"In order to absorb iron properly, you need Vitamin C."

CAUTION

Synthetic iron that is often offered to anaemic patients can constipate you.

There are only a few steps below but every person who came into my clinic with anaemia (some with quite serious conditions) has felt much better within a few weeks. Their iron levels, as measured by blood tests, were at ideal levels after they followed these simple steps.

Essential:

• Take 2 tablespoons of un-sulphured blackstrap molasses a day. Once in the morning and once at night. They can be mixed into a smoothie or can be eaten directly off the spoon.

• In order to absorb iron efficiently we need to have a good source of Vitamin C alongside our iron source. Good sources of Vitamin C are cabbage, kiwi, thyme tea, açai berries, red onions, red and yellow bell peppers, kale and papaya.

• In order to make healthy red blood cells, our systems need good sources of Vitamin B12 and folate. The most recognised source of B12 is red meat but there are equally good sources of B12 and folate from foods other than meat. Good sources of B12 are spirulina, kelp, barley grass, brewers yeast, bee pollen and alfalfa sprouts. Good sources of folate are broccoli, spinach, chickpeas and lentils.

Acupressure Points:

Sp 6, St 36 and Ren 12.

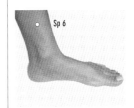

Sp 6

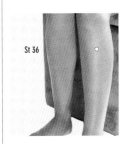

St 36

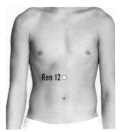

Ren 12

PUMP THAT JUICE 1

3 kale leaves
¼ red cabbage
4 carrots
1 apple
1 lime
1 beetroot
2 teaspoons spirulina

Place fruits and vegetables in a juicer.
Add spirulina.

PUMP THAT JUICE 2

1 banana
340 g pineapple
235 ml nut milk (not almond)
1 tablespoon molasses
1 tablespoon bee pollen
Ice (optional)

Place all ingredients in a high-speed
blender and blend until smooth.

IRON RICH SOUP

2 lamb chops (bones included)
1 stick celery
1 carrot
1 red onion, peeled
½ tin chopped tomatoes
170 g red lentils
3 cloves garlic, peeled
1 teaspoon dried thyme
Salt to taste
Ground black pepper to taste

Place all ingredients in a pot. Cover with water and bring to a boil
for 10 minutes. Lower heat and simmer for 1 hour. Remove lamb
bones and then place all ingredients in a food processor and purée.
Return ingredients to pot and simmer for another few minutes

ARTHRITIS

There are many different types of arthritis. The two main ones that we hear about most are osteoarthritis and rheumatoid arthritis. However, it all boils down to this: arthritis is a joint pain, it hurts and can make your life miserable.

In TCM, arthritis is seen as wind, dampness and cold in the joint issue. This happens when the qi (energy) is not flowing properly through your body and your meridians.

As arthritis is seen as a damp, cold and windy condition, it is quite important to not use 'cold' on joints when they are injured to avoid arthritic joint pain in the future. So the ICE (putting ice, compress and elevate) technique that people are often taught in sports could actually damage the joints more and cause arthritis in the future, .

Essential:
- Remove the following ingredients from your diet: the deadly nightshade family (tomatoes, aubergine, all colours of capsicums, ladies' fingers, goji berries and potatoes), milk, cheese, chocolate, alcohol, fried foods, omega-6 oils, processed foods (some of the preservatives used in processing are big triggers of arthritis), all refined foods (white flour, white sugar, white rice – these just strip us of nutrients), meats that have been grilled or barbecued at a high temperature, tobacco products and smoking should be eliminated immediately. All of the above affect our joints. Once the inflammation has calmed down, you can figure out which ones are your own triggers and start to reintroduce some of them (although you would be healthier just staying away from most of them on the list).
- White refined sugar is a huge no. As sugar feeds phlegm and dampness, both of these directly affect the joints. Replace all white sugar with honey, maple syrup, coconut sugar and molasses.
- Working on the circulation is crucial here. Start your day with a lemon, cayenne tincture and honey drink. Squeeze ½ lemon, 10 drops of cayenne tincture (pg 97) or ½ teaspoon cayenne pepper and 1–2 teaspoon of honey and pour hot water into the cup. Drink warm.
- Prepare an oil mix for the joints. I am going to list the oils that are good for osteoarthritis and rheumatoid arthritis. You can pick 3–4 oils that you have on hand and add 2 drops of each into the following base oil mix. Put your essential oils of choice into a 1 tablespoon of base oil made from 1 teaspoon each of olive oil, avocado oil and calendula oil, and 10 drops of cayenne tincture. Add in your choice of oils from the list below. Rub this mix on the joints as often as possible.

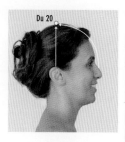

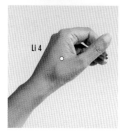

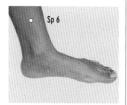

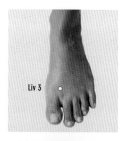

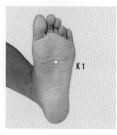

– Osteoarthritis (Osteo): lemongrass, rosemary, chamomile German, chamomile Roman, benzoin and black pepper.

– Rheumatoid Arthritis (RA): frankincense, lemongrass, rosemary, cedar wood atlas, chamomile German, chamomile Roman and peppermint.

- Add omega-3 into your diet – flaxseeds, chia seeds, flaxseed oil, sardines, mackerel, tuna (though be careful with tuna as it may contain high levels of mercury), walnuts and hemp seeds.

- Cut out coffee and black tea and instead drink 700 ml of the following teas daily: dandelion root tea (for RA) or lemongrass and ginger tea (for osteo). Dandelion root tea is readily available in tea bags but lemongrass and ginger should be made fresh. Bruise 5-cm of ginger and 1 stalk of lemongrass, pour boiling water over them in a mug and let steep for 15–20 minutes. Strain. Sweeten with good raw honey or manuka honey UMF 15+. This is also lovely drunk cold, so make a big batch and drink when it's cooled down. These teas are important as they work directly on the liver and kidneys, helping to detoxify and strengthen them. As they detox, the qi starts to flow through the joints.

- At night take an Epsom salt bath or soak the arthritic joint in a bowl of water with Epsom salts and 10 drops of a combination of the above-mentioned oils.

- Iron a red cabbage leaf (see under Sprains, Strains and Joint Pain on pg 220) and wrap the leaf around or place over the sore and affected joints. Wrap a cloth or cling film around to hold in place (ideally overnight).

Acupressure points:
Du 20, Li 4, Sp 6, Liv 3 and K 1.

Additional Information:

- People with arthritis often have high levels of mercury in their systems and this can affect the joints dramatically. Mercury is mainly found in deep sea fishes (tuna, shark, swordfish, tilefish and king mackerel), high fructose corn syrup (which is in more foods than we realise) and in some holding agents for vaccines and amalgams (mercury fillings used in dentistry).

- If you do suffer from arthritis, it is worth doing a hair analysis to see if you have high mercury levels.

- If you do have high mercury levels or suspect you do, start taking 1 tablespoon of zeolite clay daily. Mix into a water or juice.

- Coriander is also an excellent herb to eat and drink as it binds to mercury and pulls it out of us. Blend fresh coriander either into a juice or on its own and drink daily.

Supplements:

- Flaxseed oil – 1 tablespoon (daily).
- MSM – 1,000 mg (daily).
- Vitamin C – 1–5,000 mg (daily).
- Vitamin D3 – 4,000 ius.
- Zeolite clay – 1 tablespoon (daily).

ASTHMA

Asthma is a serious condition that needs great care especially when treating it naturally. With an asthmatic person, something has triggered the airways in the respiratory tract to constrict, thus causing wheezing, shortness of breath and constant non-productive coughing. The problem is that the more a person coughs, the more aggravated their lungs become and the situation gets worse.

The most important thing to note is that if a person is prone to asthma, time is not on their side. Here is our two-pronged goal.

Immediate: follow the steps below to try to alleviate the discomfort and shorten the length of the attack, and hopefully reduce the amount of medication that may be needed.

Long-term: strengthen the lungs and isolate the triggers that cause the asthma attacks in the first place.

The following methods can work alongside asthma medication.

What To Do During An Attack:

- Make and take the following mixture at the first signs of the chest tightening to help stop or relieve the wheezing. Take 125 ml of manuka honey UMF 15+ and mix with 5 crushed garlic cloves and 5-cm of fresh crushed ginger root (young or old). Note that it is important to really crush or pound the garlic and ginger so as to release the juices from both. Mix this into the honey then add ¼ teaspoon cinnamon and ¼ teaspoon turmeric powder, and mix it all together. Add 1 tablespoon of coconut oil. Give this honey mix every 1–2 hours till there is relief.
- Hold a sliced red onion as close to the nose as possible and breathe in deeply to open the bronchial passages. Before you go to bed, chop a fresh red onion and place it into a sock. Lay the sock as close to the nose and mouth as possible. This again will open the bronchial passage, making breathing easier and will also break down any phlegm.

"Turmeric helps to reduce inflammation and relieves wheezing."

- Do the acupressure points listed below three times a day.
- Drink rice milk with 5–10 drops of cayenne tincture (pg 97). This will help to open the airways rapidly.
- Drink large amounts of water, it will help loosen up the phlegm.
- Replace all black teas or coffees with the fresh infusion of ginger, garlic, lemongrass and turmeric. All these herbs help to reduce inflammation rapidly. Drinking any of these in a fresh infusion will be very important. When using fresh ingredients, either peel or clean the herb or food and bruise gently to help release the juices. Pour hot boiling water on top and let steep for 15–20 minutes. Sweeten with manuka honey UMF 15+ (optional) and drink. Make a footbath of warm to hot water with 2 tablespoons of dry English mustard. Soak the feet in the mustard bath.
- Make a breathe easy mixture out of the following oils: add the following essential oils into 1 tablespoon of base oil: 1 drop benzoin, 1 drop frankincense, 1 drop thyme *vulgaris*, 2 drops sweet marjoram (Spanish), 2 drops eucalyptus *globulus* and 1 drop eucalyptus *citriadora*. Rub this oil onto chest and back. Concentrate on the lung area either side of the spine Ub 13 (see picture), criss-crossing along the spine.

Important:

During an asthmatic attack, immediately remove all milk and dairy from the diet (including goat's milk, sheep's milk and yoghurt) and abstain from wheat, chicken, eggs and anything with refined white sugar or artificial colour especially red colouring.

Acupressure Points:

Do acupressure points St 36, Ren 17, Lu 1, Ub 13 and Lu 5. Extra points Du 14 and St 40 (see pg 235). Follow the lung-strengthening massage below but in reverse – moving in the opposite way when you are having an asthmatic attack.

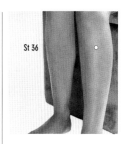

Supplements (crucial to strengthen lungs):

- MSM – 500 mg (daily for three months).
- Zinc – 30 mg (daily for four weeks).
- Foods high in omega-3.
- Magnesium – 500 mg.
- Omega-3 oils (flaxseed oil, coconut oil and good quality fish oil) – 500–1,000 mg (daily).
- Vitamin A – 5,000 ius (do not take long-term).
- Vitamin B6 – 1.3 mg.
- Vitamin C – 3–5,000 mg.
- Vitamin D3 – 4,000 ius.

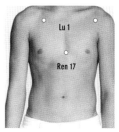

Lung-strengthening Foods:

The following foods are good for asthma as they either help open up the air passages and strengthen the lungs or help stop the excessive buildup of mucus.

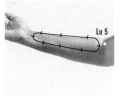

Reversing the lung meridian

Apricots	Cloves
Barley	Cinnamon
Black Currant	Courgettes
Brown Rice	Fennel
Brown Rice Milk	Garlic
Cabbage	Ginger
Carrot	Grapefruit
Chervil	Honey

Horseradish	Pumpkin (pumpkin seed butter)
Lemons	Radish
Mint	Rosemary
Omega-3 rich foods (walnuts, chia, wild rice, kidney beans, salmon, mackerel, sardines)	Savoury
	Sorrel
Papaya	Sunflower Seeds
Peaches	Sunflower Seed Milk
Pears	Turmeric
	Watercress

Asthma-inducing Chemicals:
- Anti-moulding agents used in sliced breads
- Chemicals found in certain plastic containers
- Chlorine
- Insect repellents
- Paracetamol
- Phthalates – normally listed as fragrances
- Silica – found in household scrubs

ATHLETE'S FOOT

Athlete's foot (tinea *pedis*) is a fungal infection that anybody can get. It usually begins between the toes and can spread to the whole foot. Signs and symptoms of athlete's foot include a scaly rash that usually causes itching, stinging and burning. Athlete's foot is contagious and can be spread via contaminated floors, towels or clothing.

Athlete's foot is closely related to other fungal infections and can often reoccur so you have to be committed to following the Essential steps for at least three weeks even if it seems to be gone.

Essential:
- Soak the affected area, either feet or hands, in a bucket with warm water (enough to cover the whole foot or hand). Add 85 g baking soda, 120 ml vinegar and 3 drops each of tea tree and thyme *vulgaris*. After 15–20 minutes of soaking, dry thoroughly. Repeat this everyday for three weeks. If it starts coming back immediately, do the soak again.
- Before bed, put neat tea tree oil directly onto the affected areas and let it dry.

Acupressure Points:

Du 14, Li 11, Li 4, Sp 10 and St 36. Extra points Ub 40 and Sp 6 (see pg 235).

Additional Information:

- Make a mix of 1 tablespoon of base oil (if you have coconut oil then use it as coconut is very antifungal), 2 drops tea tree, 2 drops lavender, 1 drop myrrh, 1 drop thyme *vulgaris* and 1 drop grapefruit seed extract. Rub this mix all over the area and in between the toes, even putting it on and under the nails. Do this before bed. You can put on cotton socks if you don't want to get the oil onto your bed sheets.
- During the day, apply neat tea tree directly to the area then make a mix of 85 g green clay and 85 g baking soda into which you mix 3 drops tea tree, 3 drops lavender, 2 drops thyme *vulgaris* and 1 drop myrrh. Place mixture in a bag and shake well or use a blender and blend together. Powder feet with this before putting on shoes or socks. If you wear open-toed shoes, just put the tea tree on the affected area as mentioned above.
- Whenever you feel the area starting to itch, apply tea tree. Do not scratch the area. Do not pick off the skin as it dries up and peels off. Picking the skin can also spread the fungus further.
- Add 2–3 fresh (not cooked) garlic cloves into your diet daily. You can add it to mashed potatoes, juice, salad dressings or even into tea.
- Prepare the antifungal juice and drink it daily.
- Supplements can be useful to boost up the immune system and fight the fungal infection from the inside.

Supplements:

- Grapefruit seed extract – 10 drops (daily).
- Probiotics – 10 billion cells.
- Vitamin A – 3,000 ius (only for 3 weeks).
- Vitamin C – 3,000 mg.
- Vitamin E – 400 ius.
- Zinc – 10–25 mg.

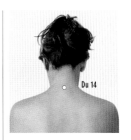

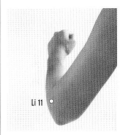

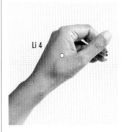

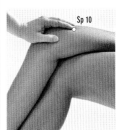

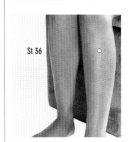

ANTIFUNGAL JUICE

10-cm fresh aloe vera, peeled
2 tablespoons coconut oil
5-cm knob ginger
½ teaspoon ground cinnamon
2 carrots
2 green apples
10 drops grapefruit seed extract

Place all ingredients except grapefruit seed extract in a juicer or blender. Add grapefruit seed extract.

AUTOIMMUNE DISEASES AND CANCERS

Each autoimmune and cancer is so different, therefore I am not going to give instructions on what to do as each disease is so complex and unique and can react very differently to different therapies. There is simply no one 'recipe' to cure all, as some herbs which might help with one can hurt another. What I will do is give suggestions and then insist that you go and seek a natural health practitioner's advice and guidance. With both autoimmune diseases and cancers, the alternative side of medicine has huge amounts to offer in the way of support and even healing, but you need to be physically seen by a practitioner who can guide and support you through your different treatments. Especially with cancers, natural health practitioners and oncologists should work closely together to support the individual, so that neither therapy negates or hinders the other. The ultimate goal is to help the individual back to good health. Remember that both practitioners need to respect and correspond with each other and keep the patients best interest at heart.

Simple Suggestions To Healing:
- The mind is probably the most powerful tool in healing. You have to have faith in yourself and your body to overcome what you have. You have to have determination and trust in yourself and the practitioners that you work with.
- All diseases start somewhere. Most often they start with emotions and stress. Emotions and stress have a huge impact on our lives and make a difference between being healthy or unhealthy. If you have been diagnosed with an autoimmune disease or cancer, it is imperative to look at your emotional

health and stress levels. This would be the time to sit back and investigate past issues or traumas. Work with a qualified practitioner and try to unearth and release the emotions or stress that you have been holding, probably for many years.

- What we eat is very important for our health, but never more so than now. You must find out which foods help you and which foods harm you. Muscle testing and kinesiology are excellent for this.
- Cancer and autoimmune diseases often occur due to toxic overload. Avoid chemicals, eat pure foods and learn to detoxify.
- Our stomachs are crucial when on the path to health. Learn how to strengthen and heal your gut especially a compromised one. Be positive. This is the time to learn how to manage your stress and worry. Start yoga, *chi gong*, *tai chi* or meditation and have faith.

BACK PAIN AND SCIATICA

Whether it's lower, upper back or sciatic pain you have, though it may sound strange, you have probably overworked your kidneys or your gallbladder meridians. And guess how you do this – stress, hormonal imbalances, air travel, too much bad salt, dehydration through excessive sports, hot weather, too much alcohol, coffee and tea, high protein diets, too much fatty foods, raw diets, pregnancy and overuse of various medications (pain killers, anti-inflammatories and blood pressure medicine). These are all things that can weaken the meridians, which in return can lead us to injure our back.

Immediate:

- Prepare a mix of the following oils. Add the following essential oils into 1 tablespoon of base oil: 3 drops sweet marjoram, 3 drops lavender and 1 drop valerian. Rub this into the area where you have the back pain.
- If it's a sciatic pain, rub the oil mix on the lower spine area. The cause of sciatica will be pressure from a bulging disc pressing on the sciatic nerve.
- Immediately do the acupressure points listed. Work on Gb 30 for quick relief.
- After rubbing in the oil put something warm (like a hot water bottle) on the area that hurts as well as on the acupressure point Ub 40.
- Get into an Epsom salt bath. Mix 3 drops of sweet marjoram and 3 drops of lavender with 170 g Epsom salts.

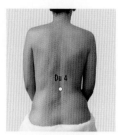

To find this point, draw a line from your belly button around to your spine

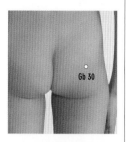

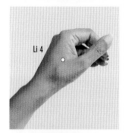

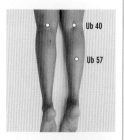

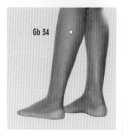

- Turmeric tea can be drunk a few times a day. Place 1 teaspoon of turmeric powder into a glass of hot water. Let sit for 20 minutes, then add ½ teaspoon black pepper and sweeten with honey.
- Start the day with a shot of pure aloe vera juice or buy the fresh plant. Peel it and blend into your juice.

Important:

- Water plays a big role in our back health. As soon as you feel your back start to twinge consciously, start to drink good quality water in large (but not excessive) amounts.
- In order to enable your body and kidneys to absorb water properly, you should take a mix of minerals that include sodium, potassium and magnesium.

Acupressure Points:

- For general lower back pain, press the acupressure points Du 4, Li 4, Ub 40 and Ub 57. These acupressure points are probably feeling quite bruised, but spend a few minutes just pressing into the pain.
- For sciatic pain, press the acupressure points Du 4, Gb 30, Li 4, Ub 40, Ub 57 and Gb 34.

Diet:

- When you have back pain, be careful with your protein intake. Too much protein will stress the kidneys and your gallbladder (cheese and dairy especially aggravate the gallbladder), which will aggravate your back.
- The same holds true for pure raw diets. If you eat raw ingredients and are experiencing back pain, gently stir-fry or steam your foods until your back feels better. Too much raw food taxes our kidneys. To break raw food down, the body has to work a bit harder to 'cook ' the food internally – this cooking energy comes from the kidneys.

BITES AND STINGS

With any bite or sting, if you are swelling or feel constricted in the throat, seek immediate medical attention.

MOSQUITO BITES

To prevent mosquitoes from biting and to calm the bites down, apply the following:

- Mix 225 ml of water with 1 teaspoon of vodka into a spray bottle and add the following essential oils: 5 drops each of citronella, geranium, lavender, cedar wood atlas and eucalyptus *globulus*. Shake well and apply all over the exposed areas that might get bitten or have already been bitten.

CAUTION

If it is a bite from a highly venomous spider, apply tourniquet and lavender oil on the bitten area and seek immediate medical attention.

SNAKE BITES

- Immediately make a tourniquet to slow the circulation of blood towards and from the bite.
- If you have an aspirator, use it to remove venom. Do not attempt to suck the poison out of the wound.
- Immediately apply neat lavender or frankincense oils onto the bitten area as this can neutralise some of the venom. Seek immediate medical attention.

ANIMAL BITES

- Wash the bitten area with water and essential oil of tea tree, then apply neat tea tree oil.
- Seek medical advice if you suspect rabies and/or do not have an up-to-date tetanus immunisation.
- Keep the wound clean and apply tea tree until it starts to heal. Apply lavender to help speed up the healing process.

SANDFLY BITES

- Apply 1 drop each of tea tree and lavender essential oils to the bites immediately. This helps relieve the itch and prevents the bites from getting infected.
- *Note*: to avoid getting sandfly bites, use the anti-mosquito spray before you go to an area where you might be bitten. Reapply after swimming.

BEE, WASP AND HORNET STINGS

- Soak the bite in a mixture made from 120 ml water, 120 ml vinegar and 5–10 drops of lavender oil. Depending on where you have been bitten, either soak the area or use a cloth soaked in the above mixture and hold to the area.
- Mix 1 teaspoon baking soda, ½ teaspoon vinegar and 3 drops of tea tree to obtain paste. Apply directly to the bite to stop it from stinging and swelling. Leave it on for as long as you can. This will calm the sting and the reaction.
- You can use the homeopathic remedy of *apis mellifica* – 30 cc every 30 minutes after the initial bite.

SPIDER BITES

Apply essential oil of lavender or frankincense to spider bites as this not only calms the bite down but also neutralises the venom.

JELLYFISH STINGS

Apply neat vinegar with a few drops of lavender oil onto the bite area. Soak or bathe the sting in this mixture until it calms down.

BOILS

Boils are painful and acute inflammations that normally start around the root of a hair. A boil usually starts off as a hot red patch that feels tender to the touch and then develops into a hard lump. Boils must not be squeezed, poked or prodded. Doing this can lead to the infection spreading. Boils are a clear indication that the body is full of toxins, so following a clean and less toxic diet along with some special cleansing foods and juices will benefit or resolve the problem.

Essential:

- Take a handful of Epsom salts combined with 2 tablespoons of zeolite clay. Make a paste by adding some water. Add the following essential oils to the paste: 1 drop each of tea tree, thyme *vulgaris* and lavender. Cover the boil with paste and let it dry onto the boil. Take a hot washcloth or flannel and hold it over the boil and the dried paste. The heat combined with the paste will help to draw the infection out whilst the oils will work on killing off the infection. Note that if you don't have both Epsom salts and clay, you can use one or the other combined with the oils. Use the washcloth to wipe the paste away. Pat dry.

- After the paste and hot compress, you should put 1 drop each of tea tree and lavender essential oil onto the boil and let them dry. Do this at least 2–3 times a day.
- Taking the homeopathic remedy of thuja helps to push the infection out very quickly, but be warned, if there is more than one boil lurking beneath the skin, the others will also be pushed out.
- Prepare a natural antibiotic: mix 100 mg of manuka honey (UMF 15+ or above) with 4 crushed garlic cloves, 1 teaspoon fresh turmeric (or turmeric powder) and 1 tablespoon coconut or flaxseed oil. Take 1 teaspoon three times a day.

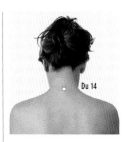

Acupressure points:
Du 14, Li 11, Sp 10, Ub 40 and Liv 3. Extra point Sp 6 (see pg 235).

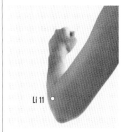

Additional Information:
- Replace all teas and coffees with echinacea, thyme or dandelion root tea. Drink any of the above three times a day.
- Make the blood cleansing juice (see pg 104).

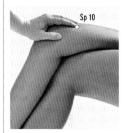

Supplements:
- Probiotics – 20 billion cells.
- Vitamin A – 10,000 ius.
- Vitamin C – 4,000 mg.
- Vitamin D3 – 1,000 ius.
- Vitamin E – 400 ius.
- Zinc – 25 mg.

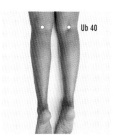

BRONCHITIS / BRONCHIOLITIS

Bronchitis is an inflammation of the lining of the air tubes in the lungs (bronchi). Bronchitis often starts virally but can turn bacterial as the mucus gets stuck in the bronchi and can get infected. Our main aim during bronchitis is to stop it from going bacterial, reduce the inflammation (which can cause wheezing) and loosen and expel as much of the phlegm as possible from the lungs.

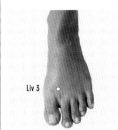

Immediate:
The top three foods that should be cut out immediately during an attack of bronchitis, or even suspected bronchitis are the following: chicken, eggs, all

forms of dairy (including cheese, yoghurt, goat and sheep milk), wheat, cold drinks or cold foods.

Essential:

- Prepare a mix of the following oils: 2 drops lavender, 2 drops thyme *vulgaris*, 1 drop ginger, 2 drops sweet marjoram (Spanish), 2 drops eucalyptus *globulus* and 1 drop frankincense. Rub on the chest and back area.
- Use these oils on the acupressure points listed.
- Make a hot onion compress on the chest and back. Slice an onion and warm it gently in the oven (do not cook). Lay a thin muslin cloth on the skin then lay onion on chest. Place a hot damp towel on top. Cover with a dry towel and breathe deeply for a while. Repeat on the back.
- Make and take the following mixture at the first sign of the chest tightening to help relieve the wheezing. Mix 125 mg of manuka honey UMF 15+ with 5 crushed garlic cloves and 5-cm fresh ginger. It is important to really crush or pound the garlic and ginger so as to release the juice from both. Mix this into the honey then add ¼ teaspoon cinnamon, ¼ teaspoon turmeric powder and 1 teaspoon coconut oil. Mix well. Give this honey mix every 1–2 hours till there is relief.
- Make a honey onion syrup. This helps to break up that thick phlegm that makes it hard to breathe. Slice up a red onion and place in a jar or bowl.

SIMPLY NATURAL HEALTH

Cover completely with manuka honey UMF 15+ or a good raw local honey. Let sit for 5–6 hours. When the honey turns into a complete liquid, add 1 teaspoon ground cinnamon and take 1½ teaspoon four times a day.

- At night, slice a red onion and place into a sock. Tie it up and put it as close to the nose as possible and breathe in deeply. This will open the bronchial passages, break down the phlegm and allow for a good night's sleep.

Acupressure Points:

Ub 13, Li 11, Lu 5, Li 4, St 36 and St 40. Hold each point for 15 seconds thrice. Extra points Liv 3 and K 1 (see pg 235). If there is wheezing, do the lung meridian massage in the opposite way.

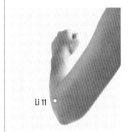

Additional Information:

- Slice 5-cm of fresh turmeric into a small pan of water and boil for 10 minutes. Strain and add equal parts of rice milk. Drink this throughout the day
- Make a footbath of warm to hot water with 2 tablespoons of dry English mustard, 5 drops ginger oil and 5 drops eucalyptus *globulus* oil. Soak the feet for 10–15 minutes.
- Good things to drink on a regular basis to strengthen the lungs include fresh ginger tea, liquorice tea or a nettle tea mixed with some manuka honey UMF 15+.

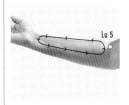

Reversing the lung meridian

Supplements:

- Magnesium – 200 mg.
- MSM 1,000 mg (daily; this helps to strengthen lungs and should be used for long-term).
- Probiotics – 10 billion cells.
- Vitamin C – 3–5,000 mg.
- Zinc – 25 mg (if there is no fever).
- Vitamin D 3 – 4,000 ius.

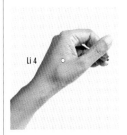

BUMPS AND BRUISES

Bumps and bruises need no great explanation. When you bump into something quite hard and you don't break the skin, there may be bleeding under the skin and a bluish black mark (bruise) appears. It normally takes a while for the bruise to appear so it is helpful to follow the steps below even if there is no sign of a bruise yet.

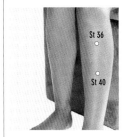

Essential:

- Take arnica pills every hour for the first few hours and rub arnica cream into the bruised area if there is no broken skin.
- Apply neat lavender essential oil directly on the bruise and rub it gently in. This will help with the pain and calm the nerves.
- Add 3–5 drops of lavender oil and 4 drops of Bach rescue remedy (pg 89) into a bowl of water. Dip a cloth in the water and place ice cubes in the cloth. Hold against the bruised area, rubbing it in circular motions.
- Children: administer 4 drops or 4 sprays of Bach rescue remedy for children into their mouths if there is any crying or anxiety.
- Into 1 teaspoon of base oil, add 2 drops lavender oil, 2 drops geranium oil and 1 teaspoon rose hip oil into a base oil of your choice. Rub this mixture onto the bruised area. Make sure to rub quite firmly into the bruise as this will help break up the accumulated blood trapped beneath the skin. The bruise will turn slightly green then yellow as it heals over the next few days.
- If the bruised area is in an area that you can bathe, get into a bath with 170 g Epsom salts and some lavender oil. Gently, but firmly, rub the bruise whilst in the bath.
- After the bath apply the above oil mixture above.

 CAUTION

If there has been a bump to any part of the head, watch for signs of concussion – dizziness, lethargy, throwing up and non-dilation of the pupils. If there are any of these symptoms, take the person immediately to the doctor and do not let them sleep no matter how tired they are.

SIMPLY NATURAL HEALTH

Additional Information:

Boil an egg till it is hard. Remove shell and rub the warm egg against the bruise for as long as you can. Repeat a few times a day. *Note*: the egg does not need to be warmed up again. Do not eat the egg afterwards.

'GOOSE EGG' BUMPS

'Goose eggs' are bumps that come up and look like an egg. Normally they occur on the head; however, they can come up anywhere on the body where there has been a strong contusion or blow. Don't panic when you see a large bump that looks like an egg on your child's head or body. It is better that the swelling comes out than if it occurs internally. Follow the same instructions as above for bumps and bruises, but here the use of the egg is quite important.

Additional Information:

If you bruise easily, you could be deficient in Vitamins C, D3, B12, B9 (folic acid) and iron.

BURNS

A burn is an injury to the skin and tissues caused by heat, friction, electricity, radiation, or chemicals.

Essential:

- Immediately run the burn under some cold running water if it is in an area that allows for that. Take some ice, wet it and hold to the skin.
- To give immediate relief, pour as many drops of pure lavender oil as necessary onto burn. Keep holding the ice to it afterwards.
- With a 1st degree burn, immediately cover the burn with flour. For example, if the burn is in an area where you can place it into a bowl i.e. your hand, fill the bowl with flour (white or brown) and place your whole hand in the bowl so it is totally covered in flour. Keep it there till the burning feeling subsides, otherwise just cover with flour and rest till the burning subsides.
- Mix together 1 tablespoon manuka honey (the higher the UMF factor, the more effectively it works) and 5 drops of lavender oil. If you have pure aloe vera gel, you can add 1 teaspoon to the mixture as well. Mix together and cover the burn area with the paste.
- Once the burn has completely calmed down, apply egg white mixed with lavender oil directly onto the burn area. This helps to repair the skin (even in the case of very severe burns).

CAUTION

If you are treating a 3rd degree burn, you can still apply neat lavender onto the burn, but do not cover it. Go seek medical attention immediately.

Supplements:

Take the follow supplements to reduce and repair the damage to the skin:

- MSM – 1,000 mg.
- Vitamin C – 2,000 mg.
- Vitamin E – 400 ius.
- Zinc – 25 mg.

"CHILLI" BURNS

These burns occur when you touch a red chilli and then rub your eye or mouth, or you drink something strong and an ingredient burns your lips. It can also occur if an essential oil is too strong and it irritates your skin and you feel like it's burning. Most of us experience this feeling at one time or another, but it is rare that someone knows what to do about it.

Essential:

- Immediately wash the area that "burns" with cold water to wash away the residual offender.
- Get some cool plain yoghurt from your fridge and apply a thick layer of yoghurt on the "burning area". Leave it on the burn until it has calmed down.
- When you remove the yoghurt, you can apply pure aloe vera gel.

SUNBURNS

Sunburns are caused by overexposure to the ultraviolet rays of the sun. This causes reddening, inflammation, and in severe cases, blistering and peeling of the skin. In the case of severe sunburn, one also has to watch out for dehydration.

After any sunburn or prolonged exposure to sun and heat, follow the steps under Sunstroke (pg 99) against dehydration to replenish the electrolytes.

Essential:

- Run cold water over the sunburnt area. If necessary, run a cold bath and add some ice cubes.
- Mix 1 tablespoon of aloe vera gel with 2 drops each of lavender, eucalyptus *globulus* oils and Bach rescue remedy (pg 89). Apply onto the sunburn. Leave it on the skin without covering for as long as possible. Reapply as necessary.
- When the sunburn has calmed down, prepare a mixture of 1 teaspoon jojoba oil, ½ teaspoon avocado oil, 1 teaspoon argan oil, 1 teaspoon sesame oil and 1 tablespoon almond oil and add the following essential oils: 5 drops

lavender, 5 drops mandarin, 5 drops geranium and 2 drops chamomile German. Use this in place of an aftersun cream, this will help repair some of the damage the sun has done to the skin. Use this at night as well.

- Make sure you cover up the sunburnt area with a UV swim shirt, a hat or trousers for at least 2–3 days after the burn. When you do return to the sun, make sure you have a good chemical-free sunscreen.
- Drinking fresh watermelon or coconut water during and after a sunburn will have a cooling effect on your internal system. Coconut water also replenishes your electrolyte balance to save you from heat stroke as well.
- If you suspect heatstroke, follow the emergency section on pg 97.

Supplements:
Take the follow supplements to reduce and repair the damage to the skin.
- MSM – 1,000 mg.
- Vitamin C – 2,000 mg.
- Vitamin E – 400 ius.

CHAPPED LIPS

Sore and chapped lips often happen due to weather change or reaction to a food or chemical. To ease the soreness, follow the steps below.

Essential:

Warm 2 tablespoons of your choice of oil very gently (do not boil or bring to smoking point). I would suggest one of the following: olive, almond or argan oil. When the oil has warmed up, add ½ teaspoon of hard beeswax. Let the beeswax melt into the oil with the oil still over low heat. Once you can no longer see the beeswax, remove from heat and let it cool for about 10 minutes. Add $\frac{1}{8}$ teaspoon manuka honey UMF 15+. When you see the mixture is starting to solidify, add 2–4 drops of any of the following essential oils – lavender, mandarin, geranium, rose or benzoin (refer to pg 76 to decide which oil you might like). Decant into a small jar that has a lid and let it set. Use as often as you like.

Supplements:
- Evening primrose oil or flaxseed oil or coconut oil – 1,000 mg.
- Liquid Multi B (which contains B3) – follow suggested dosage on bottle.
- Magnesium – 400 mg.

CHICKENPOX

Chickenpox is a viral infection caused by the herpes zoster virus. It is a highly contagious disease characterised by many itchy, red bumps and water filled blisters all over the body. Children younger than the age of 15 are most likely to get it. However, older children and adults can become infected as well. Chickenpox can be spread by contact with the affected areas or by an infected person sneezing or coughing on an uninfected person. Most children are now vaccinated against chickenpox but even with the vaccination they can still get a 'mild' case.

Essential:
- Run an oatmeal bath to ease the itch. You do this by placing 170 g oats into a cloth or clean sock, holding the cloth/sock over the tap as you run the water through the oats into the bath. Add 170 g baking soda and

SIMPLY NATURAL HEALTH

5 drops of lavender oil. Get the person affected to sit in the bath for as long as possible. Do not shower off after, pat dry instead. If you do not have a bath, follow the same instructions but collect the liquid in a bowl and sponge the patient down.

- Buy some calamine lotion from your pharmacy and add the following essential oils for each 100 ml of the lotion: 4 drops lavender, 4 drops chamomile German and 1 drop geranium oil. Shake the solution well before you use it each time. Apply liberally to all the chickenpox blisters you can see. You can reapply whenever the spots start getting itchy.
- Chickenpox is a hot disease that can come with quite a high fever, so drinking drinks that cool the system down is of vital importance as it makes the itching much more bearable. Coconut water is the best but aloe vera juice and watermelon juice are also effective.
- Give a spoonful of manuka honey UMF 15+ three times a day to help the body fight the virus

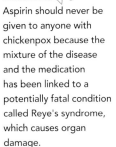

Additional Information:
- Make popsicles out of coconut, watermelon or honeysuckle tea.
- When the last blister has dried up, prepare a mixture of 1 teaspoon almond oil, 1 teaspoon avocado oil, 2 drops lavender, 2 drops chamomile German and 4 drops of pure Vitamin E oil. Rub oil on all the dried up chickenpox to avoid scarring.
- Avoid going out into the sun whilst the scars are still visible and slightly red.
- Avoid taking the antiviral drugs that claim to suppress or stop the chicken pox from coming out. It's best to let them come out. Yes, it will be uncomfortable and itchy but the worst will be over 5–7 days later.

Supplements:
- Flaxseed oil – 1 tablespoon.
- Vitamin C – 3,000 mg.
- Vitamin D3 – 2,000 ius.

CHILLS

Whether you live in the tropics or in the Arctic, getting chilled means that for some reason, be it an ice storm or a tropical storm, your body (especially your nose) gets cold. Just as we know that heat (through fevers) seems to trigger the immune system into action, the cold does the opposite. When your temperature is lowered, especially in the nose, the immune system seems to falter and we become more prone to getting cold viruses. So to avoid getting a 'chill', which can lead to a possible cold, here is what you do.

Essential:

- If your clothes are wet, get out of them and as soon as possible get into a warm bath with 170 g Epsom salts and 5 drops each of the essential oils of eucalyptus *globulus* and ginger.
- Make a ginger tea by placing 5-cm of slightly bruised ginger root in a pot with water. Boil for 10–15 minutes then strain. Add some honey and drink.
- Do a steam inhalation with 2 drops each of eucalyptus *globulus* and clove oil.
- Add 2 drops each of eucalyptus *globulus*, ginger and clove oil into 1 tablespoon of base oil. Rub onto the soles of your feet and along the spine. Put on socks and cover yourself.

"Ginger is full of zinc which is an essential trace mineral that stimulates our immune system."

"Thyme tea is extremely high in Vitamin C and stimulates white blood cells."

COLDS

The most important thing about treating colds is to begin your remedy as soon as you think one is starting. If you experience a slight sore throat, sneeze all day, feel a bit achy or have a headache, start immediately.

Immediate:

- 1 teaspoon of manuka honey UMF 15+ every 1–2 hours.
- Vitamin C – 2–3,000 mg (adults) 1–2,000 mg (children) three times a day, preferably powder form.
- Vitamin D3 – 4,000 ius (adults) 2,000 ius (children).
- Zinc – 50 mg zinc (adults) 20 mg (children) as long as there is no fever.

Li 20

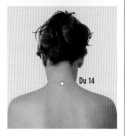
Du 14

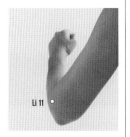
Li 11

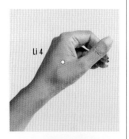
Li 4

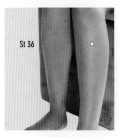
St 36

Essential:

- Make a honey, ginger and garlic tea. Into warm water crush 1 clove garlic, 2.5-cm ginger, ½ a squeezed lemon and manuka honey UMF 15+. Drink.
- Take a bath with 170 g Epsom salts and add the following essential oils: 3 drops each of lavender, tea tree and eucalyptus *globulus*. Add 2 drops pine if you are beginning to get a cough.
- If your nose is dripping, prepare a peppermint, ginger or thyme tea and add manuka honey UMF 15+.
- After the bath, do an inhalation with the following essential oils: 1 drop each of eucalyptus, tea tree, lavender and peppermint essential oils.
- Take echinacea, olive leaf extract or grapefruit seed extract three times a day.
- Drink water constantly. Do your best to help your body to flush away this cold.

Acupressure Points:

Li 20, Du 14, Li 11, Li 4 and St 36.

Additional Information:

Add 2 drops each of the flower essences of crab apple and walnut into your tea, juice or water four times a day.

IMMUNE-BOOSTING SOUP

2 pieces of organic/hormone-free chicken
2 stalks celery
1 red onion
10-12 cloves garlic, peeled
7.5-cm of ginger, peeled
6 black peppercorns
A handful of fresh thyme
A pinch of good sea salt or pink salt to taste
1–½ teaspoon of cayenne pepper (optional)

Place ingredients in a pot. Cover with water and boil for 40 minutes. Remove chicken and cut into strips. Do not eat chicken if you are coughing or beginning to cough. You may also add some noodles or macaroni (non-wheat) to the soup. Ladle into a bowl and enjoy.

COLD BUSTER JUICE

1 lemon, peeled
1 apple
1 carrot
5-cm knob ginger, peeled
1 clove garlic, peeled
A handful of mint leaves
2 cabbage leaves
2,000 mg Vitamin C
10 drops echinacea or 10 drops
    grapefruit seed extract

Place all ingredients except Vitamin C and echinacea or grapefruit
seed extract in a juicer. Once juiced add the Vitamin C, echinacea or
grapefruit seed extract. .

COLIC

Colic can be a trying time for both mother and baby. During a bout of colic,
the child normally draws his/her legs up to the abdomen and their muscles
seem to contract, which can only make the problem worse. The reason for colic
is still unknown but most of the time it can be linked to either the baby's diet
or the breastfeeding mother's diet.

Essential:

- If you are breastfeeding your baby, you must remove the following foods
  from your diet temporarily: onions, garlic, milk, cheese, cabbage, broccoli,
  green apples, beans, dried beans, cauliflower, wheat, caffeine, refined sugar,
  all soy products and spicy foods.
- Replace all caffeinated drink with fennel tea (you can sweeten this with a
  good raw honey). You can also make a very mild fennel tea for your baby
  (do not add honey). Offer this to the baby around the time that the colic
  normally starts. Fennel tea is safe for breastfeeding and very young babies.
  At many health food stores, you can find fennel tea specially formulated
  for babies from as early as birth.
- Add 1 drop mandarin oil with 2 drops Bach rescue remedy into 20 ml base
  oil (sunflower or olive oil). Massage the lower back of the baby and then
  the stomach, rubbing in a clockwise motion. Rub the soles of the baby's
  feet with the oil concentrating on the instep area. Massage this gently but
  firmly. Be warned, it might be quite tender.
- Do the acupressure points gently.

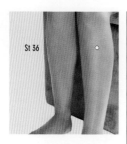

St 36

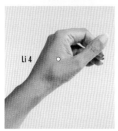

Li 4

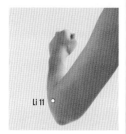

Li 11

- Putting the baby in a warm bath with a handful of Epsom salts would help the baby and the muscles to relax.

Acupressure points:

St 36, Li 4, Li 11 and rub the stomach gently in a clockwise direction with the oils.

Supplements:

- Magnesium – 400 mg.
- Probiotics – 1 billion cells (baby) 50 billion cells (mother).

CONSTIPATION

For most of us, constipation means that you have trouble going to the toilet on a daily basis. Some people will argue that their natural rhythm is to have a bowel movement every 2–3 days, but that's not ideal. Statistically, people who do not empty their bowels every day are shown to be more prone to bowel and liver cancers as the toxins from the un-expelled faeces get reabsorbed back into the system. What causes constipation? Mainly a lack of fibre in the diet, food intolerances, not drinking enough water or liquid, changes in the environment, travelling, sluggish bowels, emotions and fears.

One has to be slightly patient with constipation, as treatments will often take between 12–36 hours before you see results.

"Soaked flaxseeds stimulate the bowels to move."

Essential:

- Make a concerted effort to start drinking a minimum of 1–2 litres of good quality water a day. If you find it difficult to drink water, purchase a 1 litre bottle and squeeze some lemon or a small amount of fresh juice into the water to make sure that you drink it. Force yourself to drink this throughout the day, but not all in one sitting as you might just pee it out.

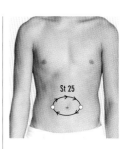

- Often people with constipation are low in the mineral magnesium. Magnesium helps to draw liquid into the bowel and relaxes muscles, which will allow for the bowels to move more easily. Take 400 mg magnesium in a liquid form before going to bed.

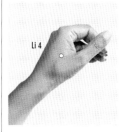

- Cut out foods that cause constipation – milk, dairy, wheat, bananas, white rice, black tea, chocolate, red meat, refined white sugar, refined grains, processed foods and caffeine.
- Add more fibre to your diet. First thing in the morning, before you have breakfast, drink a big glass of water with the juice of ½ a lemon and either 1 tablespoon of psyllium husks or 1 tablespoon chia seeds mixed in (or both).
- Soak 85 g flaxseeds overnight in 235 ml water. The next day, take 1 tablespoon of the flaxseed mix in the morning and 1 tablespoon at night after dinner.

- Mix the following essential oils: 2 drops each of fennel, mandarin and sweet marjoram into 1½ teaspoon of a base oil. Rub on the stomach and intestinal areas in a clockwise direction, pressing in firmly as you rotate. See acupressure points.
- Do the acupressure points daily until your bowels are moving regularly.
- Take high levels of good quality multi-strain probiotics. Eating a good home-made yoghurt or kefir daily or almost any of the fermented foods will also provide you with a good amount of probiotics.

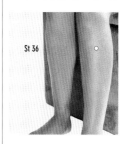

Acupressure Points:

St 25, Li 4, Sj 3, Sj 5, Sj 6, St 36 and Sp 6 (push in a downward motion). Extra points Si 3 (see pg 235).

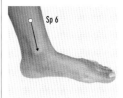

Additional Information:

- Drink 235 ml marshmallow root tea at night.
- Eat magnesium-rich foods (see pg 73).
- Prepare a warm castor oil pack to hold on the stomach area.
- Eating prunes and papayas often helps to get things started and moving, but you have to eat them on a regular basis.

- Check for other food intolerances through a blood test.
- The following chemicals and medicines are known to constipate: painkillers, thyroid medicines, antidepressants, antacids, calcium supplements, iron supplements, aluminium (found in many household products and some foods), anti-inflammatories and blood pressure medicine.

Diet:
- Add more fibre into your diet through fruits and vegetables and whole grains. Make sure you are getting a minimum of 25–35 g of fibre a day.
- Eat the following foods on a daily basis: grapes, raisins, apricots, prunes, pears, broccoli, whole flaxseeds, chia seeds, carrots, beans, peaches, pineapple juice, figs (dried or fresh), whole grains, oats, bran, plums, raspberries and strawberries.

....

MOVE YOUR BOWELS JUICE

Drink first thing in the morning on an empty stomach.

1 beetroot
1 apple, peeled
½ papaya, peeled
1 lime, peeled
1 lemon, peeled
2 kale leaves
A bunch of mint
1 teaspoon (25–30 billion cells) probiotics
1 tablespoon psyllium husks
1 tablespoon chia seeds

Place fruits and vegetables in a juicer or blender.
If you are using a blender, add 235–470 ml water,
then add probiotic, psyllium husks and chia seeds.

....

COUGHS

Coughs come in many different varieties. There are dry coughs, phlegmy coughs, wheezing coughs and barking coughs. It is in all our interests to stop spreading coughs around as fast as possible. In this section, you will find the most efficient methods that are proven to work on all the above mentioned coughs.

I will differentiate the specific treatments for each variety of cough in the next page, however, there are a few basics that apply across the spectrum.

Essential for ALL Coughs:

- Prepare a chest rub using 1 tablespoon of base oil with the following essential oils: 2 drops eucalyptus *globulus*, 2 drops lavender, 2 drops sweet marjoram, 2 drops pine, 1 drop benzoin and 1 drop frankincense. Rub the oil onto the chest and upper back area. Concentrate specifically on the Ub 13 area. Do a steam inhalation with 2 drops each of eucalyptus, pine, tea tree and lavender oils.
- Make a natural antibiotic and anti-viral honey mixture of 125 g manuka honey UMF 15+ with 5 crushed garlic cloves and 5-cm of crushed peeled ginger. It is important to really crush or pound the garlic and ginger so as to release the juices from both. When this is mixed together, add ¼ teaspoon powdered cinnamon, ½ teaspoon dried turmeric and 1 teaspoon of coconut oil. Mix well together. Give or take this mixture every 1–2 hours until there is a noticeable relief of the symptoms.
- At night, slice or roughly chop a red onion, place in a sock and put near the nose area or next to the bed. The onion improves circulation and will help break up thick mucus and phlegm.
- Make a natural cough syrup by slicing a red onion and covering it with manuka honey UMF 15+ or ½ manuka honey UMF 15+ and ½ good quality raw honey. Let sit for 5–6 hours until the onion turns into a liquid. Give or take 1½ teaspoon 3–4 times a day until the cough starts subsiding or is gone completely.
- Take 2–4 drops of oregano oil in juice or water until the cough subsides.

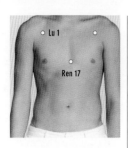

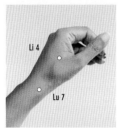

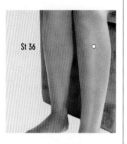

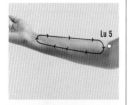

Lung meridian massage

Acupressure Points:

Lu 1, Lu 7, Lu 5, Li 4, Ren 17, Ub 13, St 36 and massage lung meridian.
Extra points K 1 and Li 11 (see pg 235).

Additional Information:

- Air-conditioning might irritate the air passage; using a fan is recommended.
- Chicken meat (but not chicken broth or soup), refined white sugar and dairy products will make you cough more. Limit these foods for the duration of the cough.
- Chlorine from pools and water systems can aggravate a cough. Limit swimming and contact with chlorinated things.
- A residual cough can last for up to 30 days which means that you will be more prone to getting a secondary infection. Prepare the immune-boosting soup (pg 138) to strengthen the immune system.
- Place an onion next to the bed every day till the cough fully subsides.
- People who are prone to coughs and lung issues are often low in zinc. Supplementing zinc or eating zinc-rich foods is important (see Mother Nature's Medical Kit pg 53).

CHESTY COUGH

- Prepare a sage and manuka honey UMF 15+ tea if you have a chesty/phlegmy cough. Use either dried or fresh sage. Take 1–2 heaped tablespoons of sage, pour hot (not boiling) water over the herbs. Let sit for 10 minutes then strain and add honey. Take two times a day until phlegm disappears.
- For thick phlegm and wheezing, do a mustard footbath. Take 2 tablespoons of dried English mustard or crushed mustard seeds and place into a large bowl of warm water. Add 5 drops each of eucalyptus *globulus* (for children under the age of 5, use eucalyptus *citriodora*) and ginger essential oils to this mixture. Soak feet for 10–20 minutes.

DRY COUGHS

- Make a thyme and manuka honey (UMF 15+ is recommended) tea. Use either dried or fresh thyme. Take 1 tablespoon dried thyme or 1 handful fresh thyme and pour hot (not boiling) water over the herbs. Let sit for 10 minutes, strain and add the honey. Take two times a day until cough disappears.
- Mix 3–4 tablespoons of manuka honey UMF 15+ with the juice of 1 whole lemon. Take a spoonful of the mixture every 3–4 hours.

- Rub a piece of fresh ginger above and below the sinus area.
- Suck on echinacea or manuka honey lozenges.

WHEEZING

Do the lung-strengthening massage on the arm but in reverse (see diagram).
- Soak the feet in a mustard bath for 20 minutes (see under Chesty Coughs).
- Make a mustard rub for the chest and feet. Mix 1 tablespoon crushed mustard seeds or ½ tablespoon ground mustard powder into 120 ml base oil. Let infuse for 30 minutes. If you are using mustard seeds, remember to strain before using.
- Rub the mustard oil on the chest and back, then place slices of red onion on the chest where the oil is. Cover chest with a warm damp cloth and cover the cloth with a dry cloth. This helps to keep the chest warm. Do not let the chest get cold. This will make the chest warm and might cause a burning sensation.
- Drink nettle tea with manuka honey UMF 15+.

Sage and manuka honey tea.

BARKING COUGHS

Please see the section about Croup on pg 147.

Supplements:
- Olive leaf extract or echinacea – 1 teaspoon (three times a day).
- Probiotics – 30 billion cells.
- Vitamin C – 1,000 mg.
- Vitamin D3 – 2,000 ius.
- Zinc – 25 mg.

CRACKED HEELS

Cracked heels can be excruciatingly painful and not to mention very unsightly. They are caused by cracking or splitting of the thickened and dry skin on an area of the foot that takes a lot of pressure daily – the heel. Walking barefoot, on hard floors and with open shoes that have little support can make this condition worse.

Mustard footbath

Essential:

- Soak your foot in a warm footbath with 85 g Epsom salts and 5 drops of mandarin oil. Pat the foot dry.
- When feet are still soft from the soak, use a natural pumice stone to rub some of the dead and dry skin away.
- In a small pot that has a cover, mix 1 teaspoon olive oil and 1 teaspoon calendula oil together. Add 5 drops benzoin oil. Rub onto the heels at night. Put socks on so the oils will be more efficiently absorbed while you sleep.
- Repeat this routine nightly. If you can't do a footbath every night, try and do it a few times a week.

Supplements:

- Magnesium – 200 mg.
- Omega-3 oils (flaxseed, coconut and krill) – 1,000 mg.
- Zinc – 25 g.

CRADLE CAP

Cradle cap is harmless but it looks unsightly. Normally found in babies but, beware, it can also affect adults. It is characterised by a thick yellow crust on the scalp. This crust can also be in the eyebrows and sometimes on the cheeks. It is due to overactive seborrhoeic glands. The one thing you should not do is pick at it and try to remove it as this is not only painful but can cause bleeding, which in turn could lead to infection.

Essential:

- Prepare a paste of baking soda and water – 3 tablespoons of baking soda mixed with equal amounts of water (or enough to make a paste). You can also add 1 drop of lavender if you would like. Wet the head then cover the whole head with the baking powder paste, rubbing gently into the cradle cap (do not pick at it.). Leave the paste on for 5–10 minutes, then gently wash off.
- Rub either olive oil or coconut oil all over the scalp and leave it on overnight before sleeping. Rinse or shampoo off the oil in the morning (make sure you use a gentle shampoo).
- Gently brush away the loosened crusts with a soft brush or a fine toothcomb.

CROUP

Croup is characterised by its loud barking cough and is caused by inflammation of the voice box. It can be particularly frightening for a child – as the voice box swells, it can get hard to breathe, and the more the child coughs, the more the voice box swells. One of the main aims here is to get the child to calm down and not panic.

Essential:

- Make a steam inhalation to ease the coughing and help with the inflammation. Add the following essential oils into a bowl of steaming hot water: 2 drops each of eucalyptus *globulus*, lavender, thyme *vulgaris* and sweet marjoram (especially good for inflammation) oils. Place a towel over your child's head and get him/her to breathe deeply. If the child is fussing, you can go into the bathroom and run either a very hot bath or shower to get the steam into the room. Add the oils into the bath or in a bowl in the shower. Get the child to breathe deeply.
- Prepare a drink of turmeric powder (turmeric helps stop inflammation) and manuka honey UMF 15+. Place ½ teaspoon of turmeric powder into 235 ml warm water. Let sit for 5 minutes then add 1 teaspoon of manuka honey UMF 15+. Alternatively mix ½ teaspoon turmeric powder with 1 tablespoon manuka honey UMF 15+ and feed off the spoon. Both should be given four times a day or more if necessary. Syringe this into young children's mouths if they are fussing.

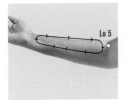

Lung meridian massage

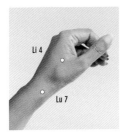

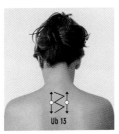

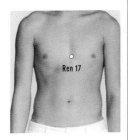

- Make an essential oil blend: 1½ teaspoon of base oil with 2 drops each of sweet marjoram, lavender, eucalyptus *globulus* or radiata (for children under 2 years of age) and chamomile (Roman) oils. Rub onto the chest, back and feet.
- Use the oils to rub the acupressure points and massage.
- Make a footbath of warm water (enough to cover your feet). Add 2 tablespoons of dry English mustard and 5 drops each of ginger oil and eucalyptus *globulus*. Soak the feet for 10–15 minutes.
- Give the child Bach rescue remedy (pg 89) if they are panicking or you can add it into the oil blend that you rub on the chest back and feet.
- Make sure the child drinks lots of warm water or drinks. Avoid giving cold drinks as this will make the coughing and wheezing worse.

Acupressure Points:
Lu 5, Lu 7, Li 4, Ub 13 (rub either side of the spine, then criss-cross along the spine), Ren 17 and lung massage.

CUTS, GRAZES AND CHAFFING

Cuts, grazes and chaffing occur all the time and normally cause no fuss. However, even the smallest and most innocent cuts or scrapes could potentially turn into something more serious. It is always important to clean and take care of cuts as our broken skin is literally left open to infection.

When to seek medical attention:

See a doctor when you cannot control the bleeding, the skin is gaping open or you can see bone or muscle. If the skin on either side of the cut curves in and you can't "close" the cut, the wound might need stitches and you should seek medical advice immediately.

If you do follow the steps below and the skin around the wound starts to turn hot and reddish and seems to be spreading or is oozing pus – seek immediate medical attention.

CUTS
Essential:

- Apply a few drops of neat tea tree oil to the cut even before you wash it. Why not wash it first? The tea tree oil has the ability to recognise and differentiate between bad bacteria and good bacteria. We need the good bacteria to help us heal and fight off infection. Allow the tea tree to sit on the cut for a few minutes to recognise the bacteria that it is dealing with.
- Get a bowl of clean water (around 1 cup) and add 3–5 drops of tea tree oil. Take a clean cloth or gauze and wash out the cut. Make sure you remove any dirt that is in the cut.
- If the cut is bleeding profusely, get some cayenne powder and sprinkle it quite liberally over the cut, then apply pressure. Leave the cayenne powder on until it stops bleeding for a good few minutes. You can let the powder just fall off or you can clean it out gently.
- Make a mix of 1½ teaspoon of manuka honey UMF 15+ into which you add 4 drops lavender oil. Cover the cut with this mixture and then cover with a plaster. Repeat the next day or until the wound has healed.

GRAZES
When you fall and the outer layer of skin comes off. This is a graze. A graze normally covers a wide surface and often has lots of dirt in it; you need to watch out for infection.

Essential:

- Apply tea tree oil before you wash the skinned area. Let sit for a few minutes.
- Add 2 drops each of tea tree and lavender oils to a bowl of warm water. Dip a clean cloth or some cotton wool in the water and then gently but firmly remove all the dirt from the skinned area.

- Apply a combination of undiluted tea tree and lavender oils onto the area and let it dry. If you want to cover it, do so with a plaster that allows for some ventilation. Try and let the skin be in the open air when you can.
- Wash the area daily with tea tree or lavender oils as above.

CHAFFING

This happens when skin rubs against skin, a rough surface (or anything really) and the skin becomes irritated, red and hurts to the touch. It often looks like a rash.

Essential:

- Wash the area with some cool water into which you have added 1 drop lavender and 1 drop peppermint oil
- Make a calming gel with either 1½ teaspoon of pure aloe vera gel and 2 drops lavender oil or 1½ teaspoon of calendula oil with 2 drops lavender oil. Rub onto chaffed area. Repeat a few times a day.

Additional Information:

To stop the chaffing from happening again, make your own talcum powder. Put 2–4 tablespoons of cornstarch into a bag and add 5–10 drops of lavender oil. Shake well to mix and use like a powder.

CYSTITIS / URINARY TRACT INFECTION (UTI)

Cystitis is a medical term for inflammation of the bladder. Most of the time, the inflammation is caused by a bacterial infection. Typically it starts with the feeling that the bladder cannot be emptied and with the sensation that one has to use the toilet very badly but urination is very scarce. There might also be a burning sensation and urinating can be very painful.

Cystitis and UTIs can be a serious health problem and must be dealt with promptly. If the infection is left to spread to your kidneys it can lead to kidney damage.

As soon as you even suspect cystitis, start following the steps below.

Essential:

- Make a drink by mixing 1 teaspoon baking soda and ½ lemon in a big glass of water. Drink every 30 minutes or every hour.

"Baking soda gives immediate relief to the discomfort of UTIs."

CAUTION

If you start feeling pain in your lower back or see blood in your urine and develop a sudden fever, see a doctor immediately.

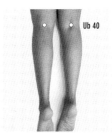
Ub 40

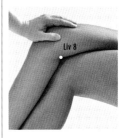
Liv 8

- Start pressing the acupressure points as often as you can.
- Follow this by drinking unsweetened cranberry juice.
- Make a natural antibiotic. Take 125 mg of manuka honey UMF 15+ and crush in 5–8 cloves of garlic, 1 teaspoon turmeric powder, 1 teaspoon coconut oil and ½ teaspoon crushed black pepper.
- Take 5 drops of grapefruit seed extract three times a day.
- After the cystitis has subsided, take 30–50 billion cells of multi-strength probiotic that is targeted at the urinary and reproductive area.

Acupressure Points:

Ub 40 and Liv 8. Press deep into acupressure point Ren 4. Hold and press for the count of 30 seconds x 4. Keep doing these points until you feel relief.

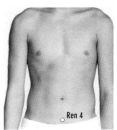
Ren 4

Additional Information (once the cystitis/UTI has calmed down):

- Do a sitz bath with warm water and 5 drops of tea tree oil.
- Do a probiotic douche: Add 5–10 billion cells of probiotic powder to some pre-boiled (but cooled to warm) water. Dissolve and put into the douche. Do the douche at night before bed.

- You can also rub neat tea tree on the area where the urethra is or you can insert a tampon onto which you have put about 8–10 drops of tea tree. As the vagina and the urethra sit very closely together, the tea tree will permeate through to the urethra and can deal with any bacteria that might be lingering there.

Supplements:
- Cranberry extract or cranberry pills (three times a day).
- Grapefruit seed extract – 5 drops (three times a day).
- Probiotics – 60 billion cells (orally). There are a range of probiotics specifically targeted at females' 'natural vaginal health'.
- Probiotics – 5–10 billion through a douche.
- Vitamin C – 1,000 mg.
- Zinc – 50 mg.

DANDRUFF

Dandruff is a very common problem that affects people of all ages and can occur for many different reasons. It can appear due to the use of harsh shampoos and hair products. It can also occur due to vitamin and mineral imbalances, poor diet or dehydration. However, the most likely cause of dandruff is actually a yeast-like fungus, *malassezia globosa*, which lives on your scalp and feeds on skin oils.

Be warned that dandruff shampoos make the condition worse. They might get rid of the dandruff but it is a short-term solution to a long-term problem.

Important:
Follow this hair routine twice a week for three weeks.

Essential:
- Cover the scalp with coconut oil. Massage into scalp and leave on for a few hours or overnight.
- A day before you start the treatment, prepare an 'anti-dandruff hair oil'. Infuse 235 ml coconut oil with 3 tablespoons of crushed mustard seeds or mustard powder. Leave overnight. Strain the mixture the next day. Add 3 drops each of tea tree and ginger oils. Whisk in 2 teaspoons of manuka honey UMF 8+ or higher and 5 drops of grapefruit seed extract. Pour into a jar. When you decide to treat your hair, pour a sufficient amount of the

'anti-dandruff hair oil' to cover the scalp. Leave on overnight. You can wrap a warm towel around your head or even run a blow drier through a towel to warm up the oils so they penetrate the scalp more fully.

- The next day, combine 120 ml apple cider vinegar, 4 tablespoons of baking soda and 235 ml warm water in a bowl. Pour this on the head, making sure the scalp is covered. Massage this mixture into the scalp and leave on for a few minutes. Rinse with water.
- Shampoo your hair with a mild natural shampoo into which you have added some tea tree, ginger and rosemary oils. Add 5 drops of each oil into 100 ml of shampoo.
- Do not over wash your hair.

Supplements:
- Grapefruit seed extract – 10 drops (daily).
- Liquid Multi B complex – follow suggested dosage on bottle.
- Magnesium – 200 mg.
- Probiotics – 10 billion cells.
- Vitamin C – 1,000 mg.
- Zinc – 25 mg.

DENGUE

Dengue fever is spread by mosquitoes and is frequently called the 'bone breaking fever' as you literally feel that your bones are going to crack when you contract dengue. Mild dengue fever causes high fever, a rash as well as muscle and joint pain. A severe form of dengue fever, also called dengue haemorrhagic fever, can cause severe bleeding, a sudden drop in blood pressure (shock) and death. The most dangerous aspect of dengue is that as the virus attacks the system and the blood platelets drop, which makes the blood vessels very leaky. This can cause damage to some of our vital organs.

Symptoms:
It is hard to diagnose dengue in the beginning as it starts very much like a viral fever with temperatures ranging between 38.5–40°C or above. Only after about 4–5 days of fever can the virus actually be found in the blood.

Once the diagnosis of dengue is given, depending on the platelet levels, the patient either goes home to rest (but has to have a daily blood test) or is hospitalised.

CAUTION
It is vital to seek medical attention if dengue is suspected.

Whether in the hospital or at home, follow the steps below: as dengue is a virus, there is little that can be done from a pharmaceutical perspective. It really is up to the immune system to fight it so it is crucial to boost the immune system and to rest.

Important:

Collect about five papaya leaves. Remove hard veins from the leaves and discard. Pound, crush or blend papaya leaves. Place the crushed leaves in a muslin cloth and squeeze the juice out. Discard the pulp. Feed 1½ teaspoon of papaya leaf juice two times a day until the platelet levels stop dropping. This works magic and forces the platelets levels to start rising back to normal levels. Once the platelets are rising, you can give the papaya juice for a few more doses and then stop.

Essential:

- Get the highest level of manuka honey and give a spoonful to the patient every two hours.

SIMPLY NATURAL HEALTH

- Give 1,000 mg of Vitamin C every 1–2 hours mixed with 1 teaspoon of molasses (the molasses and Vitamin C can be given in a drink).
- Sponge the body and pulse points with the following mixture. Add the following essential oils to a bowl of cool water: 2 drops lavender, 2 drops thyme *vulgaris*, 2 drops eucalyptus *globulus*, 2 drops lemon, 1 drop peppermint and 4 drops of Bach rescue remedy (pg 89).
- Give the patient lots of water and coconut water to drink.

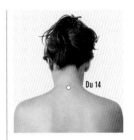

Acupressure Points:
Du 14, Li 4, St 36, Sp 6 and Liv 3. Do not press the acupressure points hard, as when platelets are low, you tend to bruise very easily.

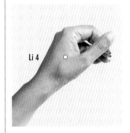

Additional Information:
- If possible, bathe the patient with Epsom salts into which you have added 4 drops Bach rescue remedy, 4 drops lavender oil, 4 drops thyme *vulgaris*, 4 drops eucalyptus, 4 drops lemon and 2 drops peppermint oils. This will help alleviate the aches and pains of the fever.
- Prepare the immune-boosting soup (pg 138).

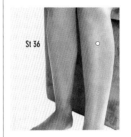

DEPRESSION

Depression is a common mental disorder, characterised by sadness, loss of interest or pleasure, feelings of guilt or low self-worth, disturbed sleep and/ or appetite, combined with feelings of tiredness and poor concentration.

There are many times in life we feel depressed due to external factors like losing a loved one, losing a job, friendship issues or post-traumatic stress. Most people can feel down and then pull themselves up again. When you are truly depressed, it is very hard to pick yourself up. Where depression comes from is again one of those things that are hard to pinpoint.

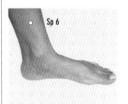

In my clinic I see a wide range of depression – from mild to severe, postnatal depression and even bipolar disorders.

In every case, and whatever the title of the depression, it is very closely linked to certain vitamin and mineral deficiencies and food intolerances as well as malabsorption issues. Hence it is quite crucial to both supplement and review diet.

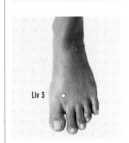

The essential oils also play a huge role in the recovery from depression as they cross the blood brain barrier and can alter our state of mind in a dramatic way.

Si 3

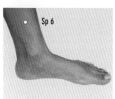

Sp 6

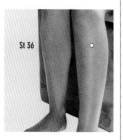

St 36

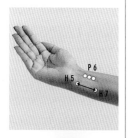

P 6
H 5
H 7

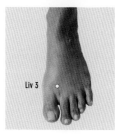

Liv 3

Many studies are now being done on the use of essential oils and depression in hospitals all over the world on the use of essential oils to treat depression.

Essential:

- Remove these foods from your diet immediately – dairy (especially milk), refined sugars, caffeine, artificial colouring (especially red and yellow) and wheat products.
- Diffuse the following oils into your home to lift the mood in the house. Place 2 drops petitgrain, 3 drops lemon, 3 drops grapefruit and 1 drop clary sage into a diffuser (I would recommend using a steam diffuser).
- For your body, make a blend of 2 drops neroli, 2 drops petitgrain, 2 drops sweet orange, 1 drop lemon oil, 1 drop grapefruit and put into 1½ teaspoon of a base oil. Use on your body especially your spine, chest and arms and on the acupressure points listed and shown.
- If your depression is due to a hormonal imbalance then you need to really watch out for your kidney, spleen and liver health. For the kidneys, do not eat too many raw and uncooked foods; for the spleen do not eat too many sweet foods (especially foods with refined sugar) and for the liver do not take too much alcohol, caffeine or medical drugs.
- Oil blend for hormonal depression – add ½ teaspoon of evening primrose, 2 drops geranium, 2 drops clary sage, 2 drops petitgrain and 1 drop fennel into 1½ teaspoon base oil.
- Supplementing is crucial for depression. See the supplements you should start taking.
- The Bach flower remedies are a very effective and gentle way to help with depression. Look at the Bach flower remedy guideline (Part 2 – Mother Nature's Medical Kit) and see which essences may apply to you. You can mix them up and take them internally but also add them into your oil blend.
- Taking an Epsom salt bath before bed will help relax the system and ensure a good night's sleep. Sleep is crucial to combating depression. Add into the bath either of the blends suggested above before adding in an extra 3 drops each of chamomile Roman and lavender. If sleep is an issue, see pg 198 for Insomnia.

Acupressure Points:

Use oil blend on the acupressure points. Si 3, Sp 6, St 36, P 6, H 5–H 7 and Liv 3. Extra points Du 20 and Li 11 (see pg 235).

Supplements:

- Calcium – 1,000 mg.
- Hydrochloride acid (HCL) directly after each meal (if you experience burning after taking HCL stop taking it).
- Digestive enzymes with each meal as you start the meal
- Extra B6 – 50 mg.
- Liquid Multi B complex – follow suggested dosage on bottle.
- Magnesium – 500 mg.
- Omega oils (alternate between flaxseed oil and evening primrose oil) – 2,000 mg each (especially if it is a hormonal depression).
- Probiotics – 50 billion cells.
- Zinc – 50 mg.

TYPE 2 DIABETES AND INSULIN RESISTANCE

Diabetes is rapidly becoming the world's second biggest health problem. This condition occurs when the pancreas stops producing enough insulin to help control our blood sugar levels. Insulin resistance is when our bodies stop responding to the insulin that is being produced. This results in high sugar levels in the blood stream. Insulin resistance is often the precursor to type 2 diabetes and if caught early can be controlled and even reversed before it worsens and makes the patient dependent on medication.

Crucial:

Chromium is a crucial mineral that helps keep our blood sugar stable. How does it do this? Chromium is needed to make the glucose tolerance factor (GTF). GTF helps improve insulin activity by binding to insulin and increasing its potential. So, when our bodies stop responding to insulin, chromium can help (see Part 2 – Mother Nature's Medical Kit for chromium-rich foods and supplementing information).

Essential:

- Remove all white refined sugars and carbohydrates especially refined wheat products at each meal.
- Avoid all trans fats and processed foods such as cookies, cakes and potato chips.

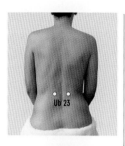

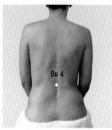

To find this point, draw a line from your belly button around to your spine

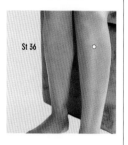

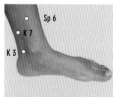

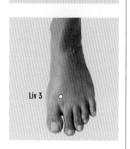

- Eat protein and a good fat (olive oil, coconut oil, avocado oil). Eat seeds and nuts such as Brazil nuts, walnuts, almonds, pecans. Avoid peanuts and cashew nuts.
- Eat 8–10 servings of fruits and vegetables per day. Avoid high sugar fruits such as mangos, bananas, watermelon, grapes and durians.
- 30 minutes of exercise daily is vitally important.
- Supplementing from the list below is also crucial to help the body to start producing and reacting to insulin properly.

Start to add in these foods either through teas or to meals on a daily basis:
- Bitter gourd – juice it fresh or have it as a tea. This stimulates the pancreas to produce insulin.
- Sage – prepare a sage tea, add sage to food or simply chew the leaves. Sage contains certain extracts and chemicals that mimic the drugs typically prescribed for managing diabetes.
- Glucose tolerance factor (GTF) is best helped by chromium-rich foods – broccoli, potatoes, green beans and apples.
- Cinnamon – ½ teaspoon of cinnamon in 235 ml hot water or sprinkled on foods (like oatmeal) helps to stabilise blood sugar levels.
- Oats – add oats to your diet wherever you can as they help to regulate blood sugar.
- Apple cider vinegar – take 2 teaspoons mixed in water just before you have your meals as it helps lowers post-meal glucose levels.
- Cayenne tincture – helps to increase our metabolism and control blood sugar levels.
- Try to change your diet and eating habits using the guidelines on pg 160.

Acupressure Points:
Ub 23, Du 4, Sp 6, St 36, K 7, K 3 and Liv 3.

Supplements:
- Chromium picolinate – 500 mcg.
- Coconut oil – 1 tablespoon.
- CoQ10 – 300 mg.
- Digestive enzymes – 2 with every meal.
- Magnesium – 500 mg.

- Olive leaf extract – 500 mg (two times a day).
- Selenium – 200–400 mcg.
- Vitamin C – 2,000 mg.
- Vitamin D3 – 2,000 ius.
- Vitamin E – 300 ius.
- Zinc – 25 mg.

DIABETES REVERSING DRINK

7.5-cm fresh aloe vera or 120 ml
   pure aloe vera juice
A handful of basil
½ bitter gourd
2 teaspoons cayenne tincture (pg 97)
1 green apple
2 carrots
85 g broccoli

Blend all ingredients in a high-speed
blender. Add some water to aid the
blades or juice in a slow juicer.

FASTING SOUP

½ red cabbage
1 carrot
1 celery
1 red onion, peeled
1 clove garlic, peeled
1 teaspoon cayenne pepper
A handful of sage
A handful of barley or millet
Salt to taste
Pepper to taste

Place all ingredients except barley
or millet in a pot. Cover with water
and bring to a boil. Lower heat and
simmer. Add barley or millet. Season
with salt and pepper to taste.

Monday, Wednesday and Friday

6 am – Drink 235 ml water with 1 tablespoon apple cider vinegar, 1 teaspoon cinnamon, ¼ teaspoon cayenne tincture (pg 97), 1 teaspoon raw unrefined coconut oil and 1 tablespoon psyllium husks.

Exercise – 20 minutes of brisk walking or running on a treadmill or outside.

Breakfast:
- 1–2 eggs cooked as desired and eaten with wheat-free bread (seed breads are good).
- Plain yoghurt (not Greek) with nuts, fruits and seeds.
- 170 g oats (simmered in a pan with some water) Add ¼ teaspoon of pink salt, ¼ teaspoon cinnamon and 1 tablespoon seed mix. You can add some berries to this if you want.
- A vegetable and fruit smoothie: 80% vegetables to 20% fruit. Blend in some nuts and seeds.

Mid-morning snack:
- A handful of seeds or nuts (no peanuts or cashews).
- Hummus with veggie sticks.
- 2 squares of dark chocolate (containing 70%–80% of cacao) eaten with walnuts, almonds, pecans or sliced fruit (apples or pears).
- Slice of cheese with a nut or seed butter.

Lunch:
A bowl of salad with a mix of vegetables. Try to add in some raw broccoli, onions, olives, peppers, and radishes. Sprinkle some seeds and nuts, add 43 g feta or goat cheese or add some grilled chicken, tuna or a hard-boiled egg. Dress with olive oil, mustard, garlic and vinegar.

Mid-afternoon snack:
Same as the mid-morning snack above.

Dinner (dinner should be eaten early):
- Wild salmon, halibut, barramundi fish or a lean piece of good quality meat with an assortment of grilled or roasted vegetables.
- Exercise – 30 minutes of walking after dinner.
- You must drink at least 10–12 glasses of water throughout the day. Replace all coffees and teas with rosehip, bitter gourd or dandelion root tea.

- First thing in the morning: drink a glass of water followed by the diabetes reversing drink (pg 159).
- Exercise – 20–30 minutes walking or running on treadmill.
- Lunch and Dinner – fasting soup (pg 159).
- You can still have the same snacks as Monday, Wednesday and Friday.
- Evening – 30–40 minutes walking.
- All supplements are to be taken daily.

DIARRHOEA

Several diseases and conditions can cause diarrhoea. Common causes of diarrhoea include viruses, food poisoning, bacteria, parasites and food intolerances.

No matter what has caused it, diarrhoea is a sign that your body is working for you – though somewhat uncomfortably. So, initially respect the process and do not try and stop diarrhoea immediately. Let your body get rid of what it is trying to purge, then step in.

Essential:

- Immediately stop eating all hard to digest foods such as meats, dairy products, fried foods and refined sugar.
- Add the following oils to 1½ teaspoon of a base oil for a tummy rub: 1 drop each of lavender, mandarin, thyme *vulgaris* and cardamom. Rub the stomach first in a clockwise direction to encourage the system to purge itself then, when the diarrhoea has stopped or is simply watery with no food particles in it, rub in an anti-clockwise direction.
- During a bad case of diarrhoea, do not worry about food intake – what is more important is the liquid intake. Offer good quality water followed by a cooled mixture of either mint or fennel tea with a teaspoon of manuka honey UMF 15+, ¼ teaspoon of pink salt or sea salt (not iodised table salt) and some acidophilus powder 10 billion cells minimum (if you have capsules, open them and mix the powder into the drink).
- If you suspect food poisoning, drink 1 teaspoon of clay every three hours (*smecta* or zeolite are normally readily available at your pharmacy).

Coconut water helps to replenish loss of electrolytes.

CAUTION

If continuous foul smelling diarrhoea goes on for more than four days, you need to check for a bacterial infection or parasites.

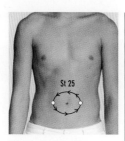

When you want the diarrhoea to stop, rub the stomach in an anti-clockwise direction.

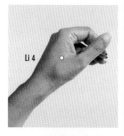

Li 4

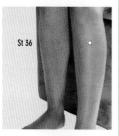

St 36

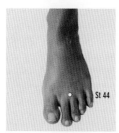

St 44

- Eating charcoal tablets can also be very effective (readily available at your pharmacy).
- Watch out for dehydration.

Additional Information:

- If the stomach isn't settling well, prepare a cumin and mustard tea. Add 1 teaspoon of cumin seeds and ½ teaspoon mustard seeds together. Pour hot water over. Let it sit for 20 minutes. Sieve. Add ½–1 teaspoon of manuka honey UMF 15+. Stir and drink.
- Offer foods that are very easy to digest – boiled rice, chicken soup, apple sauce, live yoghurt etc.
- To bind the stomach, boil 170 g white rice in 700 ml water for about 45 minutes. Drain the rice and drink the rice water.
- Small sips of carrot juice are helpful (especially for infants).
- Give small spoonfuls of an overripe mashed banana.
- Grate a carrot and green apple together and eat as a meal.
- Offer weak black tea, fennel or chamomile tea sweetened with manuka honey UMF 15+ (optional).
- Stomach cramping can often occur after a bad case of diarrhoea. In this case, rub the stomach gently in a clockwise direction with 1 drop each of lavender, mandarin and chamomile oils.
- After a bad case of diarrhoea, one needs to replenish one's electrolyte system especially potassium and sodium. A good way to do this is to drink fresh coconut water or prepare a shake of 1 banana with 235 ml non-dairy milk (rice, almond or hazelnut), 1 tablespoon molasses and ½ teaspoon pink salt or good quality sea salt. Drink this twice a day.
- Once the diarrhoea has stopped, the stomach area can still be very sensitive and in need of repair. Avoid all foods that make the stomach work harder (milk, dairy, meat).

Acupressure Points:

When you feel the body has purged itself of the virus, bug or bad food, you can then step in with the acupressure points Li 4, St 44, St 36 and St 25. Rub the stomach in an anti-clockwise direction.

Supplements:

Probiotics – 100 billion cells (daily for 1 week) 50 billion cells (daily for 2 weeks).

EAR INFECTIONS

An ear infection (acute otitis media) is most often a bacterial or viral infection that affects the middle ear, the air-filled space behind the eardrum that contains the tiny vibrating bones of the ear. Ear infections are painful because of the inflammation and the buildup of fluids in the middle ear. Following the steps below should give relief and clear the infection within 12 hours. If the pain lasts longer than this seek medical advice. You must follow all the acupressure points in order.

Essential:

- To give immediate relief to the ear, rub 2 drops neat lavender oil in and behind the ear.
- Prepare garlic-infused oil mixture. In 1 tablespoon olive oil, squeeze 1 clove of garlic with a garlic crusher. Mix garlic and olive oil and let it sit to infuse for a minimum of 15 minutes (to make it stronger, leave it for longer). Pass the olive oil through a little sieve to remove any garlic pieces.
- Whilst you are waiting for the olive oil and garlic to infuse, take a red onion and slice it in half. Place ½ the onion in the oven at the lowest temperature possible, so it just warms but does not cook. Add 2–3 drops of lavender oil into a warm bowl of water. Soak a cloth in the water, wring it out, then wrap the warm cloth around the raw onion half. Hold it directly on the ear and behind the ear for as long as possible. Keep dipping the cloth in the hot water as the heat will give relief to the ear. When the half onion that is

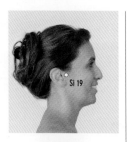

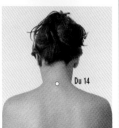

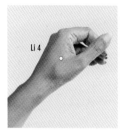

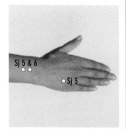

in the oven is slightly warm, take it out then wrap the damp cloth around the warm onion. Hold this to the ear for as long as possible.

- Take the olive oil and garlic mixture and add 1 drop tea tree and 1 drop lavender into the oil.
- Dip a piece of cotton wool into the garlic-infused oil (make sure that it is covered in oil) and place the cotton ball in the ear and leave it in.

Acupressure Points (do the points as often as you can until relief is felt):
Si 19, Du 14, Li 4, Sj 3, Sj 5 and Sj 6.

Additional Information:
Cut out all milk and dairy products, refined wheat and refined sugar as these foods encourage more liquid buildup in the ear.

Supplements:
- Vitamin A – 10,000 ius.
- Vitamin C – 2,000 mg.
- Vitamin D3 – 4,000 ius.
- Zinc – 30 mg.

ECZEMA

Eczema is sometimes caused, in part, by an abnormal response to proteins that are natural part of the body which the immune system usually ignores. However, for some reason the immune system starts to attach these proteins which causes inflammation. Eczema can also be linked to leaky gut syndrome prompted by stress on the intestines from ingesting too many antibiotics or medications. With leaky gut, particles of food slip through the intestinal wall and into the bloodstream. This can cause the immune system to regard common foods as the enemy, and, as a result, eating these foods will cause the system to overreact and inflammation of the skin will occur.

Common triggers of eczema flare-ups include:
- Food intolerances. Top triggers are wheat, dairy products, soy products, the protein from chicken, chocolate, eggs, red food colouring, citrus fruits and peas (but can honestly be anything).

- Chemicals found in cleaners and detergents that strip the skin of oils – e.g. foaming agents like sodium lauryl sulphates (SLF) and sodium laureth sulphate (SLS).
- Rough scratchy materials like wool
- Synthetic fabrics
- Raised body temperature
- Sweating
- Temperature changes
- A sudden drop in humidity
- Animal dander
- Stress
- Upper respiratory infections

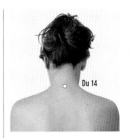

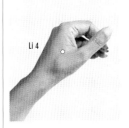

Essential:
- It is essential to eliminate the foods that might be causing the skin to inflame.
- Remove trigger chemicals from your environment as much as possible.
- Eczema is related to "toxins" in the body, whether they are from foods or environmental toxins. What is important here is to detoxify the liver. You can do this by replacing all teas and coffees with a dandelion root tea in the morning, afternoon and at night before bed. Prepare a detox tea consisting of ½ a squeezed lemon, 1 clove of crushed garlic and with some manuka honey UMF 15+ to sweeten.
- To relieve the itching, take an oatmeal bath with lavender oil. Place a handful of oats into a cloth. Attach the cloth to the tap nozzle of your bath and run the water through the oats. Add 5 drops of lavender oil, get into the bath and soak for 20 minutes.
- If you don't have a bath, follow the same procedure but collect the water in a bowl and wash your skin with the oat water and lavender.
- Prepare a mixture of the following oils: 2 drops each of chamomile German, lavender and carrot seed oil. Place the oils into the following mixture of base oils: 1½ teaspoon avocado oil and 1 teaspoon calendula oil. Make a bigger batch if you want and use this as your moisturiser.
- Use the oil on the acupressure points below. Do the points 2–3 times a day.

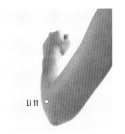

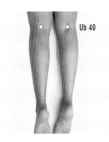

Acupressure Points:
Du 14, Li 4, Li 11, Ub 40 and Liv 3. Extra points Sp 6 and St 36 (see pg 235).

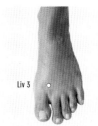

Additional Information:
- If there have been lots of antibiotics in the patient's system, watch out for Yeast Infection/Candida (see pg 234).
- Emotions can be a big part of eczema. Look at Bach flower remedies in Part 2 – Mother Nature's Medical Kit and choose the remedies that might fit your emotional needs.

Supplements:
- Digestive enzymes – 2 with each meal.
- Glutamine – 1,000 mg.
- Liquid Multi B – follow suggested dosage on bottle.
- Magnesium – 400 mg.
- Molasses – 1 tablespoon (daily).
- MSM – 500 mg.
- Probiotics – 100 billion cells.
- Vitamin D3 – 4,000 ius.
- Zinc – 30 mg.

EYE INFECTIONS / CONJUNCTIVITIS

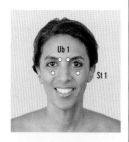

An eye infection can manifest itself in many different ways – sore eyes, swollen eyes, itchy eyes or crusty eyes. An eye infection occurs when the eyes come into contact with a virus or bacteria. The most common eye infection is conjunctivitis (also called "pink eye"). These basic steps apply for all eye infections.

Essential:
Prepare 235 ml chamomile tea and add 1 teaspoon of manuka honey UMF 15+, ½ teaspoon of baking soda and 1 drop tea tree or 1 drop thyme *vulgaris*. Using a clean cotton ball for each eye, soak a cotton ball in the tea. Start at the outside edge of the eye and wipe from the inside of the eye out.

Acupressure Points:
Ub 1, St 1 and Si 3.

"Garlic is known to reverse and repair liver damage. It is packed full of the mineral selenium – which increases the action of antioxidants."

FATTY LIVER

A "fatty liver" condition is the buildup of fat in the liver cells. It is not a dangerous condition in itself but could become dangerous as it can lead to other more harmful conditions like cirrhosis or chronic liver inflammation.

A fatty liver develops when the body creates too much fat or cannot metabolise fat fast enough. The excess fat is stored in liver cells where it accumulates to form fatty liver disease.

Symptoms of a fatty liver include fatigue, general malaise, loss of appetite, nausea, abdominal swelling and pain especially on the right side below the ribs, brain fog, mental confusion, swelling of the legs, raised liver function tests and, in severe cases, yellowing of the skin and eyes due to high bilirubin levels.

There are four main types of Fatty Liver Disease:
- **Alcoholic Liver Disease (ALD)** – which is caused by heavy alcohol consumption.
- **Non-alcoholic Fatty Liver Disease (NAFLD)** – caused by obesity, hyperlipidaemia (high levels of fats in the blood), pre-diabetes, diabetes, genetic inheritance, rapid weight loss and the side effect of certain medications (including aspirin, steroids, tamoxifen and tetracycline).

- **Non-alcoholic *Steatohepatitis* (NASH)** – Occurs when the fat builds up in the liver and causes the liver to swell. If the original cause is not from alcohol, it's called non-alcoholic *steatohepatitis* (NASH). This disease can impair liver function and if left untreated can eventually lead to liver failure.
- **Acute Fatty Liver of Pregnancy** – Acute fatty liver is a rare complication of pregnancy which can be life-threatening. Women who are pregnant will be screened for this condition. Most women improve after delivery and have no lingering problems.

The good news is that fatty liver disease is a very reversible condition, especially if caught relatively early, but treatment for fatty liver could take up to three months so be patient.

Important:
- A fatty liver tends to affect people who have high cholesterol (see High Cholesterol on pg 192).
- Reduce all saturated fats and trans fats. Reducing high-fat meat like beef, lamb and pork, whole fat dairy products, butter, cheese, ice cream. Cut back on trans fats by avoiding commercially-baked pastries, cookies, muffins, cakes, doughnuts, packaged snacks like crackers and chips, stick margarine, vegetable shortening, fried foods and candy bars etc.
- Have good fats and foods high in omega-3 oils. Some of the good oils are coconut oil, olive oil, avocado oil and sesame oil. Have more avocados, olives, nuts including Brazil hazelnuts, pecans and walnuts, sunflower, sesame, pumpkin seeds, flaxseed, seed butters and fatty fish like salmon, tuna, mackerel, herring, trout and sardines (reliably sourced from clean seas).
- Increase your intake of fresh vegetables.
- Increase your intake of fruit – though try to reduce the fruits high in sugar.

Essential:
- Cut out all alcohol from your diet until the liver repairs.
- Cut out all refined sugar. Refined white sugar, corn syrup, cane sugar, brown sugar etc. affects your liver in exactly the same way alcohol does. Replace with raw organic honey, raw manuka honey UMF 15+ and raw maple syrup.
- First thing in the morning, start your day with lemongrass water and lemon. Bruise a stalk of lemongrass and pour hot water over it, letting the lemongrass infuse into the water. When it has cooled, add the juice of ½ a freshly squeezed lemon and 1 teaspoon avocado oil.

- Prepare an apple cider vinegar drink. Add 60 ml apple cider vinegar into a 500 ml bottle of water. Stir in some manuka honey UMF 15+ to sweeten (optional). Drink throughout the day.
- At night, drink a tea made up of ½ lemon with 2 crushed garlic cloves, ½ teaspoon of turmeric, ¼ teaspoon black pepper or 1 teaspoon coconut oil Add 1 teaspoon manuka honey UMF 15+ (optional).
- Replace all caffeinated teas and coffee with dandelion root tea or a rose tea.
- Increase the amount of raw garlic that you put in your food to at least 3–4 cloves a day.
- Prepare the liver lover juice daily. Drink whenever you like or in place of that nightly glass of wine.
- Do a 7–9 day liver detox.

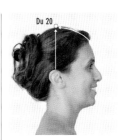

Acupressure points:
Du 20, Liv 8, St 36, Sp 6 and Liv 3.

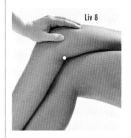

Additional Information:
People who are low on iron or anaemic are more prone to fatty liver disease. (see Anaemia to boost your iron levels.)

Supplements:
- Green tea extract daily – 250 mcg (daily).
- Milk thistle tincture supplement – 1 teaspoon or 1 teaspoon (three times a day).
- Liquid Multi-B vitamin – daily (follow suggested dosage on bottle).
- Probiotics – 30–50 billion cells.
- Turmeric or *curcumin* – 500 mg (daily).

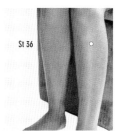

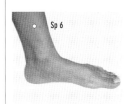

LIVER LOVER JUICE

½ head red cabbage
1 beetroot
1 grapefruit, peeled
1 apple
2 carrots
170 g kale
A handful of mint
1 stalk lemongrass
1–2 cloves garlic, peeled

Place all ingredients in a juicer. Serve.

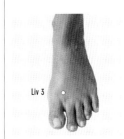

FEVERS

Unfortunately for most of us we have been led to believe from early childhood that fevers are a bad thing. Nothing could be further from the truth. As long as they are supported and treated with respect, a fever is our bodies' very natural and powerful way of fighting for us and can help us get rid of the most nasty illnesses. Given this, the last thing we should do is suppress or ignore a fever. Please read Part 1 pg 48 for more on fevers.

CHILDREN

Fevers often indicate that the child is moving into a new phase in their life. Clear a space and let them lie down as much as possible. Take this opportunity to spend some time with your child. Read books, do a puzzle, do some drawing, play a game. Remember your child is probably moving into a challenging new phase and might need to spend some time with you to know he/she is supported. Follow the steps below:

Basics – for all fevers

- Understand what kind of fever you have.
- Avoid fever suppressants such as Panadol, ibuprofen etc. as much as you can. By taking a fever suppressant, you automatically feel a bit better, which means you try to do more when all your body needs is rest. Taking medications like these will only prolong the fever and draw out the sickness.
- Do not worry if your child refuses to eat, their bodies are too busy fighting.
- Spray the room with thyme *vulgaris*, lavender, pine and tea tree spray. Add 1½ teaspoon vodka or pure alcohol and water into a 250 ml spray bottle. Then add 5 drops each of the above mentioned oils. Spray this in and around the room.
- To help with the aches and pains of fever, take a bath with 85 g Epsom salts, 4 drops Bach rescue remedy (pg 89), 3 drops each of lavender, lemon, tea tree and sweet marjoram oils. If you do not have a bath, place all ingredients in a bowl and sponge down. This will help aid sleep as well.
- Prepare manuka honey with crushed garlic. Add 200 mg manuka honey UMF 15+ to 4–8 crushed garlic cloves. Give 1 teaspoon every two hours.
- Offer lime flower tea sweetened with manuka honey UMF 15+.
- "Starve a fever, feed a cold". Offer very simple foods such as clear soups, fresh fruit juices, eggs on toast etc.
- Do the acupressure points three times a day.
- When the fever has gone, do not rush yourself or your child back into a daily routine. Let them have time to recover.

KNOW YOUR FEVERS

There are two types of fevers we normally deal with – a hot fever and a cold fever.

Cold fever – This condition occurs when you have a fever but your hands and feet are cold and your head and torso are hot. The best remedy for this is to do arnica wraps.

- Arnica wraps on the wrist and ankles: You will need 4 cotton wraps. You can use a clean tea towel or a muslin cloth and cut the cloth into 4 strips. Squeeze arnica cream onto the strip in a line. Wrap the cloth with the arnica on the skin, around the wrists and ankles, tying the wraps gently but securely. Put socks on the feet and go to bed.
- If the fever comes back within the hour, you can slice a lemon into half and warm in an oven (not in the microwave). Hold the warm lemons to the soles of the feet.
- Re-apply the arnica wraps.
- To encourage the fever to break, prepare a lemon, manuka honey UMF 15+, cayenne and ginger drink. Squeeze ½ a lemon and crush about 2.5-cm peeled and bruised ginger into a pot. Pour hot water to cover. Add manuka honey UMF 15+ to sweeten. Add 3–4 drops cayenne tincture (optional). Mix well and drink.

CAUTION

Take fevers seriously, they are good for you but they can also be dangerous. If the fever is unusually high and the patient does not respond to any treatments or has become delirious or unconscious, seek immediate medical help.

Spread the arnica cream on the wraps.

Wrap around the wrist loosely.

Do for both wrists and ankles.

- If the sufferer is cold, cover him/her till sweating begins. Monitor the temperature closely if you do this.

Hot fever – A hot fever is when your temperature is raised and your whole body is hot to the touch. Often your face can be flushed. The best remedy for this is to do a vinegar and lavender sponge bath.

- Add 60 ml apple cider vinegar and the following essential oils into 500 ml bowl of cold water: 4 drops lavender and 2 drops eucalyptus. Use a cloth and dip it in the water, wring it out and sponge all the pulse points – neck, armpits, groin, elbows, wrists, behind the knees and ankles. Re-wet the cloth, wring dry and hold the cloth on top of the head. When the cloth is hot, re-wet the cloth and repeat the above steps again five times.
- When you have sponged five times, dip a pair of socks in the vinegar mixture. Wring them out. Put on the feet. Place a dry pair of socks on top and lie down to rest. Repeat the routine when the fever goes up.

There are also three reasons why we get fevers, how do we differentiate them?

Viral fevers – Most fevers start virally. Often they are just fevers with no other symptoms. These fevers can last for five days sometimes. They can accompany coughs, colds and tummy bugs. They normally start at the same time as the symptoms, if not slightly before. Most people often run off to the doctor on the third or fourth day of a fever in a panic and are given medicines, which they will take and by the fifth day the fever goes. Coincidence? Not necessarily so. If you can wait five days and support your fever, I am sure you'll be pleasantly surprised. However, if it doesn't clear up after five days, you must go to the doctor for it might be a bacterial fever, dengue, malaria etc.

Bacterial fevers – If you don't take care of yourself when suffering from the initial virus, you may prompt something viral to become a bacteria. How do you recognise that it has gone bacterial? If a fever comes and then goes during sickness and then comes back again, it has probably gone bacterial. A bacterial fever normally doesn't start right away.

You must be aware of bacterial fevers if you have a cut, wound or burn which turns hot and, suddenly, you develop a fever. This is extremely dangerous as the bacteria may be heading into your blood system. In this case, you should seek medical advice immediately.

Changing or detoxing fevers – These fevers would normally be classified as viral fevers as they have no symptoms but the fever itself. These fevers often happen when a body needs to detoxify you of something or you need to shift, change or grow. Children often get fevers before they grow or hit certain milestones in their growth. It is vital that these fevers are not suppressed, as it will stop the change from happening.

Hopefully, you can manage the fever with the above methods. If you are worried and desperate for sleep, take a fever suppressant.

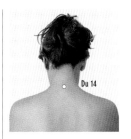

Fever Acupressure Points:
Du 14, Li 11, Li 4, Sj 3, Sj 5, Sj 6 and St 44. Extra point Ub 40 (see pg 235).

Supplements:
- Probiotics – 50 billion cells.
- Vitamin C – 1,000 (three times a day).
- Vitamin D3 – 4,000 ius.

FLU

What exactly is a "flu"? How does it differ from a cold? Well with the flu you have almost every symptom in the book. Your head hurts, your throat hurts, your eyes ache, you feel totally congested, you have a fever and some flu victims may even throw up and have diarrhoea.

What do you do? First thing you should do is acknowledge that you are sick and will probably be sick for at least 3–5 days and that you need to rest. Rest is vital when it comes to the flu.

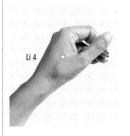

Essential:
- To get through the flu faster, try not to suppress the fever with pharmaceutical products, no matter how bad you feel. Get into bed and rest and follow the section on Fevers (pg 170).
- Take an Epsom salt bath with 2 drops thyme *vulgaris*, 2 drops clove, 2 drops lemon, 2 drops lavender, 2 drops eucalyptus *globulus* and 3 drops chamomile Roman oils.
- Mix 2 drops thyme *vulgaris*, 2 drops eucalyptus, 2 drops lemon, 2 drops tea tree and 1 drop clove essential oils into 1 teaspoon base oil of your choice and 1 teaspoon of carrot base oil. Rub this onto the spine, the soles of your feet and the acupressure points.

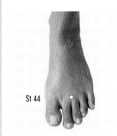

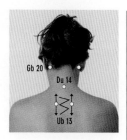

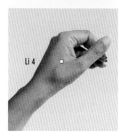

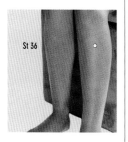

- Make a tea of manuka honey UMF 15+, ½ a lemon, 10 drops of cayenne tincture (pg 97) or ½ teaspoon of cayenne pepper, 1 crushed garlic clove and 2-cm crushed ginger. Combine all ingredients in a cup and pour boiling water over. Drink a few times a day.
- Take a spoonful of manuka honey UMF 15+ every two hours.
- You must drink lots of water. Take a big bottle of water to bed with you and drink as much as you can.
- Make and drink the immune-boosting soup (pg 138).

Once the flu symptoms have passed, which will take 3–5 days, you will probably feel weak and exhausted. This can also last for up to 5–6 extra days. Keep taking the immune-boosting soup and rest as much as you can.

Acupressure points:
Follow the fever acupressure points and add in the following points for flu: Gb 20, Ub 13, Du 14, Li 4 and St 36.

Supplements:
- Probiotics – 30–50 billion cells.
- Vitamin A –10, 000 ius.
- Vitamin C – 2–5,000 mg.
- Vitamin D3 – 4,000 ius.
- Vitamin E – 4,000 ius.
- Zinc – 30 mg.

FUNGAL INFECTIONS / RINGWORMS

Ringworms are a common and contagious skin infection. The fungus called *trichophyton rubrum* most commonly causes them and they are itchy.

The fungus loves warm, moist areas and can infect several areas of the skin from the scalp to the feet (where it's known as athlete's foot) to the groin (better known as "jock itch") and everything in between. Ringworm infections generally result in red, itchy, scaly round patches on the skin, which are not only unsightly but can cause great discomfort.

Because ringworm is a particularly contagious and stubborn, it can be hard to eliminate (particularly when it has affected the scalp, fingernails, or toenails). It is also very good at hiding, so when you think it may be gone and you stop the treatment for a few days or a week, it can come back. You must treat ringworm for quite a while even if it appears to be safe.

SIMPLY NATURAL HEALTH

When treating ringworm, be sure to keep the affected area clean and dry between treatments, avoid any additional irritants, and be sure to wash all towels, sheets and items of clothing that have come into contact with the fungus. Do not let anyone else in the house use your towels or any clothes until they have been properly washed.

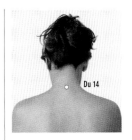

Essential:
- Make a paste with ½ tablespoon apple cider vinegar and 1 tablespoon baking soda. Add 5 drops tea tree and 2 drops geranium essential oils. Apply onto the patches or, if the fungus is on your hands or feet, do a soak. In a bowl of 1 litre of water, place 120 ml apple cider vinegar and 85 g baking soda. Add 5 drops each of tea tree and geranium oils. Soak hands and feet for 10 minutes then pat dry.
- Apply neat tea tree oil to the affected area and let it dry.
- Infuse coconut oil with garlic: take 120 ml coconut oil and squeeze in 3–5 garlic cloves. Let it infuse overnight. The next day, strain the garlic out and pour oil into a bottle. Use this oil at night before you sleep on all the fungal areas.
- Drink lemongrass tea daily.

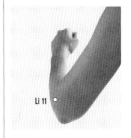

Acupressure Points:
Du 14, Li 11 and Sp 6.

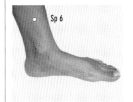

Supplements:
- Grapefruit seed extract – 10 drops (daily).
- Olive leaf extract – 500 mg (two times a day).
- Probiotics – 100 billion cells (50 billion at 1am and 50 billion taken at 1 pm).
- Vitamin A – 10,000 ius (until fungus is gone).

GALLSTONES AND GALLBLADDER FLUSH
Gallstones are usually caused by the consumption in excess of certain rich foods for example: fatty heavily fried foods, creamy foods such as milk, cheese and eggs, foods high in fat, refined sugar and refined flour, too much red meat (especially fatty meats).

People who also do not drink enough water and sleep at irregular hours are more prone to gallstones, as well as those who are or have been on any form of hormone therapy (the contraceptive pill, HRT or fertility treatment), and those on statins and blood pressure medications.

Signs of gallstones tend to be gas and bloating after eating, discomfort on the right side below the ribcage, higher back pain, sciatica, indigestion, nausea after eating and allergies which effect the sinuses.

If you know you have gallstones or you suffer from any of the above symptoms, it might be wise to do a do a gallbladder flush not once or twice but about six times (with a few weeks in between), and I can almost guarantee you that your stones will be gone.

Performing the flush:

- For five days, cut out all meat, fatty and fried foods, eggs, cheese and milk. Turn to a mainly vegetarian diet with occasional fish (steamed or grilled).
- You must drink two glasses of freshly squeezed apple juice with ½ a squeezed lemon. Once in the morning and once in the afternoon or evening, both on an empty stomach if possible. The malic acid from the apples helps to soften the stones.
- On the sixth day, drink your juice then have a light fruit breakfast (include apples) and a light lunch (not later than 2 pm) then stop eating for the rest of the day. Prepare the following mixtures at around 6 pm.
- Epsom salt mixture – Mix 5 tablespoons of Epsom salts into 800 ml of water. Place salt mixture in a clean glass bottle and cover. You can leave it in the fridge.
- Olive oil mix – Mix 120 ml of extra virgin olive oil and 120 ml of freshly squeezed lemon juice into 250 ml of water. Place in a clean glass bottle or jar and cover.
- At 6 pm – drink 180 ml of the Epsom salt mixture.
- At 8 pm – drink 180 ml of the Epsom salt mixture.
- At 10 pm – drink 250 ml of the olive oil mixture. Drink this standing up. You may have water after.
- At 8 am or when you wake up, drink the last 200 ml of the Epsom salt mixture. If nothing is happening within an hour, drink the olive oil mixture again.
- You may be feeling a bit unwell or nauseous at this point. Drink a freshly squeezed apple juice or eat some apples and fruit.
- The flush should start. When your bowels open, look for floating balls on the surface of the water. Those are the stones that are being flushed out.
- Eat light clean foods for the rest of the day.
- Repeat this every two weeks for six times or until there are no more stones floating in your stools.

Do the acupressure points daily – Gb 34 and Gb 39.

GINGIVITIS

Gingivitis is an inflammation of the gums. With gingivitis, the gums can become swollen and bleed easily. This can be due to a buildup of plaque or bacteria, poor oral hygiene, food or chemical sensitivities.

Essential:

- When your gums are inflamed, do an 'oil pulling'. First thing in the morning before breakfast, take about 3 tablespoons of pure coconut oil into your mouth and swish it around for 1–2 minutes. Spit it out. Do not swallow. Do this every morning until the condition improves, then do it periodically to keep the mouth and gums healthy.

- Oral hygiene is very important with gingivitis, however the SLS and SLF that make generic toothpastes foam aggravate gingivitis so use a natural toothpaste without chemicals or you can make your own toothpaste. Prepare a toothpaste with 1 tablespoon baking soda, ½ tablespoon coconut oil, 3 drops peppermint oil and 2 drops tea tree (you can also use myrrh or neem). Mix together. Put into a jar with a lid. Dip your toothbrush in the paste and brush.

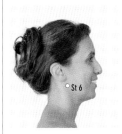

- Get some neem oil or neem bark powder (neem does not smell or taste nice so use it sparingly). Rub it on the gums for as long as you can.
- At night, rinse your mouth with the following mouthwash. Prepare a mouthwash with 200 ml of water and 50 ml of aloe vera juice then add the following essential oils: 4 drops myrrh and 5 drops tea tree. Hold the mouthwash in the mouth, swishing it against the gums for at least 30 seconds morning and night.

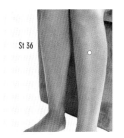

- Rub some pure aloe vera gel on the gums before bed.
- In Chinese medicine, both the stomach meridian and the large intestine meridian run through the gums; therefore diet could also affect gum health. Check for food intolerances.
- Wheat/gluten, dairy and refined foods as well as the deadly nightshade vegetables are known to aggravate gingivitis.

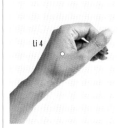

Acupressure points:
St 4, St 6, St 36 and Li 4.

GOUT

The visual image that the word gout conjures up in my mind is that of a large red-faced, meat-eating, and beer swilling man. However, nothing could be farther from the truth than this image. Gout can affect any of us – young and old – and actually often affects more women than men.

Gout is a form of arthritis. It is recognised as being the most painful form of arthritis that you can get. It is caused by the buildup of uric acids in the joints, most often the big toe (which is where the liver meridian starts from). The uric acid forms little crystals that lodge in joints and this gives a sensation compared to the pain you might experience of little shards of glass in the joint. Although the big toe is the most commonly affected joint other joints like the ankles, knees and hips etc. are also susceptible to gout. As gout is a form of arthritis, please read the section under Arthritis (pg 115) to understand this condition better.

With gout, it is vital to remove foods that are high in purines from the diet. Foods with high purines form uric acid. These foods include organ meats (such as liver, kidneys and sweetbreads), bacon, beef, pork, lamb, game, anchovies, sardines, herring, mackerel, scallops, gravy, beer and other alcohols.

Gout, like arthritis, is seen in TCM as a damp and windy condition. But unlike arthritis, which is a cold condition, gout is seen as a hot condition. Eating foods that cool you down and consciously avoiding overheating the body, can be beneficial to gout sufferers. (Please see Part 2 – Mother Nature's Medical Kit for a list of hot and cold foods).

Immediate relief:

- As gout is an acidic condition, your body would need to become more alkaline to balance it out. The best way to do this is to drink a lemon and baking soda drink. Squeeze ½ a lemon and add 1 teaspoon of baking soda into a large glass of water. Take this three times a day.
- Prepare an essential oil mix of the following oils: 2 drops pine, 2 drops juniper, 3 drops lemon, 1 drop sweet marjoram and 1 drop coriander. Mix the oils into a 1½ teaspoon base oil of olive or coconut. Apply to affected area.

Essential:

- Soak the foot or the joint in an Epsom bath or basin. Add the above oils to the warm water.
- Start your day with a fresh pure aloe vera juice followed by a glass of water
- Throughout the day, drink 700–950 ml of pure cherry juice. Cherry juice

contains powerful antioxidants called anthocyanins that help reduce the levels of uric acid in the bloodstream.

- Prepare a turmeric and lemongrass tea with honey before bed. Place 1 teaspoon of powdered turmeric or 2.5-cm fresh turmeric and 1 stick of bruised lemongrass into a pot. Cover with water and boil for 10 minutes. Let sit for a few minutes. Add the juice of ½ a fresh lemon and 1 teaspoon honey (optional). Drink before bed. Continue this until the pain has subsided and for a few days after the pain has gone.
- Get a red cabbage leaf (which contains anthocyanins), iron it to heat it up and break down the anthocyanins. Wrap the warm leaf around the painful joint. Secure with cling film or a towel and go to bed.
- Do the acupressure points three times a day.

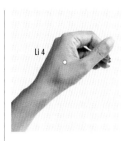

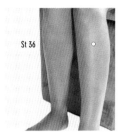

Acupressure points
Li 4, St 36 and Liv 3.

GROWING PAINS

Growing pains are mysterious and rather acute pains that occur as children are growing. They usually are felt in the legs and often occur at night. Even though it is never a pleasure to have your sleep disturbed, have pity on your child as growing pains are really painful. You can't see growing pains and they are not associated with physical changes of the area such as swelling or redness, but don't ignore them. The pains are usually easily relieved by massage, rest and a bit of tender loving care.

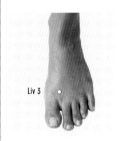

However, if the pain persists for over a week or there are physical changes, the child should be seen by a physician.

Essential:
- Prepare an oil mix as follows: 1½ teaspoon base oil with 1 drop each of sweet marjoram, lavender and ginger oils. Rub onto the area where there is pain.
- Do the acupressure points listed.
- When the child is going through a growth spurt or a growing pain episode, make sure they have a warm bath at night into which you have put 85 g Epsom salts with 2 drops each of lavender, lemon, ginger and sweet marjoram oils.
- Prepare a ginger tea – bruise 2.5-cm ginger, cover with water and boil for 10 minutes. Cool and add honey to sweeten. Drink before bed.
- Give 300 mg of magnesium if your child experiences cramps.

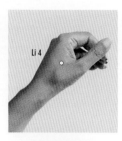

Li 4

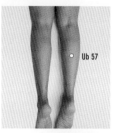

Ub 57

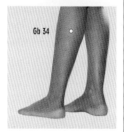

Gb 34

Acupressure Points:
Li 4, Ub 57 and Gb 34.

Additional Information:
- If the child wakes up and is in distress due to the pain, offer them some Bach rescue remedy (pg 89) and add a few drops into the oil mix next time you massage the area.
- During a spate of growing pains, make sure your child has enough iron, zinc, magnesium, calcium and potassium in their diet. One way to do this is to give 1 tablespoon a day of organic blackstrap molasses.

Supplements (daily):
- Calcium – 300 mg.
- Magnesium – 600 mg.
- Potassium – 100 mg.
- Vitamin D 3 – 2,000 ius.
- Zinc – check the dosage based on your child's age.

HAEMORRHOIDS / PILES

Haemorrhoids (also known as piles) are painful and annoying but are easily treated, especially if treated quickly.

What exactly are haemorrhoids? They are swollen veins located around the anus or in the lower rectum. Haemorrhoids can either be internal or external. Internal haemorrhoids develop within the anus or rectum. External haemorrhoids develop outside of the anus.

External haemorrhoids are the most common and most troublesome. What causes haemorrhoids? A multitude of things – chronic constipation and straining when trying to move your bowels, sitting too long (my grandmother used to say from sitting on cold floors), pregnancy (due to the extra weight one is carrying), childbirth, labour, from carrying very heavy objects, chronic diarrhoea and sometimes due to anal intercourse.

The symptoms of haemorrhoids vary from severe itching in the anal area to difficulty sitting, frequent rectal bleeding, and can sometimes manifest themselves as quite severe pain in the rectum that can spread into the abdomen.

Immediate relief for acute pain:
- If your haemorrhoids are really painful, to the point where you can't sit down, take a piece of ice, put 1 drop of lavender and 1 drop of Bach rescue

remedy on the ice. Rub over the inflamed area (for external haemorrhoids). For internal haemorrhoids, place a small ice cube or ice chips in a bag. Lubricate the bag with oil or aloe vera gel (or any lubricant you might have). Add 1 drop of lavender oil and 2 drops of Bach rescue remedy to the lubricant and gently insert into the anus for as long as you can withstand the discomfort. This will bring immediate relief and calm the pain. If you can feel the haemorrhoid popping out of the anus, gently try and push it back inside with a clean finger.

Essential:
- Prepare a haemorrhoid gel of 1 tablespoon of pure aloe vera gel and add the following essential oils: 2 drops of cypress, 2 drops of juniper and 1 drop lemon. Shake well to mix. Apply to the area where the haemorrhoids are morning and night. Keep the gel in the fridge so that it is cool when you apply. This helps to reduce the inflammation even faster.
- Drink lots of water to soften the bowels so that you don't have to strain when you go to the loo. If you suffer from constipation, look under Constipation on pg 140. When you do move your bowels, drink 235 ml water either before or when you are in the toilet.

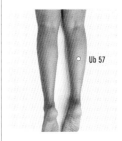

Ub 57

Acupressure Points:
Press the acupressure point Ub 57 in the morning and night.

Additional Information:

If the haemorrhoids are bleeding badly or continuously, you can put a tiny amount of dry cayenne pepper on the area.

Supplements:

- Magnesium – 400 mg (daily).
- Probiotics – 50–100 billion cells (daily).

HAND, FOOT AND MOUTH DISEASE

Hand, foot and mouth Disease (HFMD) is a normal, mildly contagious viral infection common in young children. However, adults can also succumb to the virus. It starts with a runny nose and fever and is characterised by sores in the mouth, blisters and a rash on the hands, feet and anus. Hand, foot and mouth disease is most commonly caused by a Coxsackie virus.

Coxsackie viruses belong to a family of viruses called enteroviruses. This virus lives in the gastrointestinal tract and are, therefore, present in faeces. Poor hygiene allows the virus within the faeces to be passed from person to person. After exposure to the virus, development of symptoms takes only 4–6 days but can remain in the system for up to one week after all the symptoms are gone.

As it is a virus, the only thing you can do is boost the immune system as much as you can and keep the child comfortable. The main worry with HFMD is dehydration as children do not want to eat or drink as their mouths, and often throats, are covered with sore blisters.

Essential:

- Boost the immune system by putting some neat lavender oil on and rubbing the acupressure points listed.
- Run a warm bath. Add 85 g Epsom salts with 2–3 drops lavender, 2–3 drops lemon and 4 drops of Bach rescue remedy (pg 89). Sponge the child gently or let them play in the bath as they like.
- After the bath, prepare an oil of 1 teaspoon base oil and add in 1 teaspoon each of rosehip oil and carrot oil. Add 2 drops each of lavender, chamomile Roman and mandarin oils. Rub along the spine.
- Give manuka honey UMF 15+ at least four times a day. The manuka will have a calming effect on the ulcers. If the child refuses to take the honey, make manuka honey popsicles.

- Encourage the child to drink as much as possible and add some olive leaf extract. Take 250 mg two times a day.

Acupressure Points:

Du 14, Li 4 and Lu 11. Rub Du 14 in a clockwise direction for the count of 30. Try to do this three times a day.

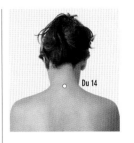

Additional Information:

- Take a handful of fresh thyme or ½ tablespoon of dried thyme and place in a cup or bowl. Cover with hot water for fresh thyme (or boiling water for dried thyme) and let steep for 10 minutes. Strain and cool, then add 1 teaspoon manuka honey UMF 15+. Thyme tea is an excellent way to boost the immune system and helps the body to detoxify from the virus. It is also full of Vitamin C.
- Offer fresh watermelon juice or fresh coconut water. This soothes the ulcers and cools the system.
- Follow the Fever steps on pg 140.

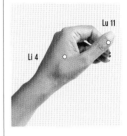

....

MANUKA HONEY POPSICLES

Juice from 3 apples (green or red)
Juice from 3 oranges
Juice from 1–2 large carrots
Juice from a handful of mint
4 tablespoons of manuka honey
   UMF 15+ (or higher), diluted in
   a small amount of warm water
1 drop clove oil

Combine all the juices together. Add honey mixture and clove oil. Pour mixture into a popsicle mould and freeze. Offer these popsicles as often as they are wanted. If this combination of fruits does not appeal to your child, use fruits that he or she likes and get them involved in making the popsicles themselves. They will love it.

....

"Probiotic foods and drinks coat your stomach and make hangovers more bearable."

HANGOVERS

This is not necessarily an illness but when a hangover strikes, it can sometimes feels like you are pretty close to death. So how can you prepare yourself if you know it's going to be a night of heavy drinking? Follow these easy preparatory and curative steps.

Essential:

- Before you leave for your evening out, coat your stomach with a good natural probiotic – kombucha, kefir or live yoghurt are ideal – or just take a probiotic supplement of 10 billion cells.
- Follow this with a glass of water into which you have added 1 teaspoon of a good liquid Vitamin B complex.
- Remember to always have a full glass of water next to you that you keep refilling and drinking alongside any alcohol you drink.
- When you get home, drink a big glass of water or juice with another 1 teaspoon liquid B and 2,000 mg powdered Vitamin C (you can make this before and leave it in the fridge). Take before going to bed.
- Take a jug of water to bed with you as you are likely to wake up thirsty in the middle of the night.
- Take a liquid Vitamin B complex the next morning; add 1–1½ teaspoons into whatever liquid you are drinking and add ¼ teaspoon pink salt and 1 teaspoon magnesium. Drink a glass of fermented kombucha tea.

HEADACHES / MIGRAINES

Headaches come in many forms and come upon us for many reasons. The five areas where a headache can originate from are the liver, gallbladder, stomach, large intestine and urinary bladder areas. It is important to isolate which area the headache is coming from.

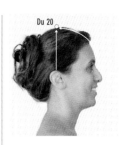

FOR ALL HEADACHES (IMMEDIATE)

- Take a supplement of magnesium between 400–600 mg when you realise you have a headache. After the headache is gone, keep taking 400 mg magnesium a day for 2–3 days then make sure you are eating magnesium-rich foods (pg 73).
- Put 5–10 drops of cayenne tincture (pg 97) into warm water and drink.

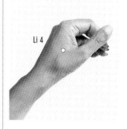

LIVER HEADACHE

- This headache starts behind the eyes and can be quite blinding.

Essential:

- Drink a big glass of water with 1 lemon squeezed into it. Add in 1 teaspoon of milk thistle tincture (pg 65).
- Sip a rose bud tea.
- Prepare a liver lover juice (pg 169).

Acupressure Points:

Press the following points Du 20, Li 4, Gb 34 and Liv 3 for 1 minute each. Repeat until you experience relief.

GALLBLADDER HEADACHE

This headache starts on the sides of the head and near the temples.

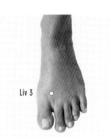

Essential:

- Drink a glass of water with the juice of ½ a lemon and ½ teaspoon of baking soda mixed in. Repeat within the hour till the headache starts to subside.
- Dab neat lavender oil onto your temples.
- Mix 1 drop sweet marjoram, 2 drops lemon and 2 drops lavender essential oils in 1 teaspoon of base oil and rub at the base of the neck, under your ears and on the acupressure points listed.

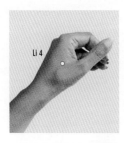

Acupressure Points:

Li 4, Liv 3, Gb 34, Du 20, Gb 8 and Gb 20. Put 30 seconds of pressure on each of these points. Repeat until you experience relief.

STOMACH HEADACHE

Stomach headaches can be felt across the front of your forehead. This headache is often caused by eating things that you may be sensitive to such as MSG, food colouring, preservatives, chocolate, oranges, wheat/gluten and red wine.

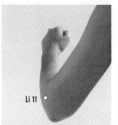

Essential:

- Prepare 235 ml peppermint tea (sweeten with some honey if you would like)
- Dab peppermint oil on the acupressure point St 8.
- Prepare a mix of the following essential oils: 2 drops cardamom, 2 drops lavender and 1 drop peppermint and add to 1½ teaspoon base oil. Rub your stomach in a clockwise direction with a small amount of the oil.

Acupressure Points:

Do acupressure point Li 4 for a few minutes continuously. Alternate between Li 4, Li 11 and St 36 (see pg 187).

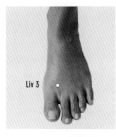

SINUS HEADACHE

Often a headache accompanies a sinus infection or a head cold, this headache can be felt along the top of the eyebrows. Please see under Sinusitis (pg 217).

URINARY BLADDER HEADACHE

This headache can start from your shoulders or the back of the neck and creeps forward and you can feel it all the way to where your eyebrows start. It can often be triggered by sunlight, bright lights, heat or exercise.

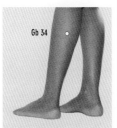

Essential:

- At the start of the headache, take a liquid mineral supplement of potassium, magnesium and sodium (follow instructions on your bottle).
- Keep drinking water throughout the day but add a little bit of salt and lemon to the water.
- Prepare a footbath of warm/hot water and add 5 drops of sweet marjoram oil. Soak your feet for as long as you like.
- Prepare a blend of 2 drops sweet marjoram, 1 drop lavender, 1 drop lemon oils and rub it on the shoulder area and on the acupressure points.

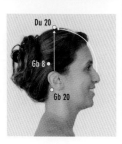

Acupressure Points:
Press acupressure points Li 4, Ub 10 and Ub 40.

CLUSTER HEADACHE
Into a glass of warm water add 2 drops frankincense and drink before bed or when the headache starts.

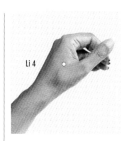

Li 4

HEAD LICE

For some reason, we tend to equate head lice with dirt and a lack of hygiene – nothing could be further from the truth. Lice are annoying and itchy but every society around the world and every school will eventually have cases of head lice. Contrary to popular belief, lice prefer clean hair to dirty hair.

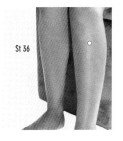

St 36

Essential:
- Get a piece of white paper and a lice comb. Bend the head in question over the piece of paper and comb the hair from the base of the skull to the tip of the hair with the lice comb. Any nits or lice that comb out, squash them onto the paper. The lice are reddish-black and often have blood in them while the nits are whitish-grey and give a convincing pop. Once you have confirmed the infestation, move on to the next step. If not, you are free from them (for the moment). Remember to keep checking regularly as a nit-free Monday can become a full infestation by Friday.

Ub 10

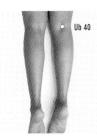

Ub 40

- If you have lice, get a spray bottle and fill with vinegar. Apple cider vinegar is preferred but any vinegar will do.
- Wet the head with the vinegar, making sure all the hair is extremely wet.
- Massage the hair shafts (this is to un-glue the nits which glue themselves on). Make sure the scalp is also covered. Be careful to avoid the eyes, especially for young children.
- Let the vinegar sit on the head for a good 10–15 minutes. You can wrap the head in a towel to avoid dripping vinegar everywhere.
- Meanwhile, add the following essential oils into a 100 ml shampoo bottle (if your bottle is bigger, increase the amount of essential oils based on the amount given for 100 ml): 5 drops each of tea tree, lavender, geranium and eucalyptus *globulus* oils. If you don't want to add all this into the bottle itself, pour the shampoo into your hand and use 1 drop each of the above essential oils and massage thoroughly into the head.
- Shampoo the hair and massage the shampoo thoroughly everywhere – most essentially at the bottom of the hairline and above the ears.
- Add 10 drops tea tree oil to 100 ml of conditioner or you can add 2–3 drops of pure tea tree oil into the conditioner in your hand.
- With the conditioner in your hair, use a lice comb and comb the hair thoroughly to get out the nits and lice. Make sure to wash the lice comb out after you brush it through your hair.
- Leave the conditioner on for a few minutes. Rinse the hair thoroughly.
- Do a final rinse with a small container full of water with 2–3 drops of tea tree oil. Do not rinse this out.

Additional Information:

Wash all sheets, pillowcases and towels in a hot wash. Add in a few drops of tea tree and lavender essential oils to the washing powder. Iron on hot. This kills all nits that might be floating around.

HEAT RASH

According to TCM principles, heat rash is an outward sign of an internal temperature imbalance. The goal here is to cool down. If you have heat rash, avoid eating spicy foods, sugar, drinking hot beverages, alcohol and taking hot showers or baths – indeed, cease all behaviour and intake that generates heat in the body.

Essential:

- Add 1 drop of lavender essential oil into 1½ teaspoon of aloe vera gel. Rub on the heat rash area and let it dry on for instant relief.
- Add 30 ml of pure aloe vera juice to 1 big glass of water. Drink a glass of this mixture three times a day.
- Prepare a cooling herbal tea with 1 tablespoon of peppermint leaves and 2 tablespoons of chrysanthemum flowers in 700 ml boiling water. Steep for 20 minutes, then strain and cool to room temperature. Drink 120 ml every few hours until the rash clears.
- To relieve the itchiness of the rash, do an oat bath. Place 170 g organic oats into a cloth. Place the cloth over the nozzle of the tap and run lukewarm to cool water through the oats. Then add 85 g baking soda into the water and 5–10 drops of lavender oil. If you do not have a bath, follow the same instructions, just collect the water in a bowl and sponge affected area.

Peppermint tea cools you down.

Additional Information:

Make a talcum powder with cornstarch or zeolite clay to "powder" the area. Place 170 g of either cornstarch or zeolite clay into a bag and add 5 drops of lavender and 2 drops of chamomile German oils. Shake the bag to mix the oils with the powder or blend in a blender. Place into a dry jar or bottle. Use as you would use a talcum powder.

HIGH BLOOD PRESSURE / HYPERTENSION

Often referred to as the silent killer, high blood pressure (HBP) has no obvious symptoms and unfortunately can go completely undetected. But, what exactly is high blood pressure?

Our hearts pump blood. Blood pressure is the force of blood against your blood vessels as it circulates. This force is necessary to make the blood flow. As it flows, it delivers vital nutrients and oxygen throughout your body. When you develop HBP, it means there is too much pressure in your blood vessels. This can severely damage your blood vessels and puts you at risk of having a stroke, a heart attack or other heart damage.

What makes blood pressure increase? Diet is a major factor – too much bad salt, fatty foods and sugar. Being overweight or obese can also raise blood pressure. Other triggers are lack of exercise, smoking, too much alcohol and stress alcohol. Finally, it also has to do with older age, genetics, family history, kidney disease, adrenal disorders, thyroid disorders, sleep apnoea as well as blocked blood vessels. Bad news, even if none of the above applies to you, anybody can develop HBP. So, remember: a regular blood pressure check is an extremely important thing to do, no matter how good you may feel and how virtuously you think you may be living.

Important:

Often people with HBP are immediately told to lower their sodium or salt intake. That is today's short answer to a long-term problem. Yes, indeed, this is very important and salt (generic iodised table salt especially) is a real killer for people with high blood pressure and, if you really do have HBP, you must try to stop using it immediately. However, what many people fail to realise is that potassium and salt/sodium work closely together in the body and that a deficiency in potassium can contribute to HBP as potassium works to counteract the effects of sodium. Therefore, as potassium levels decrease, the sodium is not balanced out and affects your blood pressure, making it go higher and higher. However, we need sodium for so many bodily functions that cutting it out completely is dangerous. We need a balance of sodium, potassium, calcium and magnesium to keep our blood pressure stable.

Essential:

- Immediately remove iodised table salt from your kitchen and house. Replace with a good quality pure sea salt, pink salt or Himalayan salt.
- Start your day with coconut water (fresh or bottled – if bottled, make sure there is no added sugar) or make coconut kefir (fermented coconut water) and add ½–1 teaspoon cinnamon. Coconut water has the perfect balance of the following helpful minerals: potassium, magnesium, calcium and sodium. If coconut water is not available take some aloe vera juice.
- Take 1 tablespoon of virgin olive oil or avocado oil daily. You can add this into smoothies, drinks, salads or soup.
- At night prepare a drink of juice of ½ a squeezed lemon, 1 crushed garlic clove and warm water. Add 1 teaspoon of good quality raw honey to sweeten (optional).
- Take 1 teaspoon of olive leaf extract three times a day for up to three months.
- Make a dessert of 1 tablespoon of blackstrap molasses mixed with 1 tablespoon of pumpkin seed butter or tahini. Molasses is an iron-rich food which helps increase oxygen levels in the system and also has a huge amount of essential materials.
- Take an Epsom salt bath 1–2 times a week with the following essential oils: 5 drops lavender, 5 drops hyssop and 3 drops ylang-ylang. If stress is

Avocados are the fruits highest in potassium

SIMPLY NATURAL HEALTH

a contributing factor, add in 3 drops of basil oil. Breathe deeply when in the bath.

- Too much coffee is not good for HBP, replacing coffee with a black or green tea helps to reduce high blood pressure dramatically.
- Drink a lemongrass and cardamom tea before bed. If using fresh lemongrass, just pound 1 or 2 stalks of the lemongrass with 3–4 cardamom seeds and pour hot boiling water over it. Let steep for 3–5 minutes. Remove the stalks and seeds and drink. Sweeten with a good quality honey (optional).
- Add in potassium-rich foods wherever and however you can into your diet (see potassium-rich foods in Mother Nature's Medical Kit on pg 73).

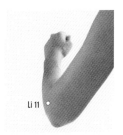

Acupressure Points:

Do the acupressure points Li 11, Ub 40, St 36, Sp 6 and K 1. Place 60 seconds of pressure on each of these points every night before bed. Once the blood pressure has gone down, keep pressing K 1, Sp 6 and St 36 three times a week.

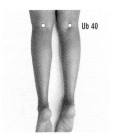

Additional Information:

- Regular exercise is crucial to keep blood pressure under control. However if you are a runner or do any sport where you sweat profusely, you must make sure you replace your electrolytes after each exercise session by drinking coconut water or taking a good mineral supplement – one with potassium, sodium, magnesium and calcium.
- The best forms of exercise to lower blood pressure are yoga and stretching.
- A good breakfast to help lower blood pressure is 170 g cooked rolled oats with 1 teaspoon powdered cinnamon, 1 teaspoon tahini, a mixed handful of pumpkin seed, walnuts and pecans and dried apricots sprinkled on top. Sweeten with a good raw organic honey or pure maple syrup.

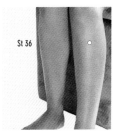

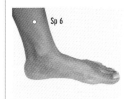

Supplements:

- Green tea extract – 250 mg (daily).
- Minerals – potassium, calcium, magnesium and sodium.
- Omega-3 oil (flaxseed or coconut) – 1 tablespoon.
- Probiotics – 20 billion cells or through fermented foods.
- Potassium – 3,000 mg (daily).
- Vitamin C – 3,000 mg.
- Vitamin D3 – 3,000 ius.
- Vitamin E – 400 ius.

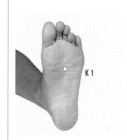

HIGH CHOLESTEROL

There are two types of cholesterol – HDL and LDL. HDL is good cholesterol (we want more of this as it protects our heart) and LDL is bad cholesterol (we want this to be as low as possible as this can cause problems for our heart).

What is cholesterol? Cholesterol is a type of fat in our blood stream that either helps us or hinders us. There are many drugs out there that can lower cholesterol – the problem with taking these cholesterol-lowering drugs is that it is dangerous to stop taking them, and they often have nasty side effects.

The following steps have been followed by many and have had very positive long-term results in reducing high cholesterol.

Essential:

- Cut out coffee, milk and dairy products, fatty foods, fried foods, refined white sugar, processed meats and animal fats.
- Start taking red yeast rice extract daily. You must take 600 mg a day for three months.
- First thing in the morning, prepare a drink of 1 tablespoon apple cider vinegar, 1 tablespoon psyllium husks, 1 tablespoon olive oil, 1 teaspoon cinnamon powder, about 2.5-cm of crushed ginger in about 235 ml warm water. Add 1 teaspoon manuka honey UMF 15+ (optional). Drink daily for three months.
- Prepare a grapefruit drink twice a week. Take a whole organic grapefruit (including the peel and pips) and blend in a high-speed blender. Add water to make it more drinkable.
- Selenium is also very important in reducing cholesterol. Eat 6–8 Brazil nuts a day to get an excellent amount of selenium.
- Take the following supplements below for three months (or until your next blood test).

Supplements:

- CoQ10 – 50–100 mg (daily).
- Green tea extract – 1 teaspoon (in the morning).
- Selenium – 400 mg.
- Vitamin E – 400 ius.

HIVES / URTICARIA

A break out of hives can happen, quite honestly, anytime and can be quite alarming. Hives is the bodies' natural response to an allergic reaction marked by raised red patches of skin and is usually, but not always, accompanied by intense itching. Hives are normally caused by contact with a specific precipitating factor such as a food, drug, animal or something environmental. The contact can be either external or internal – intense and ongoing hives are also called urticaria.

The two areas that we want to concentrate on here are the liver and the intestines.

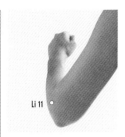

Essential:

- At the onset of hives, immediately prepare the following mixture: 1 teaspoon of turmeric and 1 teaspoon of coconut oil mixed into a little bit of warm water. Drink it every hour until the hives calm down.
- You can also put neat lavender oil onto the hives to calm the area.

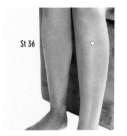

Acupressure Points:

- Do the anti-allergy acupressure massage by pressing from Li 1–Li 4, holding strongly on Li 4. Repeat until the hives start to calm.
- Then do the following acupressure points in the order that I give them to you – this does two things; it calms the hives down but also stimulates the system to accept the 'allergen' and to not see it as such an enemy:
- Acupressure points: Li 11, Li 4, Li 1, St 36, Sp 6 and Liv 3. Extra point P 6 (see pg 235). Repeat this routine five times.

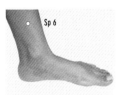

Supplements:

- ½ teaspoon of turmeric and 1 teaspoon coconut oil into warm water 2–3 times a day for two weeks.
- Glutamine – 2,000 mg.
- Probiotics – 50 billion cells (daily).
- Zinc – 20 mg (daily).

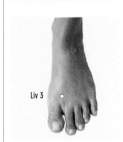

H. PYLORI

"We're talking about a bug that's been in the human gut for at least 58,000 years........There's probably a reason for that."

Dr. Martin Blaser, New York University Langone Medical Centre

Helicobacter Pylori, more commonly known as H. Pylori, are spiral-shaped bacteria that grow in the digestive tract that have a tendency to attack the stomach lining. H. Pylori infections are harmless but have been linked to causing ulcers and various digestive issues in the stomach and small intestine. What makes most people worry is that the H. Pylori bacteria seem to be linked to some stomach cancers. However, significant studies that are now being done on the gut, and the importance of the gut bacteria (the microbiota or microbiome of the stomach), seem to have scientists a bit confused about whether H. Pylori is as bad as they initially thought. It seems that more than half the world have H. Pylori in their guts. It also seems that this bacteria might actually be quite useful to our gut microbiota by protecting us against obesity and asthma. Therefore, the last thing that we should be doing is using aggressive antibiotics to kill it. It must also be noted that using antibiotics to cure conditions perhaps caused by H. Pylori won't necessarily get rid of the ailment fully but can kill other important gut bacteria.

Researchers in Switzerland and Germany have reported that mice that are given H. Pylori are actually protected against asthma and one doctor has gone so far as to say that he may foresee a time when a detoxified strain of H. Pylori might be administered as a treatment for conditions like obesity and asthma.

The most worrying thing about H. Pylori is that it can change the acidity levels of the stomach in order to survive. This is not good as we need our stomachs to be acidic to break down foods properly, and contrary to popular belief, indigestion is often caused by low acidity levels in our stomach as opposed to high acidity levels.

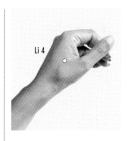

Symptoms:
Most commonly there are no symptoms, but if there is an overgrowth of H. Pylori then symptoms may include abdominal pain, especially when your stomach is empty. Other symptoms include burping, bloating, flatulence and stomach and duodenal ulcers.

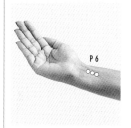

Essential:
- First thing in the morning before breakfast, drink a glass of cabbage juice with 1 teaspoon of baking soda, 1 tablespoon coconut oil and 1 teaspoon of probiotics mixed into it.
- Take 350 mg of mastic extract or mastic gum three times a day for four weeks.
- Mix 250 mg of manuka honey UMF 15+ with 8 crushed garlic cloves, 1 teaspoon of turmeric and 1 teaspoon of liquorice extract. Take 1 teaspoon three times a day for three weeks (only use liquorice extract if you do not have high blood pressure).
- After each meal, take 1 caps of hydrochloric acid (HCL) for three weeks.

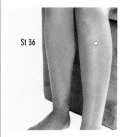

Acupressure points:
Li 4, P 6 and St 36.

IMPETIGO

The remedy for impetigo may seem short and sweet, but believe me if you start at the very beginning of this bacteria, you will not have to deal with it for long.

Impetigo is caused by streptococcus (strep) or staphylococcus (staph) bacteria. Our skin normally hosts many types of bacteria; however, when there is a break in the skin, bacteria can enter the body and grow. Breaks in the skin may occur from injury or trauma to the skin or from insect, animal or even human bites. Although impetigo is most common in children, adults can easily succumb. It can also develop as a result of a cold or other viruses.

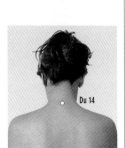

Essential:

- Take 1 tablespoon of manuka honey UMF 15+ and add 5 drops tea tree oil. Cover the impetigo sore as soon as it appears or even if it is suspected impetigo. Keep it covered. Reapply every two hours.
- You can also cover the sore with pure tea tree.
- Take 1 teaspoon of manuka honey UMF 15+ every hour.

Acupressure Points:

Du 14, Li 4, Liv 3 and St 36.

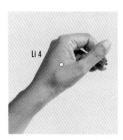

Additional Information:

- Impetigo is very contagious and spreads quickly. If there is someone with impetigo in the house, make sure the infected person washes his or her hands often. You can rub a drop of tea tree onto the hands to clean them.
- Make a spray of thyme and tea tree essential oils. Add 5 drops each of thyme *vulgaris* and tea tree oils into a bottle of 500 ml water. Shake each time before you spray and spray the rooms, counter tops and tabletops even doorknobs that infected hands might have touched.

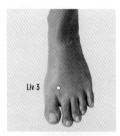

Supplements:

- Vitamin C – 1,500 mg (three times a day).
- Zinc – 50 mg (take in the morning).

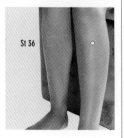

SIMPLY NATURAL HEALTH

INDIGESTION / HEARTBURN / ACID REFLUX

Indigestion, heartburn and acid reflux occur when stomach acids are forced back up into the oesophagus. This causes a burning sensation in the middle of the chest (which is why it is called heartburn) and is incredibly uncomfortable. Contrary to popular belief, indigestion is often caused by low acidity levels in our stomachs.

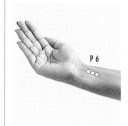

Immediate:

To give immediate relief from heartburn, drink a glass of water with ½ teaspoon of baking soda mixed in.

Essential (if reflux and heartburn are recurring):

- First thing in the morning, place 1 teaspoon baking soda into a glass of water and drink it.
- Follow this with pure red cabbage juice and manuka honey UMF 15+. Juice ½ a red cabbage. Add 1 teaspoon of manuka honey UMF 15+ and 50 billion cells of powdered multi-strain probiotics.
- Wait for about 30 minutes before you eat breakfast.
- Take some digestive enzymes with every meal.
- Even though indigestion is often seen as one's stomach being too acidic, the opposite can often be true and our stomach can have too little stomach acid (HCL), so after a meal you should take a supplement of HCL to help break the foods down. However, if you feel the HCL is making you more acidic, stop taking it.
- Remove all the following items from your diet: any hot chillies or spices, ginger, onions, garlic, cinnamon, milk products, white sugar, bread, and refrain from eating too many raw salads.
- The acupressure points are vital to stop the heartburn. Every time you feel the heartburn start, do the acupressure points.
- Supplementing is also essential.

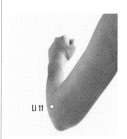

Acupressure Points:

Li 4, P 6, Li 11, St 25, Ren 4 and St 36 (press St 25, Ren 4 and P 6 whenever you feel the burning). Rub the stomach firmly in a clockwise direction to ease the burning directly after a meal.

Supplements:

To help the stomach to heal take:

- Digestive enzymes – 2 with every meal.
- Glutamine – 2,000 mg (on an empty stomach in the morning)
- Magnesium – 200 mg.
- Probiotics – 10 billion cells; 5 billion in the morning and 5 billion in the evening (powder form)
- Vitamin D3 – 4,000 ius.
- Zinc – 30 mg.

Foods to Heal:

- Pure coconut water with probiotic powder mixed into it taken on an empty stomach.
- Aloe vera juice (pure) – taken on an empty stomach.
- Papaya juice before a meal.

INSOMNIA

Sleep is such an important part of our health. It is during sleep that our organs can regenerate, rest and repair themselves. It is also a time when our brains gets to rest as well.

When patients come to my clinic whatever the problem is, the first question I ask them is "how well do you sleep?" If the answer is "not well", then no matter what they are seeing me for, I will work first and foremost on getting them to sleep soundly. That way the healing can begin.

Insomnia itself is a state of sleeplessness that can affect anyone at anytime. It takes on different characteristics. It can be the inability to fall asleep, to stay asleep, or waking at a certain time of the night. There are acute and chronic cases but all can be treated in a somewhat similar way.

Firstly, know your body clock. To help treat insomnia, it is very important to read your body clock as this will tell you which organ you need to work on. Here is a quick guide for you. If you can't sleep at the times noted – it is the fault of the organ mentioned. Please refer to Gallstones (pg 175) to see how to do a gallbladder flush if you suspect that you might have gallstones.

11 pm–1 am Gall Bladder:

- Physically, the gallbladder stores and excretes bile, but emotionally, it oversees self-esteem and decision-making. If you're not sleeping by this time, you are depleting your gall bladder's energy, which over time can lead to poor self-esteem, poor judgment and difficulty in digesting fats. This may lead to migraines, sciatica, sinus issues and/or indigestion.

1–3 am Liver:

- The liver's role is to detoxify our bodies. If you're not sleeping at this time, you can quickly become out of balance, especially if you are female, as the liver has a lot to do with hormonal balance or imbalance. The liver is also emotionally connected to anger. You may find that you wake up between 1–3 am if you are harbouring repressed anger or a long-standing resentment. Symptoms of liver imbalances include irregular menstruation, difficult menopause, anaemia, chronic fatigue and headache.
- Take a tincture of milk thistle (pg 65) before bed if you tend to wake at this time.
- Drinking rose tea or a garlic lemon tea before bed can benefit. Squeeze ½ a lemon and 1 clove of garlic. Pour warm water on top and add a good raw honey or manuka honey UMF 15+.

3–5 am Lungs:

- The lungs are responsible for moving the Qi (energy) through the meridians and to the entire body, and they also provide immune protection. The lungs are also emotionally associated with grief. You may find that you wake up during these times if you are struggling with grief or sorrow. Imbalances may also show up as wheezing, coughing, asthma or falling sick easily.
- Drinking a nettle tea and taking 1,000 mg of magnesium will help with this waking. If there is grief, look through the Bach flower remedies guideline (pg 83) to select some remedies to help you through this.

5–7 am Large Intestine:

- This is the best time to have a bowel movement. The large intestine is all about 'letting go' physically and emotionally. Symptoms of malfunction include constipation, dry stools, skin rash and feeling emotionally 'stuck'.
- Taking magnesium-rich foods and treating constipation will help with this waking. Please see Constipation on pg 140.

TIP
Making a warm lemon honey and garlic drink before bed with 1 teaspoon of olive oil added to it will help the function of the gall bladder.

TIP
Taking a cup of dandelion root tea before bed can help with this waking. For anger, look at the Bach flower remedy guideline (pg 83).

TIP
Drink nettle tea to strengthen the lungs.

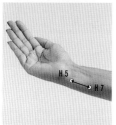

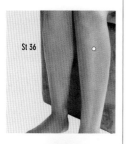

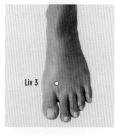

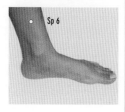

Essential:

- Take a warm Epsom salt bath at night before you sleep. Add the following essential oils to it: 2 drops each of sweet marjoram, lavender, *palmarosa* and chamomile Roman and have a long relaxing soak.
- If you don't have a bath, then take 400 mg of magnesium before you sleep or use a magnesium spray.
- Taking a good liquid Multi B complex first thing in the morning will help you sleep at night.
- Drinking a warm cup of chamomile tea sweetened with an organic raw honey can help you sleep.
- Take the Bach flower remedy of white chestnut before you sleep or when you wake up to calm a restless mind.
- Do not look at the screen of any electronic devices at least half an hour before bed. Instead, do some deep breathing with your hands placed on your chest and solar plexus areas.

Acupressure Points (use your essential oil blend on your acupressure points):

Acupressure points are crucial. Prepare the same blend of oils that you put in the bath but put them into 1 tablespoon of base oil. Use this oil on the following acupressure points *ying tang*, H 5–H 7, St 36, Liv 3 and Sp 6.

If you wake up at night

Do not get up and start to watch TV. Refrain from turning the lights on and walking around. Take your oil blend and rub it on your arms and press deeply into the H 7 point. You can rub this up and down. Inhale deeply into the oils and place your hands on your solar plexus and chest and breathe deeply into your stomach.

Fighting Fatigue

If you feel worn down or are lacking energy due to improper sleep, learn how to fight fatigue naturally.

- Liquid magnesium supplementation has been shown to improve symptoms of fatigue in persons with low magnesium levels.
- Coenzyme Q10. This vital nutrient is involved in cellular energy production throughout the body.

- The *ashwagandha* and Rhodiola herbs are adaptogenic herbs that help the body deal with stress but also boost energy levels.
- *Cordyceps*, a traditional Chinese medicinal mushroom may help fight fatigue and boost energy levels.

ITCHY EARS

Itchy ears are often due to fungal infections, an eczema or psoriasis outbreak in the ear. The thing you must not do with itchy ears is to try and stick anything inside the ear to try and stop the itch as you could pierce the eardrum.

Essential:
- Make garlic-infused oil (pg 163) in the previous section for ear infections.
- Add 2 drops each of tea tree oil and grapefruit seed extract to 1 teaspoon of garlic oil. Dip a cotton bud in the oil and gently rub the oil in the ear. Release some of the liquid into the ear canal.
- Repeat this every morning and night till the itching stops or put neat tea tree on a cotton swab and rub into the ears.

Supplements:
Drink 5 drops of grapefruit seed extract in a glass of water morning and night.

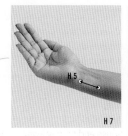

LARYNGITIS

Laryngitis is an inflammation of the voice box (larynx) which causes hoarseness, loss of voice and throat pain.

Common causes of laryngitis include upper respiratory infections, such as colds, or overuse of the voice box by talking, singing, or shouting. Other possible causes for laryngitis are reflux, chronic irritation of the vocal cords due to shouting, constant talking at a loud level, smoking, exposure to second hand smoke or exposure to polluted air.

Essential:

• Cut out all cold drinks – only drink room temperature or warm drinks.
• Prepare a drink of warm water combined with the juice of ½ a fresh lemon, 2 teaspoons of manuka honey UMF 15+ and ½ teaspoon of fresh or ground turmeric. Drink this throughout the day.
• Massage the neck area with a mix of the following essential oils: 2 drops chamomile German, 2 drops sweet marjoram and 1 drop thyme *vulgaris*.
• When the voice returns, do not overdo the talking, singing or shouting – give your voice at least a three days break.

Acupressure Points:

Press the acupressure points H 5–H 7 throughout the day. Keep pressing it intermittently until the voice returns.

MEASLES

Measles is a viral infection that was once quite common – mainly amongst children. Signs and symptoms of measles include a cough, runny nose, inflamed eyes, sore throat, fever and a red, blotchy skin rash.

A person with measles can spread the virus to others for about eight days, starting four days before the rash appears and ending when the rash has been present for four days. So if your child has measles, make sure you keep them at home so as to avoid an outbreak. Although most children and adults are immunised against measles, more and more people are opting not to vaccinate, so beware. Warn people, especially pregnant women, who have had contact with the child or person.

Measles, in general, is not a virus to be worried about as it should naturally run its viral course, but it does mean your body is weakened and needs to be supported. The worry about measles is that it can lead to other complications

like encephalitis, secondary ear infections, bronchitis and pneumonia and, statistically, 1 person in 1,000 actually die from these complications. This is why it is very important to boost the immune system and support a person through a measles episode.

Essential:
- Vitamin A is essential to prevent you from getting measles as well as helping you get through a case of measles. Make the 'A' soup.
- To help ease the rash, have an oatmeal bath. Place 170 g oats in a cloth and hold the cloth over the nozzle of the bath. Run the water through the oats or tie the oats in a cloth and place in the bath, gently squeeze. Add the following essential oils: 3 drops chamomile (Roman or German) into the bath with 3 drops lavender and 2 drops thyme *vulgaris*. Soak for 20 minutes. If you don't have a bathtub, make the oat water in a bowl. Add ½ the quantity of the oils and dab on the rash.
- Offer chamomile tea sweetened with manuka honey UMF 15+ to ease the throat and itching.
- Make a mixture of 100 mg of manuka honey UMF 15+ with 1 teaspoon turmeric and 1 tablespoon coconut oil – take 1 teaspoon three times a day.
- To calm the itching down, use some aloe vera gel with some lavender oil and apply onto the rash area. Make sure to test a patch of the rash to make sure it doesn't make the itching worse.
- Look at pg 140 to help support the fever.
- Once the fever is down and rash has stopped spreading, you can make a mixture of ½ teaspoon of Vitamin E oil and 1 teaspoon of jojoba oil with 2 drops each of lavender and chamomile (German or Roman) essential oils. Massage it on the blotches to get rid of the rash quickly and prevent scarring.

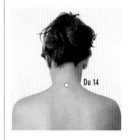

Du 14

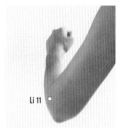

Li 11

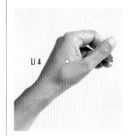

Li 4

Acupressure Points:
Du 14, Li 11, Li 4 and St 36.

Additional Information:
People low in Vitamin A are more prone to contracting measles.

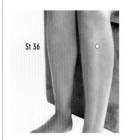

St 36

Supplements:
- Increase your Vitamin A through supplementing 15,000 ius daily until the end of the virus.

- Make a fresh carrot and apple juice daily into which you have added 2,000 mg of Vitamin C, 800 ius of Vitamin E and a liquid Multi B complex.
- Take a liquid Vitamin B.
- Make the soup below to supplement your Vitamin A intake.

....

'A' SOUP

½ red bell pepper
½ yellow bell pepper
½ a small pumpkin
2 carrots
Olive oil as needed
Amino acids as needed
Dried thyme as needed
470 ml home-made immune
    boosting soup
1 teaspoon turmeric
Salt to taste
Pepper to taste

Marinate red and yellow bell pepper, pumpkin and carrots in olive oil, amino acids and some dried thyme. Place on a roasting tray and roast until soft. Place roasted vegetables in a blender. Add home-made immune-boosting soup (pg 138) and blend. Gently warm and season with turmeric and salt and pepper to taste.

....

MEMORY – HOW TO IMPROVE IT!

It feels that, as we get older and older, our brains just get fuller and fuller of memories, information, ideas and worries. There seems to be less space and we start to forget things. This is not only very annoying but sometimes quite worrying too. Do not despair. There are many things that can help to improve our memory, so start before you forget to.

Firstly, even though your brain may feel like it is filled to capacity, it is not. Our memory is stored in our hippocampus, which has the capability to retain more as we get older. The memory can continue to grow even as we reach our 90's as long as we exercise it continuously and give it the right tools.

So what are the things that affect our brains and our memory in a negative way? Here's the list: lack of good sleep, depression, lack of exercise, anxiety, stress, medication, menopause (the memory actually gets better after the menopause), smoking, excessive sugar, alcohol and thyroid issues.

Essential:

- Sleep. It is vital to get into good sleep patterns to help the memory. If you have sleep issues, please read the section entitled Insomnia (pg 198) to understand your own sleep patterns.
- Green tea is excellent for the memory. Start your day with a green tea or add a green tea extract into your morning drink. Sip it throughout the day as you work – this can also help you to retain the information.
- Eating gingko *biloba* nuts, drinking a gingko *biloba* tea or taking a supplement helps to boost the memory.
- The B vitamins are essential for brain health and function. Getting a good liquid Multi B daily is imperative.
- B12 is the most important B vitamin as it actually slows down brain shrinkage. An excellent source of Vitamin B12 is bee pollen – add it into your porridge or cereal in the morning or into your morning drink. Black pepper helps to absorb B12 so crack some pepper into that too.
- Make a memory-boosting oil mix: 3 drops rosemary, 2 drops black pepper, 1 drop peppermint and 2 drops frankincense. Rub this on the spine, at the base of the skull and on the temples.
- Increasing your omega-3s is vital for your memory.
- Include these memory-boosting foods in your diet on a regular basis: celery, broccoli, cauliflower, walnuts, blueberries and garbanzo beans.
- Remember our brains need good fats. Including coconut oil in your daily diet is recognised as helping to increase memory.
- Vitamin D3 is also important for our memory. The best way to get Vitamin D is through exposure to the sun. This is the best excuse you can think of giving your boss when you want to go on a sunny holiday in the middle of winter – you actually need to. If you can't go on holiday then supplement Vitamin D3 2,000–4,000 ius every other day.
- Cut out all refined sugar and gluten.

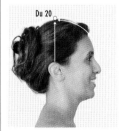

Du 20

Acupressure Points:

- The acupressure point Du 20, when pressed, activates the memory and 'switches on' all the meridians, which energises our whole system.
- Tapping the tips of your fingers and toes boosts the brain.

Additional Information:

- Major studies are being done on coconut oil and its effect on memory. It is largely believed that adding coconut oil to your diet can help to slow down – or even reverse – the onset of Alzheimer's and dementia.

- Putting 1 drop of frankincense essential oil at the base of the skull increases memory and energy almost instantaneously.
- Medical experts are now calling Alzheimer's "type 3 diabetes". In type 1 and type 2 diabetes, not enough insulin (or none at all) is produced to process glucose. This affects the organs and the body as a whole. In type 3 diabetes, the uncontrolled glucose affects the brain directly.
- Studies have also shown that people who have type 2 diabetes are more prone to getting Alzheimer's.

Supplements:
- Gingko *biloba* extract – 150 mg.
- Green tea extract – 400 mg (daily; green tea is an anticoagulant so be careful if you are taking blood thinners).
- Liquid Multi B vitamin daily – 1 teaspoon (daily).
- Omega-3 oil – 400 mg (daily).
- Vitamin D3 – 2,000–4,000 ius (every other day).

NOTE

Drinking a red date and longan tea throughout your period really helps to warm up the womb and replenish the blood that is being lost.

MENSTRUAL CRAMPS

Menstrual cramps are generally accepted as an occasional or normal part of the monthly process or "part of being a woman". However, in TCM, they believe cramps indicate a cold in the womb, which therefore cramps up and causes pain. This is why TCM advises women not to drink very cold water, or have too many cold foods in general, especially during their menstrual cycle. Women of childbearing age should, in particular, take note of period cramps as often women who suffer from bad menstrual cramps can have trouble conceiving.

Essential:
- If you know when your cycle is likely to start, and you suffer from period cramps, try to make a conscious effort to stop drinking cold water, iced drinks, ice cream and the "cold foods" a few days before your period starts. Refer to the list in Mother Nature's Medical Kit section of this book (pg 53).
- Start drinking ginger tea either before the cramps start or when the cramps start. To make ginger tea, take 5-cm of peeled fresh ginger and pound lightly.

Put in a pot of boiling water and boil for 10 minutes. Remove from the heat and strain. Add some honey to sweeten and drink.

- Make a mixture of the following oils to ease the cramps. Add the following essential oils into 1½ teaspoon base oil: 3 drops clary sage, 2 drops ginger and 2 drops sweet marjoram. Rub this onto the womb area and on the lower back area.
- Doing the acupressure points daily leading up to your period is very important.

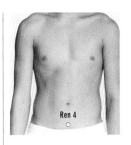

Acupressure Points:
Ren 4, Li 4 and Sp 6.

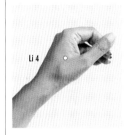

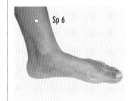

MILIA

Milia are very small, raised, pearly-white or yellowish bumps on the skin. People often mistake them for pimples, but they are quite different to a spot, as milia do not come from a pore but are just a pocket of normal skin that somehow became indented, then sealed over and the dead cells get trapped. They are most often seen on the skin around the cheeks, nose, eyes and eyelids, forehead and chest. However, they can occur anywhere on the body. Milia are very common in newborn babies but can affect people of any age. They are nothing dangerous, but they can be quite annoying if you have great clusters of them. The cause of them seem to be overactive sweat glands.

Essential:
- Scrub the area. Blend 170 g oats with 85 g baking soda. Blend until fine. Take enough to use on your face. Add water to make a paste and scrub the area gently.
- Dab jojoba oil on the spots every night until they disappear. The healing usually takes 2–4 weeks but can also last for up to three months.

MOLLUSCUMS / WATER WARTS

Molluscums or water warts are a highly contagious viral skin condition that cause small flesh-coloured little 'warts' to pop up in certain areas, often in clusters, but they can be spread across a wide area. With molluscums, there may be many treatments suggested – like burning them off or using strong topical drugs. I believe that the most effective way of getting rid of molluscums is to let the immune system fight internally as you attack them externally.

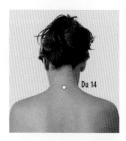

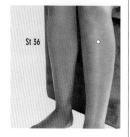

Treatment:

- At night dab undiluted tea tree onto each molluscum. After a few days to a week you will see that one molluscum will start to turn very angry and red – this is the 'mother' molluscum. Some doctors will actually advise to try and gently dig it out. This can be quite painful but it is really up to you to decide if you want to follow the advice. Otherwise, just keep on putting the neat tea tree on all the warts, especially the 'mother' molluscum. When this one eventually drops off and dies, all the others will soon disappear.
- Whilst doing the tea tree, you can take the homeopathic remedy of thuja three times a day. This will encourage all the molluscums to come to the surface so don't panic if more appear, just keep applying the tea tree. (Advice: See a homoeopath or go to a homeopathic pharmacy to inquire on dosages for thuja.)

Acupressure Points:

Du 14, Li 11 and St 36.

Supplements:

It is essential to boost up the immune system to fight the virus, prevent it spreading, as well as prevent further outbreaks. You must take the following supplements:

- Grapefruit seed extract or echinacea – 5 drops (two times a day).
- Probiotics – 10–30 billion cells.
- Vitamin C – 1–5,000 mg.
- Zinc – 15–30 mg.

MOUTH ULCERS / CANKER SORES

Mouth ulcers or canker sores are lesions on either the cheeks, tongues or along the gums. They often start small but can grow larger and are very painful. Ulcers on the cheek or tongue are normally caused when you accidentally bite into the cheek or onto the tongue, or when you knock your mouth against something hard. However, recurrent mouth ulcers along the gums can mean a few things:

- You may have intolerances to different foods that you are eating.
- Your immune system is under stress.
- Your system is overheated. This can happen due to not drinking enough water when hot or from eating foods that are too 'hot' (see hot and cold properties of food in the Part 2 – Mother Nature's Medical Kit pg 53).

- Sleepless nights and being over tired.
- Another thing that causes mouth ulcers will be sensitivity to the foaming agents in toothpastes.

Strange Advice:

As opposed to eating food away from your ulcer, eat foods near or on the ulcer. This does two things: firstly, it stops you from re-biting the ulcer, which often happens, and which makes the ulcer grow; the nutrients from the foods, which are released when being chewed, actually help the ulcer to heal faster. Initially it might sting but work through this and it will, unbelievably, feel better.

Essential:

- Make a mouth wash of sea salt and essential oils. Into 250 mg of warm water, stir in ½ teaspoon sea salt, 1 drop tea tree, 1 drop geranium and 1 drop myrrh oils. Make this in a clean jar or bottle. Swish 20 ml in your mouth three times a day.
- In a blender, blend a handful of coriander with 120 ml water. Strain through a muslin cloth. Rinse the mouth with the coriander water three times a day. This needs to be made fresh daily.
- Measure 1½ teaspoon of pure aloe vera gel into a small pot and blend in the following essential oils: 1 drop myrrh, 1 drop geranium, 1 drop benzoin. Add ¼ teaspoon manuka honey UMF 15+. Mix together vigorously. Apply this gel to the ulcer 4–5 times a day.

Acupressure points:

St 4, St 6, Du 14 and St 36.

Supplements:

- Probiotics – 10 billion cells (daily).
- Liquid Multi B complex – follow suggested dosage on bottle (daily).
- Liquid mineral supplement – follow suggested dosage on bottle (daily).

Diet:

- If you have frequent mouth ulcers, look at your diet. Intolerances to foods can often cause recurrent mouth ulcers. It is worth getting a muscle test or a blood test to see which foods may be causing the problem.
- People who are deficient in Vitamin B often have mouth ulcers.

CAUTION
If a mouth ulcer does not clear up after about 10 days, seek medical advice.

St 4

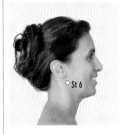

St 6

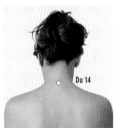

Du 14

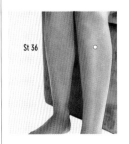

St 36

MUSCULAR CRAMPS

Muscular cramps can happen anywhere on your body and are normally caused by a painful and involuntary contraction of a muscle or muscle group. They are typically caused by fatigue, strain or a deficiency in minerals.

Essential:

- When you feel an area cramping, rub it. Do not ice the area as this will make the cramp worse. Prepare an oil mix of 1½ teaspoon base oil with 3 drops each of sweet marjoram and ginger essential oils. Rub in until the cramp starts to release.
- Drink a glass of water with ½ teaspoon of baking soda.
- Soak the area in a concentration of Epsom salts.

Supplements:

- Take extra 400 mg magnesium before you sleep if you are waking up with cramps.
- Often the reason why our muscles start to cramp is due to a lack or imbalance of the minerals potassium, magnesium and sodium.
- Find a liquid mineral which has a balance of potassium, magnesium and sodium. Take as instructed for three weeks.
- After three weeks, make sure your mineral balance is on track by either taking a spoonful of molasses daily or at least a few times a week.
- Coconut water is also a good thing to drink regularly if you feel like your minerals are going out of balance.

MYCOPLASMA

Mycoplasma is hard to deal with. It is primarily regarded as a bacteria, it also has viral and even parasitic-like qualities. Due to this ambiguous nature, antibiotics rarely eradicate mycoplasma completely. As it has virus-like components to it, the only way to truly deal with mycoplasma is to let the immune system combat it. Sadly, it is treated with very strong antibiotics, which then affect one's stomach. This in turn weakens the immune system. So, the crucial thing to do with mycoplasma is to allow our body to fight it. At the same time boost the immune system – once the immune system conquers mycoplasma, it will not come back.

Essential:

- Supplementation is essential with mycoplasma.
- Make a mix of 200 mg of manuka honey UMF 15+, 8 crushed garlic cloves, crush 5-cm of ginger, 2 teaspoons turmeric powder and 1 tablespoon of coconut oil. Take 1 teaspoon four times a day.
- Take an Epsom salt bath daily. Add 170 g Epsom salts and the following essential oils to the bath: 2 drops thyme *vulgaris*, 5 drops tea tree, 3 drops lemon and 3 drops eucalyptus.
- Prepare a thyme, clove and ginger tea. Bruise about 5-cm of peeled ginger and put into a pot with about 470 ml water and 10 cloves. Boil for about 10 minutes. Remove from heat and add a handful of fresh thyme or 1 teaspoon dried thyme and let it infuse. Strain and add manuka honey UMF 15+. Drink at least three times a day.
- Prepare a blend of the following oils. Mix 2 drops thyme *vulgaris*, 2 drops tea tree, 3 drops lemon, 1 drop cardamom, 1 drop black pepper, 1 drop clove and 1 drop myrrh. Mix into 1½ teaspoon of a base oil of your choice and add ½ teaspoon carrot oil and ½ teaspoon rosehip oil.
- Use this blend and rub on the spine and the acupressure points twice a day.

Acupressure Points:

Du 14, St 36, Liv 3, Li 4 and Li 11. Extra points P 6 and K 1 (see pg 235) if there is brain fog and anxiety.

Supplements:

- CoQ10 – follow instructions on your bottle.
- Green tea extract – follow instructions on your bottle.
- Olive leaf extract – 1 teaspoon three times a day.
- Oregano oil – 4 drops in the morning and 4 drops in the evening.
- Probiotics – 30 billion cells.
- Vitamin C – 5,000 mg.
- Zinc – 30 mg.

Diet:

- Cut out all refined foods.
- Cut out all dairy, wheat and sugar.
- Increase bone broths and easily digested nutritious foods.
- Add in to the diet wherever possible garlic, ginger and spices.
- Eat a lot of immune-boosting soup (pg 138).

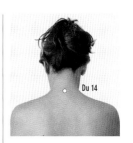

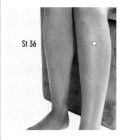

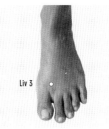

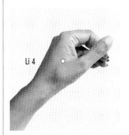

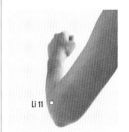

NAUSEA

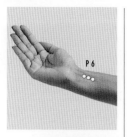

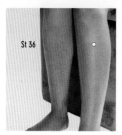

We all know what it feels like to feel sick to our stomach or nauseous – no matter what the reason – indigestion (from eating too fast or from stress around mealtime), food poisoning, motion sickness or even pregnancy – it is a horrible feeling and you just want it to go away. Well here is how you can make it go away, quickly and easily.

Essential:
- Hold or massage the acupressure point of P 6 for 3–5 minutes. This point will do one of two things: if you need to get sick it will make you physically vomit or if your body does not need to actually vomit, it will calm the system and the feeling of nausea will subside.
- You then press the point of St 36 to recover.
- Put a drop of pure peppermint oil on the acupressure point P 6.
- If you suspect food poisoning, take activated charcoal or 1 tablespoon of zeolite clay mixed into water or juice.

Acupressure Points:
P 6 and St 36.

Additional Information:
- Prepare an anti-nausea blend of oils. Mix 1½ teaspoon base oil with 1 drop cardamom, 2 drops mandarin, 1 drop peppermint and 2 drops lavender oils. Rub the oil on the stomach in an anti-clockwise direction.
- Drink either peppermint or ginger tea with a 1 teaspoon manuka honey UMF 15+.
- Drink 1½ teaspoon of vodka with ½ teaspoon crushed black pepper. This has stopped many stomach viruses/bacteria and also relieves the nausea that may be associated with it.

Pregnancy Sickness:
- Do the acupressure point of P 6.
- Drink coconut water or an electrolyte drink.
- Chew some candied ginger or drink some ginger tea – pound 2.5-cm of ginger, boil in some water and sweeten with manuka honey UMF 15+.
- Every morning, make sure you drink a balance of minerals – potassium, magnesium and sodium, coconut water, electrolyte drink or liquid minerals.

OEDEMA / WATER RETENTION

Water retention is caused by an excessive buildup of fluids in the body. This is linked to a mineral imbalance – mainly an imbalance of sodium. We need sodium, but not too much sodium. So people with diets high in salt are usually more prone to water retention and swelling than others. Water retention also means our lymphatic system isn't draining well and is getting a bit congested.

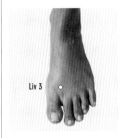

Immediate:

To start the 'drainage' system working again, replace all teas and coffee with dandelion root tea 2–3 times a day.

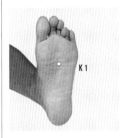

Essential:

- Do dry skin brushing daily before your shower or bath. Always brush towards the heart. Concentrate on the areas that are the most swollen.
- Take the cayenne tincture (pg 97). Add 5 drops into water once a day and drink.
- First thing in the morning, drink 1 tablespoon of pure aloe vera juice mixed in water.
- Eliminate iodised table salt from your diet. Throw out any that you may have in your house and replace with a good sea salt or pink salt.
- Reduce your intake of alcohol.
- Prepare an essential oil blend of 3 drops each of lemon, cypress and grapefruit oils in 1½ teaspoon of a base oil. Use on the acupressure points and the lymphatic drainage points.

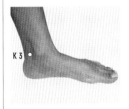

Acupressure points:

- Gb 39 – press this in a downward motion.
- Press Liv 3, K 1 and K 3 for 30–60 seconds each. Repeat for three rounds.
- Lymphatic drainage – on the outside of the leg. Use the base of your palm and push firmly from below your hip down to the outside of your knee.
- Under the collarbone, using your fingers press deeply in and drag your fingers towards the shoulders.

TIP

If flying makes your ankles and fingers swell; take a few dandelion root tea bags with you on your flight and instead of tea and coffee or alcohol.

NOTE

Black walnut hulls are safe for occasional use of up to two weeks at a time, but black walnut heartwood is not. Avoid herbal remedies that contain heartwood.

PARASITES

Around 4 billion people are infested with parasites, and they come from all walks of life. Some live in Third World countries but a large amount live in the most developed countries of the world. Parasites come in so many different forms and affect us in so many different ways that we often have no idea that we are infested with them.

These are the different ways we can be affected by parasites:

Acute parasite infection – This infection is usually characterised by stomach pain and distress along with diarrhoea and sometimes vomiting. Only rarely is there any visible evidence of infection. Moreover, many laboratories fail to detect the presence of parasites even when presented with specimens from an infected person. It is therefore necessary for the patient to determine whether infection is likely and to self-administer some remedy since allopathic medicine requires a diagnosis before prescriptions can be written.

Chronic parasite infection – This infection may be recognised from alternating periods of constipation and diarrhoea, abdominal distension and bloating, intestinal cramping followed by burning sensations and the sudden urge to eliminate. Generally, there is malabsorption of nutrients. Irritable bowel syndrome, blood sugar fluctuations, sudden food cravings and sudden weight loss or weight gain are all possible symptoms – but, as stated, not necessarily proof of parasitic infection.

Again, one can have these symptoms without being infected with parasites. However, if you have recently travelled or had a meal somewhere and do not feel well after it, you might want to try to do a parasite cleanse just in case.

Immediate:

- If vomiting occurs, let the body vomit out all the food but when the vomit turns to bile or water, drink a glass of room temperature water into which you have added ½ teaspoon sea, pink or Himalayan salt and 1 teaspoon of manuka honey UMF 15+. Administer in small sips or by the spoonful.
- Once the vomiting has stopped, prepare a mix of 100 ml of manuka honey UMF 15+, juice from 2 garlic cloves , ¼ teaspoon cinnamon and ¼ teaspoon ground cloves. Take this mixture 1 teaspoon at a time every hour (if the garlic is too strong at first, omit this and add it in later).
- Do the acupressure points listed.

Essential – to kill the parasites:

- Get a tincture of black walnut and take 1½ teaspoon three times a day for up to one month. If symptoms are milder, but still there, you can take it for up to three months.
- Drink the juice of a red cabbage daily on an empty stomach. Add 10 billion cells of probiotic powder, 1 tablespoon coconut oil and 1 drop of clove oil or ½ teaspoon of ground cloves and 5–10 drops of cayenne tincture (pg 97).
- Prepare a mix of 100 ml pumpkin seed butter with 2 tablespoons manuka honey UMF 15+, 3 garlic cloves, ½ teaspoon ground cinnamon and ½ teaspoon ground cloves. Eat 1 tablespoon 2–3 times a day for three weeks.

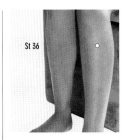

Acupressure Points:

- Press the acupressure points St 36, Ren 12, St 25, Ren 6, Sj 3, Sj 5 and Sj 6 gently. Extra points P 6 and Li 4 (see pg 235).
- If diarrhoea is also a symptom add the acupressure points Li 11 and Sp 10.

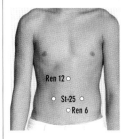

Additional Information:

Parasites can cause sleep disorders (such as insomnia) and, for some children, hyperactivity. They can also cause depression, anxiety and memory issues.

Prevention:

- When travelling to places where the food may not be as clean as usual, or you are not able to drink the water, take a supplement of hydrochloric acid after every meal. This acid, which is naturally found in our stomachs, helps to kill any parasites that may be trying to find a home in your system. By boosting the HCL levels, you are fortifying your stomach.
- Cracking black pepper into your food also increases the HCL in our stomachs.

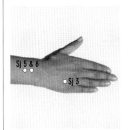

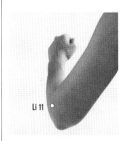

PSORIASIS

Psoriasis is a common, non-infectious – and some believe inherited – skin disorder, which occurs when the production rate of new skin cells is accelerated. The result is raised patches of pink, thick, new skin covered with flakes of dead skin. This acceleration seems to occur in connection with stress, emotional problems, infections or other illnesses. It commonly occurs on elbows, chest, knees and scalp. The reddish lesions are slightly raised and covered with silver-white scales, and the coverage can range from a single patch to covering

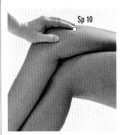

the entire body. The rash is better when exposed to sunlight and may recur over a period of years.

Medical science has not yet solved the mystery of psoriasis nor identified what causes it. The main treatment doctors are able to offer for psoriasis is the application of cortisone-based products. Although cortisone may relieve symptoms for periods of time, the side effects normally include damaged skin and patients are faced with using cortisone for the rest of their lives. Because of this, it may be to your advantage to never use cortisone products in the first place. If you are already using cortisone products, you may try to gradually decrease the use of cortisone (to avoid the reaction which can occur if the cortisone is stopped suddenly) and then to continue treatment with essential oils.

Psoriasis is a stubborn and difficult problem to treat. It requires patience, long-term treatment and commitment to get lasting results. The whole picture needs to be considered (stress management, detox of the liver, no exposure to chemicals of any kind and so on).

Crucial:
Do the acupressure points three times a day.

Essential:
- Detox your liver and gall bladder.
  Milk thistle – take 1 teaspoon of milk thistle three times a day.
  Garlic – add raw garlic into your liver lover juice (pg 169) or prepare a lemon garlic tea before bed. Pour warm water over one crushed garlic clove and ½ a squeezed lemon. Sweeten with 1 teaspoon manuka honey UMF 15+ if you need to.
  Turmeric – Prepare a turmeric tea by adding 1 teaspoon powdered turmeric and 1 teaspoon coconut oil to warm water.
- Prepare a turmeric paste. Mix 1 tablespoon turmeric and 1½ teaspoon coconut oil to make a paste. Apply it on the psoriasis patches.
- Cut out all fragrances in toiletries.
- Cut out *solanaceae* vegetables (tomatoes, potatoes, aubergine, okra and peppers), dairy and gluten.
- Cut out alcohol.
- Check your PH levels. You can buy PH kits in most pharmacies. If your system is too acidic, drink ½ teaspoon of baking soda in a glass of water every other day.

- Mix 5 drops chamomile German, 5 drops lavender, 3 drops carrot seed oil and put into a mix of the following base oils: ½ teaspoon rosehip, ½ teaspoon evening primrose oil, ½ teaspoon calendula and 1 tablespoon avocado oil. Mix all together and put in a clean bottle. Use on the psoriasis patches as often as you would like.

Acupressure points:
Du 14, Li 4, Lu 7, Li 11 and Ub 40. Extra points Liv 3 and St 36 (see pg 235).

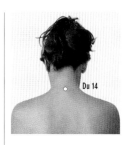

SINUSITIS

Sinusitis can be painful and extremely frustrating. Even more frustrating is that it is often a recurring problem. Technically, it is an inflammation of the sinus cavities located around and above the nose and eye area. When you have sinusitis, all these cavities, which are normally filled with air, fill with thick mucus, which causes pain, swelling and discomfort. It can also be very distressing as one's sense of smell can be very badly affected. The key to treating sinusitis is again to start as soon as you think you are getting a sinus infection.

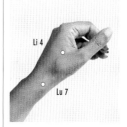

Essential:
- Start taking olive leaf extract three times a day.
- Do a sinus rinse with salt and garlic 2–3 times a day. Place ½ teaspoon of good sea salt or rock salt into 235 ml warm water. Squeeze ½–1 clove fresh garlic (start with ½ first) into the water. Let the garlic sit in the water for 15–20 minutes. Remove all garlic from the water. Place in a bowl and sniff it up into the sinus area, one nostril at a time. Blow out the water quite strongly (do not blow too strongly as you can hurt your eardrums.)
- Do an inhalation. Put 1–2 drops each of the following essential oils into a bowl of boiling water – tea tree, peppermint, geranium, clove, black pepper and eucalyptus *globulus* essential oils (if you don't have all the listed oils just use what you have though eucalyptus *globulus* and geranium are quite essential). Pour hot boiling water into the bowl and cover your head with a cloth whist bending over the hot bowl and breathe deeply.
- Prepare sinus tea: place 6 cloves, 1 stick of cinnamon, 5-cm of peeled ginger and 6 black peppercorns into a pot with 700 ml water. Bring to the boil and boil for about 10 minutes. Remove all the ingredients and sweeten with manuka honey UMF 15+ or above. Drink this 2–3 times a day.

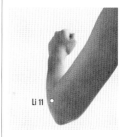

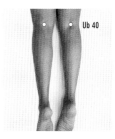

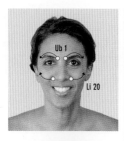

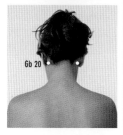

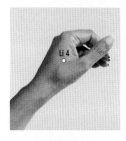

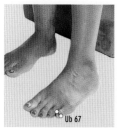

⚘ **CAUTION**
If doing this with young children observe extreme caution with the hot water.

- Prepare a natural antibiotic and antifungal mix of 100 mg manuka honey UMF 15+. Mix in 5 crushed garlic cloves, 7.5-cm of fresh ginger, ½ teaspoon cinnamon, 5-cm crushed fresh turmeric or 1 teaspoon turmeric powder and ¼ teaspoon ground black pepper. Mix together. Take 1 teaspoon 3–4 times a day.
- Do Sinus acupressure points 2–3 times a day.
- Avoid all dairy products, alcohol, yeast and refined sugar.

Acupressure Points:
Ub 1, Li 20, Gb 20, Li 4 and Ub 67. Extra points St 36, St 40 and Ub 10 (see pg 235).

Additional Information:
- Replace all tea and coffee (especially coffee) with either peppermint, fresh ginger tea or the sinus tea.
- Rub a piece of fresh ginger above and below the eyes on the sinus area.
- Most sinus infections are not bacterial or viral but are actually more of a fungal problem. Add antifungal foods to your diet wherever you can (e.g. garlic, onions, cloves, ginger and cinnamon).

Supplements:
- Oil of Oregano – 4 drops in the morning and 4 drops in the evening.
- Olive leaf extract – 450 mg (three times a day).
- Probiotics – 30 billion cells.
- Vitamin C – 5,000 mg.
- Zinc – 20 mg.

SORE THROATS / TONSILLITIS / STREP THROATS

We all have a sore throat at one time or another. It is often the first sign we are getting sick as the throat is one of our first lines of defence. As soon as you start getting a sore throat, follow the advice below.

GENERAL SORE THROATS

Essential:

- Take 120 ml warm water and add ½ teaspoon salt (sea salt is preferable) and 1 teaspoon apple cider vinegar. Add 1–3 drops of tea tree oil to it and gargle with this mixture 3–4 times a day.
- Mix 1 tablespoon of manuka honey UMF 15+ (or above) with ½ a lemon and 1 tablespoon apple cider vinegar. Take 1 teaspoon of the honey lemon mixture every hour.
- Rub 1–2 drops of undiluted tea tree oil on your neck around the area where your glands are three times a day.
- Wrap a silk scarf around your neck especially at night (making sure it is not too tight and will not get tangled while you sleep).

STREP THROATS AND TONSILLITIS

Essential:

- Take 235 ml warm water and add 1 teaspoon salt, 1 teaspoon apple cider vinegar and the following essential oils: 2 drops tea tree, 1 drop geranium and 1 drop myrrh. Gargle every 1–2 hours.
- Mix 100 mg manuka honey UMF 15+ with 5 crushed garlic cloves and the juice of 1 whole lemon. Take 1 teaspoon every hour.
- Make a tea with 120 ml apple cider vinegar, 1–2 teaspoons manuka honey UMF 15+, 1 teaspoon of coconut oil and 5 drops of cayenne tincture (pg 97). Drink 2–3 times a day
- Prepare a natural antibiotic of 100 mg manuka honey UMF 15+. Add 5 crushed garlic cloves, 2.5-cm of fresh turmeric or 1 teaspoon of turmeric powder and 1 tablespoon coconut oil. Mix together and take 1 teaspoon every two hours.
- Combine 1 drop of neat tea tree with 1 drop of neat frankincense and rub on the throat and gland area.
- Wrap a silk scarf loosely around the neck.

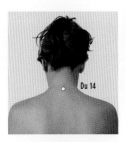

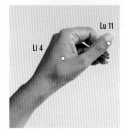

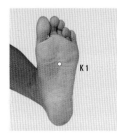

Acupressure Points:
Press Li 4 and Lu 11 with your fingernail and as you press, force yourself to swallow for about 30–60 seconds. Put 1 drop neat tea tree on the Du 14 and K 1. Press and rotate three times a day.

SPLINTERS

Splinters are when a foreign body like a piece of wood, plant matter or a sliver of glass embeds itself in the epidermal layers of our skin and gets lodged there. It is important to remember to keep the area clean when you try to remove the splinter so as to avoid infection. Wash your hands and sterilise anything you might use to help break it out.

Essential:
- If the splinter is on an area where you can soak it, get a bowl or bucket and fill enough to cover the soaking area with warm water. Add 85 g Epsom salts and 85 g baking soda. Soak the area for 20 minutes.
- Prepare a thick paste of 85 g Epsom salts and 85 g zeolite clay with enough water to make a paste. Add 1 teaspoon manuka honey UMF 15+. Cover the splinter with the paste then cover the paste with a cloth.
- Slice a red onion and place on top of the cloth. Leave on for 30 minutes.
- The splinter should start to work its way out.

SPRAINS / STRAINS / JOINT PAINS

Most people have been taught the ICE – Ice, Compress and elevate method of dealing with strains and sprains. This is the total opposite of what TCM feels one should do for any area that is under stress. If you put ice on a stressed or weakened area, it may make the swelling go down temporarily but it will also cause that joint or muscle to become too cold which might cause more problems in the long run. Do not use ICE unless the area is very hot to the touch and red – in which case you should put a cool cloth over it to cool it down. The most important thing to do with a sprain or strain is to encourage the circulation to keep flowing to this area.

Essential:

- When you have injured yourself, first rub the area vigorously to encourage the circulation to flow.
- Prepare an anti-inflammatory oil. Measure 1 teaspoon of a base oil of your choice and add 1 teaspoon of sesame oil to it. Add 2 drops sweet marjoram, 2 drops ginger, 2 drops black pepper and 1 drop frankincense into the base oil.
- Iron a piece of red cabbage and place it over the sprain/strain or joint. Get a warm cloth and wrap it around the cabbage to fix it in place. Leave it on for as long as you can (ideally overnight). Repeat as often as you can.
- Press the following acupressure points at least three times a day.

Acupressure Points:

Press the following acupressure points for 2 minutes each.

Ankle Pain – Gb 34, Gb 39, Li 4, Ub 57, Ub 60, K 3 and Sp 6.

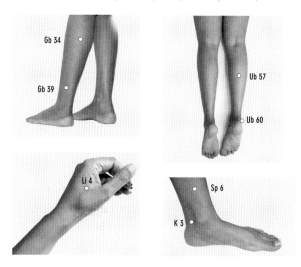

Elbow Pain – see also Tennis Elbow on pg 226.

Hip Pain – Ub 40, Ub 57, Gb 30, Gb 34 and Li 4.

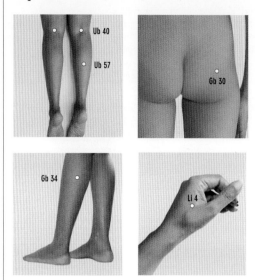

Knee Pain – Gb 34, Gb 39, Li 4, Ub 40, Sp 6, Sp 9 and Liv 8.

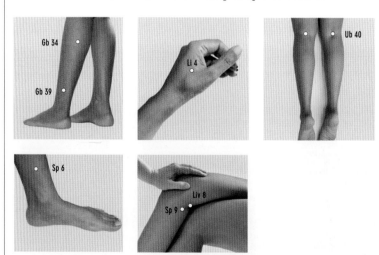

Neck Pain – Sj 3, Sj 5, Sj 6, Lu 7, Li 4, Li 11, Ub 10, Gb 20, Gb 34, Ub 60, Ub 61 and K 5. Hold Ub 60 and K 5 together and rotate the ankle whilst holding them.

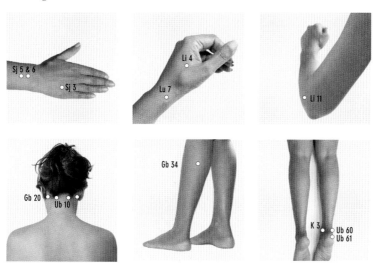

Shoulder Pain – Sj 3, Sj 5, Sj 6, Si 6, Gb 20, Gb 21, Ub 10, Ub 13, Li 4, Li 11, Ub 40 and Ub 57.

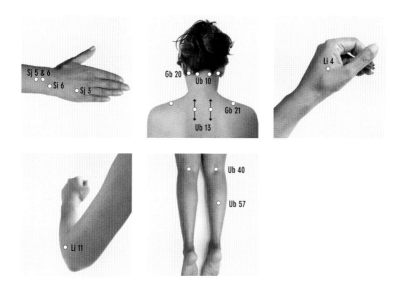

Wrist Pain – Gb 34, Li 4, Lu 7, Sj 5, Sj 6, Si 6, H 5–H 7.

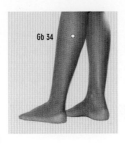
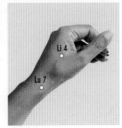

STYES

A stye is a small painful lump on the inside or outside of the eyelid. It is tiny but can make your life miserable. Now the next remedy is one that I learnt from my mother. It is so simple yet so effective.

Essential:

• Find a ring or a piece of jewellery that is pure yellow gold. Clean and sterilise it, then rub it on top of the stye for at least five minutes. Often the stye will come to a head when you are rubbing it or shortly thereafter; and sometimes it might burst then go away.
• Wash the eye with chamomile tea mixed with 1 teaspoon manuka honey UMF 15+.

Acupressure points:

Ub 1 and St 1.

Supplements:

Boost up the immune system with
• Olive leaf extract – 500 mg.
• Vitamin C – 2–3,000 mg.
• Zinc – 30 mg.

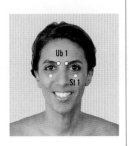

TEETHING

Teething is a trying time for both adult and child. The main sympathy however must go to the child as, as an adult, we will never have consciously experienced the discomfort of having sometimes as many as four teeth pushing through unbroken skin – normally at night, to make things worse. The symptoms of teething are sometimes hard to figure out.

Symptoms of teething:
- Teething normally starts around four months or as late as 18 months. Sometimes it can take months for the teeth to actually appear so patience is the key here.
- Raised temperature, not higher than 39°C normally.
- Clear runny nose.
- Irritability and clinginess to parent or caregiver.
- Pulling at the ear.
- Red cheeks (sometimes with a slight rash).
- Excessive drooling.
- Constantly putting fingers and toys in the mouth.
- Loose stools often slightly green in colour.
- Nappy rash.
- A dry ticklish cough especially when child is lying flat in a sleeping position.

Essential:
- Give the child Bach rescue remedy (pg 89) to help settle, reassure and soothe him/her. Place 4 drops of Bach rescue remedy in anything the child is drinking and rub 4 drops onto his/her jaw area.

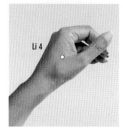

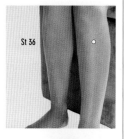

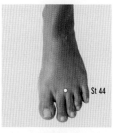

- Into 1 tablespoon of olive oil, add 4 drops Bach rescue remedy (pg 89) and 1 drop of clove oil. Rub this onto the gums as often as you need with a clean finger or a piece of cotton.
- A good old-fashioned teething ring made of anything but plastic is worth investing in at this time. There are safe metal, wooden, silicon and cotton alternatives.
- Amber necklaces have historically been said to really help alleviate the pain of teething. Amber children's necklaces are easy to find in a health food shop.

Acupressure Points:

St 6, Li 4, St 36 and St 44. Press them gently 2–3 times a day and again if the child wakes up in the night.

TENNIS ELBOW

A tennis elbow has nothing to do with tennis but is the inflammation of the tendons of the elbow (epicondylitis) caused by overuse of the muscles of the forearm. You can get a tennis elbow by pulling a rope or even stirring a pot. It simply means that the tendon has become inflamed and needs to be treated.

Essential:

- Try to rest your arm as much as possible.
- Prepare an anti-inflammatory oil: add 4 drops of sweet marjoram, 3 drops of ginger, 1 drop of lavender, 1 drop of chamomile German and 1 drop of frankincense into 1½ teaspoon of the base oil of your choice. Rub this oil into the elbow at least three times a day. At the same time press the acupressure points.
- At night, after applying the anti-inflammatory oil, iron a piece of cabbage. Place the hot cabbage over the elbow and wrap a bandage around the elbow and cabbage to keep in place. Try to sleep with this on.
- Make a turmeric tea and drink twice a day. Place 1 teaspoon of dried turmeric or 2.5-cm freshly pounded or juiced turmeric into a mug. Pour hot water over the ingredients and let infuse for about 15 minutes. When slightly cooled, add 1 tablespoon of coconut oil (you can add in some honey if you would like). Drink two times a day.

Acupressure Points:

Press the points Li 4, Sj 5, Li 11, Lu 5, Gb 34 and Ub 57. Extra point Gb 21 (see pg 235).

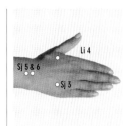

Supplements:

- Glutamine – 1,000 mg.
- Probiotics – 2,000 mg.
- Vitamin C – 1,000 mg.
- Zinc – 50 mg.

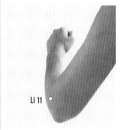

TINNITUS

Tinnitus is an annoying, high-pitched sound in the ear that either comes and goes or is continually there. The sound varies from a high-pitched whine to a clicking noise and can sometimes manifest itself as a roaring sound. Tinnitus is very unpleasant and can drive people slightly crazy depending on the level of the noise. It can also cause other problems like insomnia, depression, anxiety, decreased hearing and ear pain.

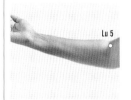

Medicine and science have not figured out exactly what happens in the ear to make these sounds and why some people are affected and not others. The conventional way of handling it is by managing the symptoms and side effects. One common medicine that is given is antihistamine.

In TCM, the approach to tinnitus is different. It is seen as a condition of the kidney. It is often taken as a warning sign that your kidneys' energy is depleting or is already deficient. What depletes the kidneys of energy? Normally stress, anxiety, over working, over worrying, extreme and continuous fear, too much alcohol, too many medications, insufficient water and too many raw foods are to blame.

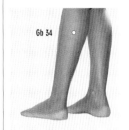

The kidneys also control the lower back pain, so people who have chronic lower back pain are more prone to tinnitus.

Using the acupressure points indicated is very effective if you have tinnitus, especially if you start early. If you have been suffering from tinnitus for years, it might take a few months of massaging the pressure points to make it go away.

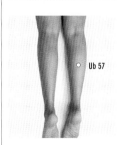

Essential:

- You must drink more water. Dehydration can be a big contributing factor to tinnitus as insufficient water weakens the kidneys even more. Cutting back your consumption of tea, coffee and alcohol, which dehydrate the body, is also crucial until the ringing subsides.

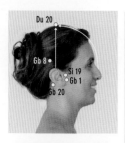

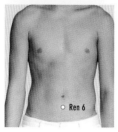

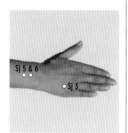

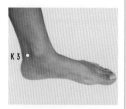

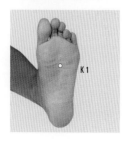

- Prepare the following mixture: add 3 drops geranium and 2 drops ylang-ylang to 1½ teaspoon of a base oil. Rub on the lower back area (where the kidneys are located). Rub the oil on the acupressure points also.

Acupressure Points:

The acupressure points here are the key to getting rid of tinnitus. Learn them and do the points three times a day minimum, but you can do them throughout the day and specifically before you go to bed.

- Du 20, Gb 1, Gb 8, Gb 20, Si 19, Ren 6, Sj 3 and 5 and 6, K 3 and K 1.
- Do these points throughout the day – Li 4, Sj 5 and 6, Gb 20, Du 20 and Si 19.
- When you hold Ren 6, lie down and massage the point whilst taking some deep long breaths. Try to equalise your in breath and out breath to the same length of time.

Additional Information:

- At night take an Epsom salt bath with 170 g Epsom salts into which you add in 5 drops geranium, 3 drops ylang-ylang and 5 drops lemon essential oils. If you do not have a bath, use the same oils on a cloth and rub them on your skin during your shower.
- Add 4 drops of Bach rescue remedy (pg 89) into water and drink four times a day.
- Put 1 drop of Bach rescue remedy on your hand and rub it gently into and around your ear.
- Apply Bach rescue remedy onto the acupressure points Si 3 (see pg 235) and Si 19.
- If you are suffering from stress refer to Part Two (Mother Nature's Medical Kit) under Emotional Healing and see if any flower essences listed (pg 84) might help you through this stressful time.
- Drinking liquorice tea once a day is strengthening for the kidneys. Do not drink this if you suffer from high blood pressure.
- Avoid salty foods, fried foods, too much alcohol, too much caffeine, too much raw food and check any medications that you might be taking and their effect on your kidneys.
- All our organs need salt/sodium to function properly (especially our kidneys), but avoid over salting and iodised table salt. Instead make sure you either take a liquid mineral that has sodium or dissolve ⅛ teaspoon of pink salt or good organic sea salt in water and drink in the morning or after exercise.

- Drink coconut water that has the perfect balance of minerals – magnesium, potassium and sodium.

Supplements:
- Gingko *biloba* – 150 mg (daily).
- Liquid minerals – most importantly, potassium, sodium and magnesium.
- Take extra 100 mg magnesium at night before bed.
- The herbs of Rhodiola and *ashwagandha* can help. Take them in powder form or as a tea.
- Vitamin C – 1–5,000 mg daily

ULCERATIVE COLITIS / INFLAMMATORY BOWEL SYNDROME

I treat ulcerative colitis and inflammatory bowel syndrome (IBS) in exactly the same way. These are both inflammatory bowel diseases that causes long-lasting inflammation in your digestive tract. Ulcerative colitis affects the innermost lining of your large intestine (colon) and rectum, IBS affects the entire digestive system. Ulcerative colitis and IBS are heavily linked to food intolerances, but symptoms usually develop over time.

Crucial:

Immediately remove from your diet all forms of wheat and gluten such as bread and pastas, all dairy products, coffee, eggs, refined white sugar, tomatoes, aubergines, peppers, okra, chilli, almonds and all soy products. Instead eat anti-inflammatory foods (see anti-inflammatory foods on pg 72).

Essential:
- First thing in the morning, drink 20 ml of pure aloe vera juice diluted in 1 glass of water with 1 tablespoon of flaxseed oil on an empty stomach. Wait 30 minutes before eating or drinking anything else.
- Just before breakfast, drink 235 ml freshly juiced red cabbage into which you have added 1,000 mg glutamine (powder) and 30 billion cells multi-strain probiotics (powder).
- Take 2 digestive enzymes at the start of every meal.
- It is vital to take the supplements listed.
- Drink gut healing soup broth throughout the day for at least two months. This helps to repair and calm the whole digestive system.

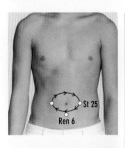

St 25
Ren 6

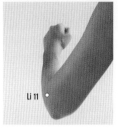

Li 11

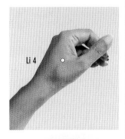

Li 4

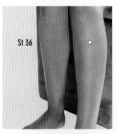

St 36

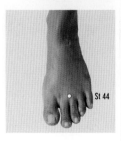

St 44

- Make a blend of the following oils to stimulate the gut to heal: 1½ teaspoon of base oil with 2 drops each of peppermint, fennel, ginger and myrrh oils. Rub on the stomach and middle back area. Use on the stomach strengthening massage and on the stomach and intestine points.
- Do the acupressure points listed using the oil blend.

Acupressure points:
St 25, Ren 6, Li 11, Li 4, St 36 and St 44.

Additional Information:
- Have 170 g slippery elm powder or tea every day.
- Drink unsweetened barley water.
- Fresh coconut juice can help to cool your system down.
- Increase your intake of water to two litres a day.
- Reduce your intake of meat.
- Soak all nuts and seeds before you eat them.
- Replace all coffee or tea with rooibos or liquorice tea (do not drink liquorice tea for more than three weeks).

Supplements:
- Glutamine – 1,000 mg (in juice).
- Liquid Multi B – 1 teaspoon.
- Magnesium – 400 mg.
- MSM – 1,000 mg.
- Multi-strain probiotics – 60 billion cells (in juice).
- Vitamin C – 5,000 mg (powder form).
- Zinc – 30 mg.

....

GUT-HEALING SOUP

1 whole red cabbage
1 stick celery
1 carrot
1 clove garlic, peeled and sliced
1 red onion, peeled and sliced
5-cm knob ginger, peeled
1 tablespoon liquid aminos
1 lime

Place all ingredients except lime in a pot and boil for
45 minutes. Strain. Season with lime. Drink the broth.

....

VOMITING

The two main reasons one vomits are due to contracting a virus or due to a poisoning (food and chemical etc.). The best thing to do is let the body naturally expel what it feels it needs to. The last thing one should do is try and stop it prematurely. We should only try and stop the vomiting when the body has gone into overdrive and doesn't seem to be able to differentiate between what's good and what's bad. So, whilst there is still food coming up, let it come up. If it's just bile and liquids, it's time for you to take preventive action.

Coke mixed with salt can work wonders to stop vomitting.

Essential:

- Do not drink water. You must drink liquids to avoid dehydration – but water tends to be too hard and will just come back up. Instead, offer small spoonfuls of 1 teaspoon manuka honey UMF 15+ diluted in 235 ml room temperature warm water with ¼ teaspoon of good quality pink salt or sea salt. The sugar and salt are essential here for the mineral and electrolyte balance of the body. This will also calm the system down as the body absorbs the necessary minerals to make the vomiting stop.
- Alternatively, use some coca cola or sprite. Stir to take the fizz out and add ¼ teaspoon salt. Take 1 teaspoon at a time.
- Make a mixture of 1 tablespoon of base oil, 1 drop each of lavender, mandarin and cardamom essential oils and 4 drops Bach rescue remedy. Rub on the stomach in an anti-clockwise direction and also along the spine.
- If there are stomach cramps, hold a warm water bottle on the stomach and on the lower back area to relax the muscles.
- To disinfect the environment, spray the room with lavender and thyme *vulgaris* to kill off any virus or bacteria to avoid others getting sick.

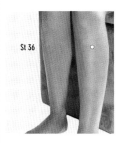

FOOD POISONING

If you suspect food poisoning, mix 1 teaspoon of zeolite clay into a rice milk and drink two times a day for two days.

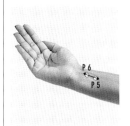

PARASITIC VOMITING – SEE UNDER PARASITES (PG 214)

Acupressure Points:

Press the acupressure points of St 36 and P 6 and P 5. Rub the above essential oil mixture on Du 3 first in an anti-clockwise direction then in a clockwise direction a few hours later.

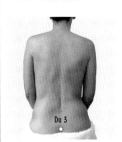

Additional Information:

- After a bout of vomiting, it is not uncommon for the stomach to feel uncomfortable after food for about 7–10 days. Do not worry about this. During this time, avoid all heavy foods especially milk and all dairy products, red meat (unless made into a broth), fried or greasy foods, heavily refined foods and sugar.
- A good thing to eat when the stomach is feeling tender is a grated carrot and apple.
- Prepare rice water. Place some rice in a pot and cover with twice the amount of water than one would normally use to make the rice. When the rice is tender, pour the water off the top of the rice and drink it. This is very binding for the stomach.
- Eat foods that are easy to digest like dry crackers.
- Prepare a carrot soup or an immune-boosting soup (pg 138).
- Prepare a ginger tea from fresh ginger if you still feel nauseous when confronted with foods.
- Fresh mint tea is very calming for the stomach and helps us to digest foods – which occasionally is an issue after a tummy bug.

....

CARROT SOUP

1 onion, peeled and sliced
3 cloves garlic, peeled and sliced
Olive oil, as needed
250 g carrots
2.5-cm ginger, peeled and sliced
1 stick celery
Salt to taste
Pepper to taste

Sauté onion and garlic in olive oil. Add carrots, ginger and celery. Cover with water or a bone broth and simmer until carrots are soft. Season with salt and pepper, then purée all the ingredients together.

....

WARTS

Warts are small, hard, benign growths on the skin caused by a variety of different viruses. There are many different types of warts: plantars, verrucas, flat warts etc. The following advice goes for all warts (except Molluscums/ Water Warts – see pg 207).

I am often asked why some people get warts and others don't. Nobody really knows the answer except that it often has to do with the state of your immune system when you come into contact with the virus that causes them. So it is important to boost the immune system when working to get rid of warts.

Warts most commonly occur on the hands and feet, but can quite honestly occur anywhere.

Essential:

- If the warts are on your hands or feet, you need to soak the area every night. Into a bowl of 470 ml warm water and add 85 g baking soda, 120 ml apple cider vinegar and 5 drops each of tea tree and thyme *vulgaris* essential oils. Soak for 20 minutes.
- If your wart is somewhere difficult to soak, prepare a paste of apple cider vinegar, baking soda with 2 drops of tea tree oil and some water. Apply the paste to the wart, leaving it on for at least 20 minutes.
- Before bed, soak some cotton wool in the water mixture above. Add an extra drop of apple cider vinegar and 1 drop tea tree oil onto the cotton. Place cotton on the wart. Leave it on overnight, securing with a plaster if you need to. Do this for 3–6 weeks or until the wart is completely gone.
- The wart will turn red and angry then brownish and finally almost black. It will then fall off or just disappear.
- This method works but the reaction period is different for each individual. Be persistent.

Supplements:

Take steps to boost the immune system by supplementing daily:

- Magnesium – 200 mg.
- Probiotics – 5 billion cells.
- Vitamin C – 2,000 mg.
- Vitamin D3 – 2,000 ius.
- Zinc – 50 mg.

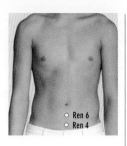

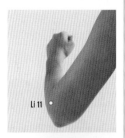

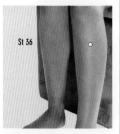

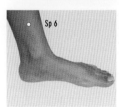

YEAST INFECTIONS / CANDIDA

Yeast infections, also known as candida, are caused by microscopic fungi or yeasts that are generally felt in the vaginal area for women but can also effect our stomach, intestines, gum, breasts, nipples, nail beds, ears, anus and any skin folds where it is damp and moist.

Yeast and candida loves needs sugar. To kill off candida you have to starve it. Immediately remove all forms of sugar, including fruits, (with the exception being some berries, lemons and limes), grains, rice, potatoes, yams, beetroots, mushrooms, synthetic vinegars and coffee. Apple cider vinegar is an exception here.

Essential:

- Start your day with 235 ml fresh water into which you have squeezed 1 lemon (or 2 limes). Add 1 tablespoon psyllium husks, 3 drops of oregano, 5 drops grapefruit seed extract and 1 tablespoon of coconut oil. Do this two times a day.
- Following this, take 100 billion cells of probiotics.
- Make a black tea with fresh ginger and cloves infused into it. Get loose black tea and put 1 teaspoon into a pot. Cover with 235 ml water. Peel and bruise 5-cm of ginger and put in the tea and add 5 cloves. Boil and drink.
- To relieve the discomfort of the vaginal itching, crush 1 whole clove of garlic into 1 tablespoon of coconut oil. Let this infuse for around 60 minutes. Remove all garlic pieces. Add 4 drops of tea tree. Cover a tampon with the oil and insert into the vagina. Leave overnight.
- Squeeze garlic into whatever food you can and before bed, drink warm water with squeezed lemon and 1 crushed garlic clove.
- Do a sitz bath with 85 g baking soda, 120 ml apple cider vinegar along with 5 drops each of tea tree, lemongrass and geranium.

Acupressure Points:

Ren 4–Ren 6, Sj 3, Sj 5, Sj 6, Li 11, St 36 and Sp 6.

Supplements:

- Chromium – 200 mcg (to help calm the sugar cravings).
- Grapefruit seed extract – 10 drops (daily).
- Magnesium – 400 mg (to help calm the sugar cravings).
- Oregano oil – 10 drops (daily).
- Probiotics – 100 billion cells.

Extra Acupressure Points

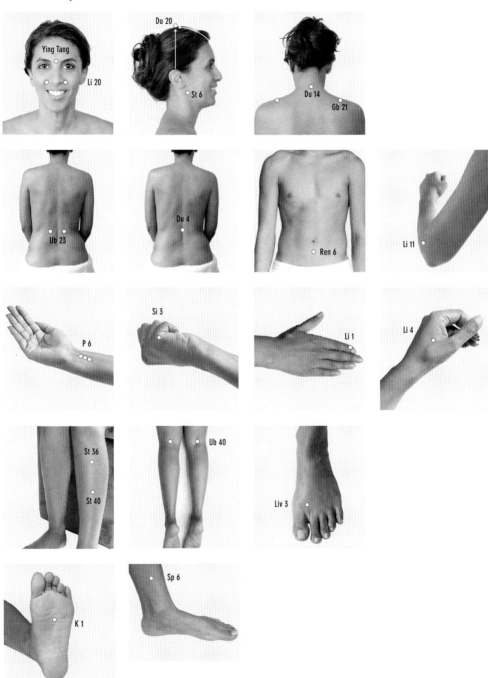

Testimonials

"Every few years I suffer from a bout of cluster headaches which leaves me with no choice but to see a doctor who then prescribes strong pain medication to help me through it. After speaking to Juliet, she suggested that I take a couple of drops of frankincense in water (twice a day) and within two days the cluster headaches, which usually last well over a week, were gone. I have not had any since but if they come back, I'll certainly be using Juliet's remedies."
Steven – *Sri Lanka*

"I was suffering from a sudden onset of painful heartburn and unbearable stomach pain. Juliet suspected an ulcer and suggested that I juice red cabbage and drink it twice a day, and to eat a good quality yoghurt. The pain reduced immediately and completely disappeared within two days. She is honestly the best diagnostician I have ever met and I would highly recommend her."
Simone – *Germany*

"I have been treated for two years for a mycosis between two toes. After seeing three different dermatologists in France, I came to visit my daughter in Singapore. Juliet recommended a very simple footbath made of white vinegar and essential oils. The mycosis disappeared after three weeks!"
Jacqueline – *France*

"I was struggling with yet another UTI episode and after two different courses of antibiotics I was not feeling any better. I bumped into Juliet at our children's school and she told me to take a mixture of natural antibiotic foods for several days every two hours and to do three specific acupressure points. After one day, I was already starting to feel better, with all my symptoms gone the next day! I even cancelled my doctor's appointment! How amazing that we can heal ourselves like this with natural remedies!"
Karen – *Holland*

Bibliography

Ang, Tee Tong & Teo S.K.H. *Ang's Method Acupuncture Therapy*. Singapore: Chinese Nature Cure Institute, 1982.

Beare, Sally. *50 Secrets of The World's Longest Living People*. United Kingdom: Da Capo Press, 2003.

Bragg, Paul C. & Bragg, Patricia. *Apple Cider Vinegar, Miracle Health System*. Santa Barbara: Bragg Health Sciences, 2007.

Dean, Richard. *Your Health Is In Your Hands*. Australia: Superior Health Products, 1995.

Gath, Michael Reed, Henning, Beth Ann. *Acupressure for Emotional Healing*, New York: Bantam Books, 2004.

Holford, Patrick. *Good Medicine: Safe, Natural Ways to Solve Over 75 Common Health Problems*. United Kingdom: Piatkus Books, 2014.

Howard, Judy Ramsel. *The Bach Flower Remedies Step by Step: A Complete Guide to Selecting and Using the Remedies*. United Kingdom: Ebury Publishing, 2005.

Low Dog, Tieraona. *Healthy at Home: Get Well and Stay Well Without Prescriptions*. Washington D.C: National Geographic Society, 2014.

Lu, Henry C. *Traditional Chinese Medicine: An Authoritative and Comprehensive Guide*. Toronto: Key Porter Books Limited, 2005.

Rose, Sara. *Vitamins & Minerals: How to get the Nutrients Your Body Needs*. London: Hamlyn, 2003.

Sherwood, Paul & Haggard Claire. *Get Well Stay Well*. London: Thorsons, 2001.

Sullivan, Karen. *Commonsense Healthcare for Children, How to Raise Happy, Healthy Children from 0 to 15*. London: Piatkus Books, 2,000.

Reader's Digest. *Food That Harm - Food That Heal*. London: The Reader's Digest Association Limited, 1996.

Worwood, Valerie Ann. *The Complete Book of Essential Oils & Aromatherapy*. United Kingdom: Macmillan London Limited, 1990.

WEBSITES

Rattue, Grace. "Autoimmune disease rates increasing." Medicalnewstoday.com. http://www.medicalnewstoday.com/articles/246960.php. (22 June 2012)

Ryman, Lori. " 10 best all natural remedies for acne." Healthextremist.com. http://www.healthextremist.com/10-best-all-natural-remedies-for-acne/ (19 February 2013)

The Well Being Team. "How to listen to your body clock." Wellbeing.com.au. https://www.wellbeing.com.au/body/health/understanding-your-body-clock.html (15 March 2015)

Rohland, Tracy. "The dirty dozen: most heavily sprayed foods." Downtoearth.org. https://www.downtoearth.org/environment/organic-vs-conventional-farming/dirty-dozen-most-heavily-sprayed-foods (14 November 2014)

Renter, Elizabeth. "Top 10 worst GMO foods for your GMO foods list." Naturalsociety.com. http://naturalsociety.com/top-10-worst-gmo-foods-list/ (28 July 2012)

Schoffro, Michelle. "Top 15 cleansing foods." Care2.com. http://www.care2.com/greenliving/top-15-cleansing-foods.html/3 (21 August 2016)

World Health Organisation. "Diabetes." Who.int. www.who.int/mediacentre/factsheets/fs312/en/ (28 November 2010)

Index